EVA AND ADOLF

Other books by this author available from New English Library :

BIG WEEK!
DISASTER AT BARI

Eva and Adolf

GLENN B. INFIELD

NEW ENGLISH LIBRARY
TIMES MIRROR

First published in the USA by Grosset and Dunlap Publishers in 1974
First published in Great Britain by New English Library in 1975
© by Glenn B. Infield, 1974

*

FIRST NEL PAPERBACK EDITION OCTOBER 1976

*

NEL Books are published by
New English Library Limited from Barnard's Inn, Holborn, London EC1N 2JR.
Made and printed in Great Britain by Hunt Barnard Printing Ltd., Aylesbury, Bucks.

45002919 0

Contents

Part 4. THE FINAL YEARS

Preface

Eva Braun was the mystery woman of the Third Reich, the stunning beauty Hitler kept hidden from public view. Only his closest associates were aware of her. Now, more than a quarter of a century after her death, her role in Hitler's life can finally be told accurately.

After the end of World War II, I began gathering the intimate details of the love affair between Eva Braun and Adolf Hitler by patient, frustrating, and sometimes adventurous investigation. In the 1950s many people did not want to talk about the Third Reich years, Hitler, Eva Braun or anyone associated with this period of death and destruction. It was too soon; they were still living with the fear. Later, however, many of these same people asked to talk with me, as though they wanted to share their thoughts with an outsider.

Others who knew both Eva Braun and Hitler intimately I was unable to interview because of their personal situations. Albert Speer spent twenty years in prison after being convicted at the Nuremberg Trial. When he was released from Spandau in 1966 I visited him at his home high on a hill above Heidelberg and we discussed Eva Braun and Hitler. Otto Skorzeny walked away from an Allied prisoner-of-war camp and took refuge in Spain. For many years he refused to talk about his experiences with Hitler but one winter day in Madrid recently Skorzeny told me many previously unknown details about this secret love affair. I also talked to many other former Nazi officials and German military officers who wish to remain anonymous even today.

In Berlin, Munich, Paris, London and many other cities I spoke to men and women who had known Eva Braun and her family before and during World War II. Many of them did not know that she held a special position in Hitler's 'court' until after her death in 1945. Their personal viewpoints helped me greatly in understanding just what type of a woman this mysterious blonde was and how she managed for years to ward off all feminine competition and retain her position as Hitler's mistress.

I was privileged to have access to material gathered by Michael A. Musmanno during the years 1945–1948 when he interviewed over two hundred persons who had been associated with Hitler. Musmanno was designated by the U.S. Navy as an official observer at the International Military Tribunal in Nuremberg and later was appointed by President Harry S. Truman as a judge at the Nuremberg war crime trials which followed. These interviews were invaluable source material since the adjutants, cooks, secretaries, waiters, chauffeurs and others interrogated gave their eyewitness impressions while they were still fresh in their minds and unbiased by the changing times.

Recently official military files in the United States and Great Britain became available as classification time limits expired. The intelligence branches of both countries had dossiers on Eva Braun based on reports from underground agents – dossiers that included facts not known to the public.

Who was Eva Braun, the woman who achieved such a strong sexual hold on Adolf Hitler? Did Hitler really love her? How did he treat her when they were alone? Was she an influence on this man who caused such widespread agony in the world? Was Hitler a sexual 'monster'? Why did Eva Braun decide to die with Hitler in Berlin when she could easily have escaped the final holocaust?

The details of this secret love affair are sometimes strange, often surprising, but always fascinating.

Acknowledgements

This book has had many contributors for whose advice and help I am grateful. The late Michael A. Musmanno, Judge, Supreme Court of Pennsylvania, was of invaluable aid throughout my years of research, and after his death his nephew, William F. Cercone, Judge, Superior Court of Pennsylvania, continued to help by permitting me access to the Musmanno Archives.

Albert Speer and Otto Skorzeny, both of whom were very well acquainted with Eva Braun and Adolf Hitler, spent many hours discussing the events they witnessed personally during the rise and fall of Hitler. The details they provided were not available from any other sources. Dr Werner Maser spent considerable time at his home in Speyer, Germany, discussing Eva Braun, Hitler and the Third Reich with me.

Franz G. Lassner, Director of Archives, Hoover Institution on War, Revolution and Peace, provided many documents for study. Arthur G. Kogan, Historical Office, Department of State; Angus MacLean Thuermer, Central Intelligence Agency; Charles E. Flinner, United Press International; Mrs Nadia Popov, Secretary, Soviet Embassy; Dr Robert Wolfe, National Archives; and Frederick C. Oechsner, former Central European Manager for United Press, all gave me a generous and constant supply of information.

The Institut für Zeitgeschichte, Munich; German Federal Archives, Koblenz; Bundesarchivs-Militärarchivs, Freiburg; and the Munich Institute for Politics, Munich, were German sources of information that I used in addition to the many persons in Germany that I interviewed. In France I was welcomed to the Ministère des Anciens Combattants, the Ministère de l'Economie, and the Ministère des Transports where, surprisingly, material and documents were available for study. In England I had the special help of David Irving, who took time out from his own writing to discuss this book with me, and Mrs C. Wichmann of the Wiesner Library.

Dr T. Johnson of Geneva College spent many hours translating German documents, letters and other materials for me.

As always, my wife, Peggy, guided me during the research and writing of the book, and my editor, Robert Markel, constantly encouraged me.

One last thanks goes to those persons who told me their personal stories but, because of a lingering fear that former Nazi officials may still be alive, refused to be identified.

Part 1
THE EARLY
YEARS

I
A Capricious Child

When Eva Braun was born in 1912, Adolf Hitler was twenty-three years old. He was living in Vienna, where he was painting scenes to be reproduced on postcards to make enough money to buy food.

Eighteen years after Eva Braun was born in Munich she would 'take a bath, put on her best underclothes' and go to meet the man who would later become Führer of Germany and the greatest despot of modern times.

Fritz Braun, a schoolteacher, and his wife were highly respected middle-class citizens of pre-World War I Munich. They were the parents of a three-year-old daughter and devout Catholics who attended mass every week. His neighbors considered Fritz Braun's morals impeccable. Though he liked his beer, he never flirted with other women – in fact, his male friends at the local *bierhaus* considered him something of a prude because he objected to their lewd stories and obscene jokes.

Franziska Katharina Kranbürger Braun, known to everyone in the neighborhood as Fanny, was the most beautiful woman in the northeast section of Munich. Twenty-seven years old, with a slender waist, shapely legs and full breasts, she had more than enough appeal to keep her husband from straying. She was also a very athletic young woman, especially adept at swimming and skiing. Many who knew the couple wondered why this beautiful Dresden doll was so devoted to the gruff, rough-featured Fritz; but devoted she was and their family life was happy.

When his wife became pregnant the second time Fritz Braun was confident that she would bear a son. He loved his three-year-old daughter Ilse but he wanted a son to carry on the Braun name. There was no doubt in his mind on the cold evening of February 6, 1912, that he would soon have one. As midnight approached, his mother-in-law, who had come to Munich from her home in the province of Oberpfalz to oversee the birth of the baby, looked at the nervous Fritz and nodded. 'It won't be long now!'

At twenty-five minutes past two on the morning of February 7, 1912, the baby was born. A girl. After his initial disappointment because the baby was not a boy, a disappointment that disappeared as soon as he looked at the small bundle his mother-in-law handed him to hold, Fritz Braun tried to think of a name for the new arrival. He had selected a name for the son he had expected – Rudolf, in honor of Crown Prince Rudolf of Austria who had been found slain in his hunting lodge near Vienna in 1889, a man Fritz had always admired and respected even though when he was murdered the Baroness Maria Vetsera had been with him. Now that it was obvious Rudolf could not be used, after considerable thought he decided to name the baby Eva Anna Paula. He completely forgot that European custom meant her birthday would be celebrated on her patron saint's day, and since Saint

14

Genevieva's Day was one day before Christmas, his new daughter's birthday and Christmas presents would always be combined.

Eva was a healthy baby who soon had father, mother and three-year-old sister busy keeping her out of trouble. She was a pink-cheeked, robust child who laughed often and, as was the German custom, long enjoyed the privileges of being the 'baby' of the family. Even her father's stern warnings seldom kept her out of mischief until he had emptied his next stein of beer. Ilse spent a great deal of time watching her younger sister for her mother and the two girls became very close. When Eva was three years old another child was born to Fanny Braun – another girl, who was quickly named Gretl. This time Fritz Braun was not around to comfort his wife during the birth or to show his momentary disappointment that he still had no son. He was in the German Army.

On June 28, 1914, Gavrilo Princip, an Austro-Hungarian student, shot and killed Archduke Franz Ferdinand of Austria and his wife in the Bosnian capital of Sarajevo. Fritz Braun immediately recognized the seriousness of the assassination. He knew of the antagonism between Austria-Hungary and Serbia over the territorial demands of Serbia, and that while the assassin was of Austro-Hungarian nationality, he was a Serbian by nationality. This indicated to him that Princip had been abetted by persons or agencies of the Serbian government. He believed the murders would cause serious trouble between the two countries and he was correct. The German government, represented by the Emperor, the Chancellor and the acting Foreign Secretary, quickly relayed a message to Vienna that Germany would support Austria-Hungary if other nations attempted to interfere with her right to punish Serbia for the assassination of the Archduke. With this assurance from Germany, Austria-Hungary declared war on Serbia on July 28, 1914, and when England, France and Russia sided with Serbia, Germany – and Fritz Braun – entered the conflict which later became known as World War I.

Eva was too young to understand where her father had gone but not too young to miss him. She adored her father, whose harsh words and occasional slaps on the behind couldn't hide his affection for her. For several weeks after he left for Flanders Eva was so quiet and subdued that her mother was convinced she was ill. The old doctor who examined Eva, however, just shook his head and said he couldn't find anything physically wrong with the girl. 'I think she misses her father,' he told Fanny Braun. 'She is young. She will soon get over it and be as lively as ever.'

It was an accurate diagnosis because Eva was soon running around the house and laughing as she had before her father left for the army. After Gretl was born in 1915 Eva and Ilse tried to help their mother as much as they could, and though they were only three and six years old, they were a comfort to the lonely Fanny Braun. It was a difficult four years for the mother. From the beginning of the conflict Germany was handicapped because her food, manpower and raw material resources were more limited than those of the Allies and her citizens were forced to make sacrifices that had not been anticipated. Germany had no prepared detailed plans for the management of her wartime economy and paid the price for this neglect. She was unable to maintain her agricultural production at the prewar level because the military drained a large segment of manpower and horses from the villages and farms, and fertilizer became scarce when nitrogen, one of its components, was diverted to the manufacture of explosives. While Fanny Braun did not know the details of such military and agricultural problems, she did know they seriously affected her and her three small daughters. Meat, butter, potatoes and other foods were in short supply and she had to hunt daily to find enough to eat. One winter she and the girls lived primarily on turnips since other foods were available only on the black market and she didn't have the money to buy these. It has been estimated that about three quarters of a million Germans died of hunger that winter, but Fanny Braun and her small brood survived. She made army uniforms and other items that brought in a small amount of money and she took in lodgers. By being very frugal, she and the girls managed to eat and keep warm during the four years Fritz Braun was gone.

Eva, who was six years old when her father returned home from the war, changed very little in disposition despite the hardships. She remained a fun-loving, mischievous child and was the one bright spot in the life of the Braun family during the miserable years immediately following World War I. Inflation in postwar Germany wiped out all savings and insurance policies, and government bonds were not worth the paper they were written on. Though Fritz Braun resumed his teaching career, his salary was inadequate to maintain his wife and three daughters in prewar comfort. Deprived of their sense of security, he and thousands of middle-class citizens like him felt betrayed by the government and deeply resented the immoderate demands of the triumphant Allies at Versailles. It was against this background of economic breakdown and bitterness that the numerous political parties of the country jockeyed for power. One of these parties was the National Socialist German Workers' Party (NSDAP) led by Adolf Hitler. Fritz Braun refused to have anything to do with the Nazi organization, whose leader he considered 'a jack-of-all-trades, an imbecile who thinks himself omniscient and who wants to reform the world'.

The child Eva was too young and too busy enjoying life to be concerned about political parties or the men who led them. In 1925, when she was thirteen years old, her father inherited a modest amount of money from a distant aunt and the fortunes of the Braun family took an immediate upswing. They moved to a new apartment, much larger and more modern, at 93 Hohenzollernstrasse, about six blocks north of where Eva was born. From their new home Eva and her two sisters often walked west a few blocks on Hohenzollernstrasse, cut north on Tengstrasse and went into Luitpold Park to play. If they tired of that park they went a similar distance in the opposite direction to the huge, famous Englischer Garten (English Gardens) which had a lake, horseback riding areas and several playgrounds. Eva was quick to follow in her athletic mother's footsteps and soon became an excellent swimmer and ice skater. In the winter she learned to ski in the mountains south of Munich where the family often went on long weekends. Both her parents were proud of her athletic achievements but Fanny Braun wanted her daughters to learn more than how to do the Australian crawl in the water or a figure eight on the ice. She recognized that Eva was going to be a problem as far as formal education was concerned. 'She has a graceful figure, holds herself well and has a fine disposition,' she told her husband, 'but she is too frivolous to study hard in school. She will only learn as long as she is being amused.'

Fanny Braun's analysis of her daughter's attitude toward school was confirmed when her teacher, Fräulein von Heidenaber, told her that Eva was 'intelligent but spends much of her time in class being a troublemaker'.

Actually, Eva's attitude was influenced by her times. The cultural decline that followed defeat in the war, the rampant inflation and unemployment, the severe restrictions put on Germany by the victorious Allies, the political confusion as the various German officials struggled for power, and the defeatist attitude in general affected her whole generation. To a young, impressionable girl it seemed best to 'live today because tomorrow may never come'. Why study the music of staid Johannes Brahms or Richard Wagner when American jazz tunes were much better for dancing? The writings of Ernst Monism, Wilhelm Dilthey, Friedrich Nietzche and Thomas Mann did not interest Eva nearly so much as the *Tales of Oscar Wilde* and the Wild West novels of Karl May. Consequently, by the time she was fifteen years old Eva had the primary and secondary education expected of a girl her age but had made no effort to delve into the classics of either literature or music. All she wanted was to have a good time, enjoying herself to the full and learn only the facts of life that would enable her to do so.

Yet her Catholic upbringing and her father's stern discipline did have some effect on Eva. When Carl Anson, a schoolmate, offered her a cigarette when she was fifteen years old, Eva refused to smoke it. She didn't accept a cigarette until a year later when several of her girlfriends gathered in the English Gardens one evening and dared each other to smoke. Eva would never back down on a dare, and besides, she had wanted to smoke ever since Anson had offered her a cigarette the year before and laughed when she wouldn't take it. Unfortunately, her first cigarette made her sick and when she returned home, pale and holding her stomach, her mother gave her a spoonful of castor oil and put her to bed. But the foul-tasting medicine didn't discourage her and she was a constant smoker for the remainder of her life.

At fifteen Eva naturally became interested in boys, which infuriated her father. He occasionally permitted her to invite a boy to the Braun apartment while he and Fanny were present, but when Eva asked to go dancing or to a movie with a boyfriend he usually refused to even answer her. Her mother understood her much better and because of her intervention Eva now and then managed to go out for a few hours with a schoolmate or a neighborhood boy whose reputation Fanny had thoroughly checked. It soon became evident to both her mother and father that the fun-loving Eva could not be kept in the apartment constantly, nor could one of them accompany her every time she stepped outside, so they made a decision. They sent her to a convent school.

Fanny Braun was convinced that a convent school would give Eva the education and social graces required of a real lady. It was then considered prestigious for a young woman to say she had been educated in a *Kloster*, and Fanny was ambitious for her vivacious daughter. She hoped that Eva would become a well-known dressmaker, or better, marry a man whose money and social status would lift her above the humdrum life of an ordinary married woman burdened with children and bills. She wanted her daughter to travel, to meet people in other walks of life who were successful and well known, to achieve the prestige that she herself had never had except in her own intimate circle. It was an ambitious objective but she was sure it could be accomplished if Eva was guided correctly during her early years.

In the small town of Simbach, approximately sixty miles east of Munich, the English Sisters, a Catholic order founded by a fugitive from English persecutions, operated a school for young girls and it was there that Eva Braun was sent at the age of sixteen. Simbach was directly across the Inn River from the Austrian town of Braunau, which was gaining fame as the birth-place of the political upstart Adolf Hitler. Eva found the rigors of the Catholic Young Women's Institute difficult to accept despite the fact that her family was Catholic and strict. Sister Marie-Magdalene, though, took a special liking to her, and helped ease her into the disciplined routine of the school. Before long, Eva was going to confession twice a week as required, attending all other religious services without protest and adhering to the rules and regulations of the convent. She wasn't happy, however.

'I will never stay here two years,' she told Nina Garnier, a classmate, less than a month after she entered the convent. 'This is not the life for me.'

The one activity at the school that Eva found congenial was the amateur theatricals that were staged periodically. Eva had always been interested in acting, although her only previous experience consisted in studying her favorite actor, John Gilbert, on the screen. At the convent she was permitted to take part in the productions, although she was never a 'star', only a supporting actress. She was an excellent dancer, probably the best among the student body, but there was not much opportunity for a dancer in a convent. Once she was caught putting on a private dancing exhibition for a group of girls when they were all supposed to be in their rooms studying and was given a month's restriction to the convent area for her disobedience. She didn't complain nor did she attempt to put any blame on the others.

'I asked them to watch me,' she told the Mother Superior, 'because I have just learned a new dance. It is my fault.'

Eva found the repetitive, dull routine of convent school life unbearable, and instead of subduing her, as her parents had hoped, the year she spent there only strengthened her resolve to have an exciting life. Smoking a cigarette or dancing on the sly and acting in a few amateur theatricals did not fulfill her craving for adventure, and when she finally took her leave of school in the fall of 1929 Eva was determined that her future was going to be very different.

All her exciting plans faded when she reached the Braun apartment in Munich. Fritz Braun was unhappy that his daughter had left the convent school a year early and displeased with the report he had received from the faculty. It stated, in part: 'Your daughter is intelligent and ambitious. She regularly attended the religious services. Yet she was not interested in the curriculum and thought that the regulations were unduly restrictive.'

Her father was intelligent too, and he realized that the Sisters were politely telling him that Eva was too rambunctious for the convent, that her ideas and the ideas of the English Sisters were entirely different. He decided to take immediate steps to bring his daughter into line. He checked on every letter Eva received and every telephone call she made or got at the apartment. She had to be in her room at ten o'clock every night, and just to make certain that she didn't read books or magazines that might not meet his approval, he shut the electricity in her room off at that hour. Eva managed to read anyway by using a flashlight and hiding under the blankets. It was an austere life for a seventeen-year-old girl, one that was designed to break her of what her father considered to be frivolous habits. Instead it made her more determined than ever to find an exciting life outside the Braun apartment.

Lack of money gave Eva the excuse she needed to get away from the family circle. Despite Fritz Braun's inheritance and his promotion to full professorship at the school where he was teaching, he didn't give Eva any personal spending money. Her purse was usually empty unless her mother managed to slip her a few *pfennigs* from her household money, and after a few weeks of such poverty Eva decided to look for a job. When she first suggested the idea to her father, he just shook his head, but after thinking it over he reconsidered. He had read about the severe depression in the United States and knew that if history repeated itself Germany's economy would feel the effects of the American depression within a year. Therefore he decided it would be a good idea if his daughter did bring in some money to help with the family bills. Eva, of course, was not thinking of the Braun family debts. She was planning on using the money for clothes, jewelry, cosmetics and other personal items.

While her father had been concentrating on revamping her outlook toward life, Eva had been concentrating on revamping her physical appearance. When she returned from the convent school she noticed that her sister Ilse, three years her senior, was using

20

cosmetics. Ilse, who was working as a receptionist for a doctor, knew that her appearance was of vital importance. She watched her weight, bought clothes that were in fashion and made herself up to look more attractive. At first Eva thought that applying lipstick, powder and eyebrow pencil was a waste of time, but when she began to look for a job she discovered just how important her appearance was to prospective employers – especially if they were male. Little by little she learned the art of makeup, studied fashions to determine which styles were best for her and spent many hours rearranging her hair. She decided that she was too heavy, although actually she was only a little on the plump side, which was considered ideal for a German girl of her age. Immediately she started dieting, but since she knew her father would consider that 'a foolhardy girlish stunt', pretended that she had an upset stomach so he wouldn't force her to eat. Eva complained about an 'upset stomach' so often that her mother sent her to a doctor, who couldn't find anything wrong with her. When Eva told him the truth the doctor sided with her and told Fritz Braun that it would be best if his daughter limited her food intake because of a 'nervous stomach'.

After three months of dieting and experimenting with clothes and makeup, Eva had changed from the round-faced, pig-tailed schoolgirl of the English Sisters' convent into a fashionable young woman. She lacked the stylish clothes she wanted so much and her mannerisms were still more giddy than sedate, but all her acquaintances noticed the difference. When Hilda May, a neighbor girl who lived on Kaiserstrasse, teased her about her cosmetics, Eva had an answer ready. 'If a few *pfennigs* of cosmetics will get me what I want,' she said, 'it is money well spent.'

Now she began to learn about a more sophisticated life from another of her acquaintances, Klara Oster, a beautiful darkhaired girl who worked as a secretary at the offices of the Industry Club in the Park Hotel in Düsseldorf. While Klara was home on vacation Eva met her walking in the English Gardens. They spent the afternoon together and Klara explained that in her position she often met wealthy and influential industrialists and, with a laugh, told Eva how they would give her expensive gifts.

'Why?' Eva wanted to know. 'Are you an excellent typist?'

At first Klara thought Eva was teasing her, but when she discovered her friend was serious, she explained a few facts of life to her.

'I am an excellent typist but so are hundreds of other girls in Düsseldorf. No, they don't give me the gifts because of my typing. They do it because I am nice to them. I go to dinner with them when they are lonely, laugh at their jokes and try to keep them in good humor as much as possible.' Seeing the shocked look on Eva's face, Klara grinned. 'Now don't get any wrong ideas, Eva. I don't go too far.'

Later that evening, when Eva told her sister Ilse about her conversation with Klara Oster, the older Ilse warned her that it was a dangerous game Klara was playing but one that was often effective. This was a lesson Eva Braun would not forget.

Shortly after Klara returned to Düsseldorf, Eva answered an advertisement in the *Münchener Neueste Nachrichten* concerning a position at a photography shop at 50 Schellingstrasse. The owner of the shop was a short, heavyset Bavarian named Heinrich Hoffmann, a vulgar man who loved drinking and women equally. Still, he was an excellent photographer who had apprenticed under his father and uncle, both of whom had photographed many members of royalty. After his apprenticeship he had joined Hugo Thiele, court photographer to the Grand Duke von Hessen in Darmstadt, for a period, moved on to Heidelberg the next year to work for Langbein, the university photographer, and in 1902 was in Frankfurt taking pictures of military officers for the Theobald studio. Later Hoffmann worked in London, where he also began publishing art books. By 1910 he was back in Germany and opened a studio of his own in Munich. Within a few years Hoffmann had established himself as one of the best photographers in the city and was a moderately wealthy man. He was also supremely confident; so when he was offered a fee of one hundred dollars to provide a picture of the radical politician Adolf Hitler to an American agency in 1922, he thought it would be just another easy assignment.

Hoffman, who had joined the Nazi Party two years earlier because he approved of its platform for the recovery of Germany, did not know Hitler when he accepted the assignment. When he approached him about the photograph he discovered that Hitler had a fetish against having his picture taken, that he believed an important factor in his hypnotic hold on an audience was that they had never seen a photograph of him. Surely, Hoffmann insisted, Hitler was no better than the emperors, kings, queens and other famous people who had permitted him to photograph them? His pleas were completely ignored, he didn't get the photograph, but during the next two years he became good friends with Hitler and Hitler spent many hours at his home relaxing. It wasn't until 1924, when Hitler was released from the prison at Landsberg, that Hoffmann got permission to take his picture, and from then on he was known as 'Hitler's photographer'. At the time the title didn't signify much, but later it brought Hoffmann worldwide fame and millions of dollars.

When Eva entered his shop late in 1929 Hoffmann was delighted with her 'pretty' appearance and her youthfulness. He liked young girls (and older women also), not only for personal reasons but also because they were good for business. He hired her immediately to work as a clerk, part-time bookkeeper and assistant in the darkroom developing films. Later Hoffmann proposed another duty for young Eva, one that was to change her life. He asked her to entertain his friend Hitler.

At approximately the same time that Heinrich Hoffmann hired Eva, Adolf Hitler rented a luxurious nine-room apartment in a fashionable section of Munich several blocks southeast of the photography shop. He wanted a more appropriate place to invite his associates and friends.

2
The Austrian Drifter

During the year 1889 nineteen-year-old Lenin and ten-year-old Stalin were still unheard of in Russia, while in Italy six-year-old Mussolini spent most of his time scrounging for food. At Geiselhoering, in the Bavarian province of Oberpfalz, four-year-old Fanny Kranburger played happily, unaware that in the small Austrian village of Braunau, only a few miles away, a baby boy had been born who would have a vital influence on her life in later years, after she married Fritz Braun and gave birth to a daughter named Eva.

Throughout his public life Hitler constantly tried to conceal the true facts about his early years, telling only those stories that projected the image he so badly wanted, often disregarding the truth in behalf of this planned image. Consequently, his family tree is shrouded in mystery. It is known that he was born at half-past six on the evening of April 20, 1889, at an inn called Gasthof zum Pommer in Braunau. His mother was Klara Pölzl, a twenty-nine-year-old former domestic servant from the village of Spital. She was the third wife of Alois Hitler, Adolf's fifty-two-year-old father, and, in all probability, his second cousin. The reason there is no conclusive evidence that Adolf Hitler's parents were cousins is that Alois Hitler was an illegitimate child. He was born in 1837 to a peasant girl named Maria Anna Schicklgruber from the village of Strones. Five years after his birth his mother married Johann Georg Hiedler but Hiedler did not acknowledge Alois as his son. Hiedler's brother took young Alois into his household and raised him until the boy became a cobbler's apprentice at the age of thirteen. Five years later Alois joined the Imperial Customs Service and served as an officer until 1895. He legally changed his name from Schicklgruber to Hitler in 1877 and during the remainder of his life was known by this name. The mystery of Alois Hitler's lineage was never solved conclusively and caused his son a great deal of tribulation.

Before he married Klara Pölzl, Alois had two other wives, an illegitimate son and a legitimate daughter. Adolf was the third child of Alois and Klara and their only son to survive to adulthood. An older brother, Gustav, and a sister, Ida, both died at two years of age, and a brother born after Adolf, Edmund, died when he was six. The last child born was a daughter named Paula, who was mentally retarded. Paula's affliction and the tragic deaths of Adolf's brothers and sisters were blamed on the 'blood curse' of cousin marrying cousin.

Perhaps because of the conflicting stories he heard about his father's origins and previous marriages, Adolf Hitler was much closer to his mother than to the unpredictable, hard-drinking, woman-chasing Alois. When Alois died at the age of sixty-six while on his way to a *bierhaus* in Leonding, a village just outside of Linz, his son was definitely not heartbroken. Three years before his father's death Hitler had enrolled in the Linz Realschule, a technical school, but by 1904 his academic record was so poor that he transferred to another educational institution at nearby Steyr to avoid being suspended. He didn't do any better at this school and did not obtain a graduation diploma. This seemed immaterial to Hitler, although it was a worry to his widowed mother, who worshipped her son. Nor did he try to find a job after he withdrew from the school at Steyr. He was content to allow his mother to buy his food and provide his other needs from her inheritance and the pension his father had left her rather than go to work himself. He fancied himself an artist and in 1907 convinced his mother to finance a trip to Vienna so that he could apply for admittance to the Academy of Fine Arts. He was turned down. The reason: 'Test drawing unsatisfactory.'

Two months later his beloved mother died of cancer, and the loner returned to Linz long enough to attend her funeral but went back to Vienna immediately afterward. In 1908 Hitler once again sought admittance to the Academy of Fine Arts, but this time he was not even permitted to take the examination. With this second failure on his record he gave up all hopes of attending the school. He was living as a down-and-out bohemian at a men's hostel in the Twentieth District in 1912 when Eva Braun was born. Though he came into contact with men of all classes at the hostel on Meldemannstrasse, he never became like any of them. He didn't smoke, didn't drink, and was apparently too shy and clumsy to have any success with women. His main passion was discussing politics. Often he would turn a discussion into a heated argument and his voice would get so loud that the porter in the hostel would make him quiet down so others could sleep.

In 1913 Hitler slipped out of Vienna to avoid forced military service and went to Munich, where he brooded over his radical theories of race, anti-Semitism and anti-Communism. He was living with a tailor's family in the Schleissheimerstrasse when he heard the news of the assassination of Archduke Franz Ferdinand. Unlike Fritz Braun, who immediately understood that war was imminent, Hitler was at first confused about the incident and blamed Ferdinand for keeping Austria independent of Germany. When he realized that Germany and Austria were joining forces against Serbia, however, he wrote a formal petition on August 3, 1914, to King Ludwig III of Bavaria requesting permission to volunteer for a Bavarian regiment even though he was an Austrian. Ludwig never saw the letter, but permission was granted, and Hitler joined the 1st Company of the 16th Bavarian Reserve Infantry Regiment.

His former friends (of whom he had very few) and acquaintances were shocked that the shy and indolent Hitler had volunteered for combat duty when only a year earlier he had slipped quietly out of Vienna precisely to avoid military con-

27

scription. They thought he would make a poor soldier, but Hitler surprised them. He became an excellent soldier, serving as a runner during most of the war. In October, 1914, the 16th Bavarian Reserve Infantry Regiment reached Lille as a reinforcement unit and was soon engaged in the First Battle of Ypres, one of the fiercest combat actions of World War I. By the time the fighting at the Ypres ended, Hitler's regiment had dwindled to six hundred men from a total of three thousand. The regiment later fought in battles in the Neuve Chapelle area on the Somme and at Bapaume, where Hitler was shot in the leg. After recuperating in a hospital in Munich he returned to the front in time to participate in the Battle of Arras, the Third Battle of Ypres, action around Lizy on the Aisne and the last large German offensive near Werwick. Once again he was a casualty. During the night of October 13, 1918, he was gassed and temporarily blinded. He was under treatment in the military hospital at Pasewalk, near Stettin, when the war ended on November 11, 1918. Though he was never promoted higher than corporal, he received both the Iron Cross, Second Class, and the Iron Cross, First Class, and was commended by his commanding officers for bravery many times.

Despite his courage as a soldier in combat Hitler's relations with his comrades were troubled. For one thing, he was considered eccentric because of his habits. He would sit in the corner of a tent or mess for hours by himself, his head down, never speaking a word. Whereas the others sought girls in the nearby towns, Hitler ignored women altogether, yet he ignored the homosexuals in the unit just as studiously. He seemed to have no interest in sex.

After Hitler was released from Pasewalk on November 21, 1918, he returned to Munich and to the barracks of the List Regiment to recuperate. He discovered that Bavaria was in the midst of a revolution. More distasteful to him than anything else was the fact that a Jew, Kurt Eisner, was in charge of the Bavarian Socialistic Republic, since his Independent Socialist Party was the strongest political organization. Eisner was not a Bolshevik but Hitler's anti-Semitism placed him in immediate opposition to the man. Hitler's friend Ernst Schmidt told a friend who asked him what Hitler thought about the revolution, 'He hadn't much to say about it, but it was plain to see how bitter he felt.'

During this period Hitler and Schmidt were sent to Traunstein as guards for a prisoner-of-war camp, but this duty lasted less than two months and they returned to the List Regiment barracks. On February 21, 1919, Eisner was assassinated and once again Bavaria was thrown into turmoil between Socialists, Communists and right-wing advocates. Hitler, still in the German Army, sided with the rightists. When the Reichswehr (regular army) and the Freikorps (armed volunteers) took control of Munich he was assigned to the Commission of Inquiry of the 2nd Infantry Regiment, which was a polite, formal title for a group of informers. It was his duty to tell his superiors which soldiers sympathized with the Communists so they could be 'eliminated'. During his work as an undercover agent in the German Army he was ordered to take an indoctrination course at the University of Munich, a course designed to give soldiers an education in the political philosophy favored by the military. It was at these sessions that Hitler first discovered he could sway an audience with words, that he could think on his own feet, voice his opinions about Jews and Communists in a direct manner, and make a speech that impressed his superiors as well as his classmates despite his lack of a formal university education. By the time the course ended on August 25, 1919, Hitler was recognized as an expert on the 'Jewish question'.

That same August Hitler appeared at the office of Dr Kurt Krueger, a physician in Munich recommended to him by Ernst Schmidt. After swearing the doctor to secrecy which, Krueger informed him, was unnecessary since as a physician he lived by the Hippocratic oath, Hitler confessed that he suspected he had syphilis. Ignorant of his patient's avoidance of women, the doctor was hardly shocked. He had witnessed many cases of neglected venereal disease and fully expected to find Hitler in the second stage of syphilis. Instead he discovered that his patient still enjoyed a healthy growth of hair, there were no blemishes on his skin and his complexion was that of a healthy man. There was no chancre on the genital organs, a certain sign of the disease. When he told Hitler that there was no outward sign of syphilis, and although he would take a blood test he didn't think the disease was present, Hitler seemed shocked. He asked one question: 'If I don't have syphilis why am I totally impotent?'

When Krueger explained that there were many reasons a man could be temporarily impotent, Hitler seemed relieved. He quickly made another appointment when the doctor told him that the sexual block could be removed once the reason for it was discovered. Over the next fifteen years Krueger learned so many intimate details about Hitler's sexual life that it was impossible for him to stay in Germany after Hitler came to power. Within a short time after their first meeting, however, he had cured Hitler's temporary impotence.

Krueger was one of the first persons to realize that Hitler's apparent disinterest in women was a pretense, that his impotence and a minor physical problem that circumcision could solve made him feign such a disinterest. Actually, his suppressed sexuality was warping his thoughts and hindering his fledgling political career.

One of the first women whose friendship he won was Hélène 'Lotte' Bechstein, the wife of the wealthy piano manufacturer Carl Bechstein. Frau Bechstein was domineering and possessive and thought she could tell the retiring, shy Hitler how to dress, how to act and even how to conduct his political career. She, as so many women after her, made the mistake of underestimating his determination and independence and the strong revulsion he felt toward anyone who tried to govern his life. He was of the 'old German school' and believed that women existed to be admired, fondled and cared for, but should not express opinions on political matters. Frau Bechstein spent large sums of money on Hitler as he struggled to establish his own political organization. He sat at her feet for hours, his head resting in her lap, telling her about his plans while she stroked his hair. He had already become a member of the small German Workers' Party organized by Anton Drexler – member number seven – and was determined to take complete control of the organization and use it for his own purposes. For this he needed money, and therefore he was willing to listen to Frau Bechstein call him *mein Wölfchen* and make plans for him to marry her unattractive daughter in return for her lavish checks. She also gave parties which enabled him to meet other wealthy and influential Munich families, and many of these new supporters contributed substantial sums to his party. Since Frau Bechstein was considerably older than Hitler, she was content for him to merely smile at her or kiss her hand or compliment her on her clothes or hair style. She was also very protective of her daughter, so Hitler was never forced into a position where his temporary impotence would embarrass him.

He was still seeing Dr Krueger on a regular schedule when he met Elsa Bruckmann, formerly Princess Cantacuzene, who was also considerably older than Hitler. She was the wife of Hugo Bruckmann, a millionaire Munich publisher. Hitler was impressed not only by her financial resources but also by her family title, and for a period the two were inseparable. When he wanted

30

a weekly newspaper for his party organization, Elsa Bruckmann was one of the contributors to the fund raised by Major Ernst Röhm – an army officer who believed in Hitler's political platform – to purchase the *Völkischer Beobachter*.

With the help of Frau Bechstein, Frau Bruckmann, Frau Gertrud von Seidlitz (the wealthy owner of a Finnish paper mill) and other women and their husbands, Hitler began to gain a foothold in Bavarian politics. After getting control of the German Workers' Party and ousting Anton Drexler from the chairmanship, he left the army and devoted himself full time to the organization. The same year that he bought the *Völkischer Beobachter* Hitler changed the name of the party he had taken over to the National Socialist German Workers' Party (the shortened form Nazi derives from the German words *National* and *Sozialist*) and began his reign of terror that was to last for so many years. The women who had helped him slowly became disillusioned after he supported the fearsome brown-shirted stormtroopers known as the SA (*Sturm Abteilungen*) under the initial command of Hermann Göring, a World War I pilot hero. They couldn't understand how their 'sweet, adorable Adi' (their nickname for Adolf Hitler) could sanction the bloody attacks his supporters made on Jews and Communists in the streets and beer halls of Munich. Yet as the Nazis grew stronger and stronger, these same women found excuses for Hitler's violent excesses, wishing to stay in the good graces of the man they had decided could lift Germany from the depths of defeat. Even after Hitler tried to seize control of Bavaria at gunpoint on the night of November 8, 1923, and failed, Frau Bechstein and Frau Bruckmann remained loyal to him.

Nineteen persons died – sixteen Nazis and three policemen – during the attempted *putsch* that started in one of Munich's largest beer halls, the Bürgerbräukeller, and ended at Odeonsplatz. Göring, who was seriously wounded, was smuggled across the Austrian frontier by his wife. Hitler injured his shoulder in the mêlée but managed to elude the police and reach the home of Ernst Hanfstängl's sister in Uffing where he took refuge. Ernst 'Putzi' Hanfstängl was a close associate of Hitler's, and his sister Erna, a slim, beautiful girl, was another woman whose friendship Hitler coveted. Not for her money, however, but for her beauty, which he said 'made all others pale by comparison'. Erna was attracted to her brother's friend and they had attended the opera together several times prior to the putsch. She had also spent many hours talking with him when he visited her brother's home.

Consequently, when he appeared in Uffing after the disastrous attempt to overthrow the Bavarian government, Erna took him in and he spent the next forty-eight hours with her until the police located him and took him into custody.

The Beer Hall Putsch did two things for Hitler: it gave him the notoriety that he wanted and it put him in jail. On February 26, 1924, Hitler went on trial in Munich for high treason and the details of the attempted coup were spread across the front pages of newspapers in Europe, the United States and Asia. The Nazi Party and Hitler himself received worldwide publicity and the fact that he was found guilty and sentenced to five years in jail in no way diminished his popularity. On the contrary, it made him a hero to his followers and a name to thousands of others who had never heard of him before the trial.

Hitler's stay in the Landsberg prison, fifty miles west of Munich along the River Lech, was more a holiday than an ordeal. He had a large room instead of a cell, plenty of good food, magazines, books and newspapers to read, and could receive visitors whenever he wished. Among his visitors were Frau Bechstein and Frau Bruckmann, both of whom ignored the stigma of visiting a prisoner despite their prominent social positions. Frau Bruckmann was particularly generous with her gifts of food and money while Hitler was in Landsberg. Frau Bechstein did everything she could to make his stay comfortable. His room was usually crowded with chocolates, fruit, flowers, wine and other presents. Winifred Wagner, the wife of Siegfried Wagner and daughter-in-law of the composer Richard Wagner, who was extravagantly admired by Hitler, was another frequent visitor at Landsberg. In 1924 she was just another follower of the Nazi Party leader, but later, as Eva Braun learned to her despair, she became much more.

Hitler served less than a year in prison. He was released a few days before Christmas, 1924, and immediately returned to Munich. While in prison he had written his political biography, *Mein Kampf,* which eventually became an international bestseller. Using this book as a blueprint for his struggle, Hitler continued his efforts to gain control of Bavaria. His parole terms prohibited him from making public speeches so he spent most of his time personally contacting loyal followers and seeking new members for the party. At no time did he forget to court his female benefactors and later it was estimated that Frau Bruckmann and Frau Bechstein between them poured as much as twenty-five million gold marks into the Nazi treasury. The money was badly needed because the party had lost its momentum while Hitler was in Landsberg, and the Bavarian government, fearful that he might once again try to seize power, had placed severe restrictions on his organization. These obstacles did not deter Hitler, however. Using a new supercharged Mercedes-Benz which cost the party twenty-eight thousand marks, he traveled constantly during these postprison years, making the contacts that would eventually lead him to the Chancellery in Berlin. He must have passed the Braun home at 93 Hohenzollernstrasse many times during these years, but if he saw young Eva playing on the street he certainly took no notice of her.

One of the predominant criticisms directed at Hitler during this period from both outside and inside the party was that homosexuality was rampant among Nazi leaders. While Hitler himself was not accused, and his friendships with Frau Bechstein, Frau Bruckmann and other prominent women, plus some who were not so prominent, were well known, many of his associates were notorious homosexuals. Captain Ernst Röhm, the Nazi connection with the Reichswehr, had been publicly chastised in the German newspapers for his 'peculiarities', which he revealed in several letters to a friend while in Bolivia. In these letters Röhm had complained that he was lonely and 'in La Paz they know nothing of this kind of love'. Every newspaper opposing the Nazis published the letters but Hitler remained a strong supporter of the army officer, calling the articles 'disgusting and dirty slander'. Another officer, Lieutenant Edmund Heines of the SA, was a homosexual, as were many of his associates. Hitler defended them all, saying that when a fight was in the offing these men were the bravest of his supporters. He had no illusions about their reputations but he was confident of their value to the party and to his ambitions.

'Such elements are unusable in time of peace but in turbulent periods it is quite different. During the war they fought with the bayonet and the handgrenade. They wouldn't permit the country to be sold out to the scum who were the product of defeat. From the beginning I knew that one could make a party only with elements like that,' he said.

He himself continued to pursue women, and not all those he met were prominent or wealthy. Jenny Haug, a party chauffeur's sister who worked in a toy shop near the Viktualien Markt, was one of the young girls Hitler spent time with for reasons other than filling the Nazi treasury with gold marks. She was slim, dark-haired and beautiful, an adventurous young woman who was thrilled to be associated with the radical politician who was challenging the established government of Bavaria. Jenny was deeply in love with Hitler – or thought she was – and after they had been friends for a period she decided she had a duty to protect him as well as entertain him. So one night she showed up wearing a small pistol in an armpit holster. 'I will be your body-guard,' she announced to the startled Hitler.

Their 'romance' ended shortly after that incident. Hitler had no intentions of associating with any woman who carried a gun regardless of how attractive she was!

There were others, such as Mathilde von Kemnitz, who later became the second wife of General Erich Ludendorff. When she insisted that persons of Nordic blood (meaning Scandinavians) were superior to all others, Hitler's personal interest in her waned. Later, however, he used her friendship as an aid in getting Luden-dorff to collaborate with him on certain political intrigues. For a time he visited former schoolteacher Carola Hoffmann in the Munich suburb of Solln quite often, but all he received from her were kind words and homemade cookies. Additional 'passing fancies' absorbed a great deal of his time and he was often criticized by his associates because he spent long hours with attractive or influential women. But Hitler ignored their com-plaints. He knew exactly what he was doing, and in a conversation with Hanfstängl in 1923 he explained his tactics: 'Do you know the audience at a circus is just like a woman? Someone who does not understand the intrinsically feminine character of the masses will never be an effective speaker. Ask yourself: "What does a woman expect from a man?" Clearness, decision, power, and action. What we want is to get the masses to act. Like a woman, the masses fluctuate between extremes. The crowd is not only like a woman, but women constitute the most important element in an audience. The women usually lead, then follow the children, and at last, when I have already won over the whole family, follow the fathers.'

At approximately the same time that Fritz and Fanny Braun sent Eva to the convent school at Simbach, Hitler rented a villa, Haus Wachenfeld, on the Obersalzberg. The rent was a hundred marks a month and Frau Bechstein provided most of the money. Later she and her husband built a home nearby. Haus Wachen-feld was a modest wooden house with a wide overhanging roof. The dining room, small living room and three bedrooms were all furnished in the German peasant style. The view from the north-east slope of the mountains overlooking the Salzburg plain was magnificent. At the foot of the mountain was the village of Berchtesgaden, and on the other side of the peak was the Königssee, a mecca for swimmers and boaters. Since Hitler stayed at Haus Wachenfeld often, he needed someone to look after it for him. His choice for this duty nearly ended his political career.

Angela Raubal was the only member of his family that Hitler kept in contact with, although he did not see her often until he rented the house on the Obersalzberg. She was his half-sister, six years older than he and a widow. When Hitler's friend Putzi Hanfstängl visited her home in Vienna during the early 1920s and saw the abject poverty she and her daughter Geli were living in, he suggested to Hitler that he do something to help her. Hitler's answer was to bring the pair to Haus Wachenfeld.

Geli Raubal was a vivacious, buxom, blue-eyed blonde who caused men's heads to turn when she entered a room. Before long, Hitler's head turned too, and his trips to the Obersalzberg became more and more frequent. When he decided to move to the luxurious apartment on Prinzregentenstrasse in 1929 he made certain that the bedroom next to his was reserved for Geli, the same arrangement he had had at Haus Wachenfeld.

A few blocks away, in the photography shop where she worked, seventeen-year-old Eva Braun heard her new employer tell a friend about Hitler's new residence and the pretty 'niece' who lived there with him.

3
The Meeting

For a reason he never adequately explained, Adolf Hitler
changed his living habits drastically in 1929. Prior to
this time he had stayed in a sparsely furnished two-room
apartment, spent little money on clothes, and lived
quietly and abstemiously. In 1929, however, his attitude
toward luxury changed. He moved into a large, plush
apartment on Prinzregentenstrasse, one of Munich's
most fashionable streets, bought a new and expensive
wardrobe, acquired a fleet of modern automobiles and
hired twelve people to take care of his living quarters
and his belongings.

One of the frequent visitors to Hitler's new apartment on Prinz-regentenstrasse was Heinrich Hoffmann. Hoffmann was undoubtedly the best known photographer in Munich in 1929. His close association with Hitler and the Nazi Party had earned him large sums of money and prestige, but this was not his only source of revenue. He periodically published illustrated books such as *A Year of Revolution in Bavaria*, which brought him a gross profit of half a million marks. He also was in demand by wealthy and socially conscious Germans who wanted their photographs taken by 'Hitler's photographer'. By 1929 he had branch studios in Berlin, Vienna, Frankfurt, Paris and The Hague and employed more than a hundred persons. His wife, who had been a great help to him, had died during the flu epidemic that swept Munich in 1928, and by the time Eva Braun applied for a job at his Schellingstrasse studio he desperately needed an assistant. Not so desperately, however, that he didn't appraise the young girl for more than the mere ability to handle a clerking job. Hoffmann considered himself an expert judge of feminine beauty and most of his female employees had been selected as much for their appearance as their work habits and abilities. He was attracted to the young, naïve Eva immediately. In some ways she reminded him of his daughter Henriette, who, he discovered later, was only three days older than Eva. He hired Eva at a small salary and she went to work the following day in his studio.

Eva was delighted with her new position. Her commercial studies at the Catholic Young Women's Institute qualified her for bookkeeping chores, but within a few weeks she was doing a variety of tasks for Hoffmann. She clerked, inventoried stock, ran errands and even learned how to develop film. She enjoyed this work in the darkroom more than any of her other assignments and became very proficient at it. During the remainder of her life she was an avid amateur photographer and always developed her own pictures. Since she worked long hours in the studio, usually in close proximity to Hoffmann, she soon learned about politics and the struggle that was in progress in Bavaria and Germany for control of the government. She noticed the attention Hoffmann paid to certain of his clients when they appeared at the studio to have their photographs taken, but thought it was because they were wealthy and their business added to his already substantial bank account. Instead, she learned later, they were associates of Adolf Hitler, one of the politicians trying to gain control of Bavaria. The names Rosenberg, Hess, Bormann, Himmler and Goebbels meant nothing to her; neither did the name Adolf

Hitler. Politics was not one of Eva's interests in 1929.

Hoffmann, on the other hand, was vitally interested in Hitler. He was well aware that most of the success he had enjoyed during the past few years was the direct result of his close association with Hitler and he had no intention of permitting this association to deteriorate. He was convinced that Hitler's political platform would eventually lead him to power in Bavaria, and when his friend reached that pinnacle Hoffmann wanted to be at his side. Consequently he plotted every move in his progressing friendship with Hitler as carefully as Hitler himself plotted his political path to power. Hoffmann made certain that every photograph he showed to Hitler was flattering; the negatives of unflattering pictures were destroyed before they left the studio. He would travel across Germany at a moment's notice on an assignment if Hitler requested it. If Hitler was in Munich, Hoffmann made certain that he went to the Café Heck, Hitler's favorite restaurant at the time, to have lunch with him. He knew that the more often he was included in Hitler's intimate circle, the more influence he would have. There was one other duty he performed for Hitler from time to time, a duty Hitler never directly requested but appreciated nonetheless. Hoffmann kept a list of attractive women whom he could introduce to his friend whenever Hitler was lonely or bored or both.

There had been a lull in this particular activity ever since Geli Raubal had moved into Hitler's apartment, so the rotund photographer was mildly surprised when he noticed Hitler staring at his new employee one day, several weeks after she started to work in his studio. Hitler was an infrequent visitor to the studio in the latter part of 1929 because he was engrossed in politics, and it took Hoffmann a minute or two to realize that this was the first time he had seen Eva. The timing could not have been better as far as Hoffmann was concerned because he felt that Hitler's interest in him had waned recently and he needed something to reawaken his friend's appreciation of his worth to him. A new woman would be an ideal contribution!

Eva was standing near the top of a ladder getting a box of film from one of the high shelves when Hitler first noticed her. Hoffmann watched his eyes slowly move up her slim legs, appraise her rounded but firm hips, and finally center on her neatly brushed hair. He could tell that Hitler was eager to see her face so he called to the girl.

'Come down, Eva, I want you to run an errand.'

She looked back over her shoulder at Hoffmann and the man

standing beside him and smiled at them both. Hoffmann saw immediately that Hitler was delighted with Eva's appearance, that he was interested. He watched her come down the ladder, but as soon as she touched the floor and headed toward them, Hitler pretended to be busy looking at some photographs on the counter.

'Run across the street and get us some *Leberkaes* and beer,' Hoffmann told Eva, handing her a few marks. 'Herr Wolf enjoys a second breakfast about this time in the morning.'

Leberkaes was a Bavarian sausage that Hoffmann loved. He knew that Hitler wouldn't eat the sausage or drink the beer, since he didn't like either, but he wanted an excuse to introduce the girl to him. Hitler, ever conscious of his image, would resent associating in public with a mere 'clerk', unless he had a logical excuse to do so. The sausages and beer provided a legitimate reason for him to join Eva and Hoffmann at the small table in the back of the studio, where he could become acquainted with the young girl at leisure.

'*Ja.*' Eva looked at the man standing beside Hoffmann, smiled and turned away.

Hoffmann was disappointed. He had anticipated that Eva would be overjoyed to meet the celebrated Hitler, and when she didn't even change expression it puzzled him. He finally decided that she was confused because he had called Hitler by the pseudonym 'Herr Wolf', which Hitler often used in Munich during this period because the Bavarian government had restricted his actions. The photographer didn't understand that the man he idolized meant nothing to Eva Braun.

When she returned a few minutes later with the beer and sausages, Hoffmann invited her to join Hitler and himself at the small table. Eva took the chair next to Hitler and accepted a small glass of beer and two of the sausages. Hitler tried to hold a casual conversation with her but he sounded stiff and formal. He was always unable to engage in light banter with anyone, male or female. Fortunately, Eva could and did. With unusual tact for a girl her age, she quickly realized that the 'old man' sitting beside her was attempting to be friendly but didn't know how to go about it, so she took over. At that moment she had no real interest in the stranger except that he was a client of her employer, and what was good for her employer was indirectly good for her. She told Hitler about an incident that had occurred earlier in the morning when she had been trying to get another box of film down from one of the high shelves and had accidentally knocked it off the shelf. It had fallen on Hoffmann's cat, which, frightened, scurried toward the main door, reaching the entrance just as a bakery clerk carrying bread for Hoffmann entered. The cat knocked the feet out from under the boy, who promptly fell head-long into a display of camera tripods. The way she described the scene made the usually sober-faced Hitler laugh and the tension was broken. Hoffmann encouraged her to tell more stories, and by the time the sausages and beer had disappeared, they were all laughing and enjoying the conversation. Hitler relaxed as he and Eva talked about a play at the Staatstheater, about music they both enjoyed and American movies.

After Hitler left the studio Hoffmann called Eva aside and asked, 'Do you know that man?'

'Herr Wolf? All I know is that he is a friend of yours, Herr Hoffmann.'

The photographer smiled and shook his head. 'His name is not really Herr Wolf. That is Adolf Hitler!'

Once again Hoffmann was disappointed. Eva gave no indica-tion that she had ever heard of Adolf Hitler before that moment.

'Who is Adolf Hitler?'

Hoffmann was mystified how anyone in Munich – or in all of Bavaria, for that matter – could be ignorant of the importance of Adolf Hitler. He just shook his head and walked away. The young girl watched him go and frowned. She couldn't understand why he was so upset with her.

Hitler was indeed well known in Bavaria in 1929. The number of due-paying members of the Nazi Party had reached nearly 180,000 and was increasing rapidly. Besides the party members who spread the name of Adolf Hitler across the country into every small village, Dr Joseph Goebbels had been appointed Minister of Propaganda in 1928 for the express purpose of publicizing Hitler's name. He was an excellent choice. The son of a factory foreman and a blacksmith's daughter, Goebbels was born in the town of Rheydt in 1897, eight years after Hitler. His parents were devout Catholics and as a boy Goebbels attended Catholic schools. Since he had a deformed foot, he was rejected for military service in World War I, so he took advantage of a number of Catholic scholarships and attended eight famous Ger-man universities – Freiburg, Cologne, Berlin, Würzburg, Munich, Bonn, Frankfurt and Heidelberg. At Heidelberg he majored in art, history and literature, and took his Ph.D. degree in 1921. After one unsuccessful novel and two unsuccessful plays Goeb-bels tried to obtain a job as a reporter on a Berlin newspaper, the *Berliner Tageblatt*, but he failed in this also. A year after his graduation from Heidelberg he heard Adolf Hitler speak at a rally in Munich and for the first time in his life he discovered a cause that really excited him. Immediately he attempted to interest university students in the message of Nazism and thus discovered his own gift for public speaking. It was a talent that he used to good advantage for himself and Hitler until they both died.

Despite the growing importance of the Nazi Party and the excellent propaganda work of Goebbels, Eva was unimpressed by Hitler when they first met. She thought his slouch hat and small mustache made him appear comical and she was critical of the fit of his suit. The collar of the jacket extended out from the back of his neck nearly an inch and she compared him to a 'turtle sticking its head out of its shell'. Yet she couldn't forget the look in his eyes when he stared at her in the studio. It wasn't their color (they were a deep blue) but their hypnotic quality that impressed her. Hitler's eyes had the same effect on many others in Bavaria; even enemies had capitulated when they met him because of his strangely affective eyes. Eva still hadn't forgotten his stare when she reached the Braun apartment that evening.

'*Vati*,' she asked Fritz Braun that night at the dinner table, 'who is Adolf Hitler?'

That was the wrong question to ask in the Braun household in 1929. Fritz Braun considered Hitler a fanatic and was opposed to most of his political program. Fanny Braun's father, who often visited the Braun apartment in Munich, was violently opposed to the Nazi doctrines and he had convinced Fritz that of all politicians on the Bavarian scene in 1929, Adolf Hitler was the worst. A personal matter made Eva's father dislike Hitler and the Nazi Party even more. He had been proposed for promotion to assistant master of the technical school where he taught, but when the school officials learned that he was not a member of the Nazi Party they refused to recommend him for the advancement. Fritz Braun had always disliked politics and after this rebuff he was really disgusted. So when Eva innocently mentioned Hitler's name at the dinner table that evening, her father exploded.

'Hitler? I would not walk on the same side of the street with him. He is a fanatic!'

Realizing the question had irritated her father, Eva dropped the subject immediately and began talking about other matters with her mother. But her father's angry remarks had made her curious to learn more about the man with the 'slouch hat and little mustache'. The following day, instead of going to a nearby café for lunch, she stayed in the studio and studied the photograph file on

Adolf Hitler. Hoffmann had the largest picture collection of Hitler in existence, mainly because he was the official photographer and had an exclusive franchise to sell Hitler's pictures to outside sources. Eva was fascinated by the file photographs. Some of the pictures showed women trying to break through guard lines to touch him, throwing flowers in his path, reaching for him as he passed in his Mercedes-Benz. There were photographs of him at the theater and the opera with glamorous actresses and fashionably dressed older women who were obviously wealthy and influential. In some of the photographs Hitler had exchanged his slouch hat for a top hat; in others he wore a uniform and brightly polished boots. By the time her lunch hour was over and she had finished examining the file, Eva had revised her opinion of Hitler. She realized now that he was much more than a slightly comical 'old man' who enjoyed talking with young girls. He was a celebrity. She hoped he would come to the studio again.

Hitler was extremely busy in 1929, however, and his visits to Hoffmann's were rare. Now firmly established in Bavarian politics, this year he had his first opportunity to break into the national scene and become famous throughout Germany. The Allies had agreed to renegotiate the reparations settlement first outlined by the Dawes Plan of 1924 and Hitler saw a chance to oppose the German Chancellor, Gustav Stresemann. He recognized that Stresemann was in a difficult position, that regardless of what settlement he obtained during the conference – unless reparations were canceled completely, which was improbable – the German people would complain. That was exactly what occurred. After long talks with a committee of financial experts under the chairmanship of an American banker named Owen D. Young, Stresemann agreed to their terms, which required the German government to pay a reduced amount of reparations yearly for the next fifty-nine years. He gained one small victory when he was able to get the French to agree to start withdrawing their forces from the Occupied Rhineland immediately and to complete the evacuation by the end of June, 1930.

Hitler immediately moved in with propaganda forces headed by Goebbels and himself, determined to use the issues generated by the Young Plan to overthrow or damage the Stresemann administration. He was joined in the fight by Alfred Hugenberg, a German nationalist who had large financial resources at his disposal. The Hitler-Hugenberg alliance, one partner providing the mass support, the other the money, conducted a hard fight against the Young Plan but lost when the Reichstag approved the plan on

March 12, 1930, and President Paul von Hindenburg signed it the following day. This defeat was not nearly as serious for Hitler as it was for Hugenberg, who, as part of the establishment, lost a great deal of prestige. During the six months he had agitated against the terms of the reparations, Hitler's name became known to millions of Germans who had never paid any attention to him previously. His speeches were carried in all the important newspapers of the country and over most of the radio stations. Among those most adamantly opposed to the Young Plan were the owners of German heavy industry, and they were pleased with the way this new radical Adolf Hitler had agitated their enemies. They decided to back him financially if he would cooperate with them, and in 1929 Hitler needed money for the Nazi Party badly enough to quickly agree to their terms. He knew that once he was in power he could do exactly as he pleased without worrying about any promises he had made to the industrialists.

Eva saw very little of Hitler during this period but it hardly mattered to her, for aside from his 'celebrity' status, he was of little interest to her. She had inquired discreetly about his age and discovered that he was forty, which in her seventeen-year-old mind made him an 'old man'. The young men who came into Hoffmann's studio and flirted with her were much more lively and able to offer her the fun she was always seeking, so by the time Hitler visited the studio the second time she had nearly forgotten him. Not until he stopped at the counter directly in front of her and spoke did the vivid memory of his eyes come back to her. She looked up directly into his eyes and for a moment she was confused.

'Is Herr Hoffmann in the studio?'

After she summoned the photographer from the darkroom, Hoffmann and Hitler went into a back room of the studio and she returned to her task of inventorying the items stored under the counter. Both men emerged from the room an hour later. Hitler bowed slightly in her direction and walked out the front entrance to the Mercedes-Benz waiting for him. Hoffmann watched him drive away and then joined Eva at the counter.

'I would like to have you come to the house tonight, Eva,' he said. 'Hitler is going to stop by and he asked that you come too.'

That evening at Hoffmann's house in the Schnorrstrasse was the first of many for Hitler and Eva. Hoffmann's home was one of Hitler's favorite hideaways during this period in his life, a place where he could find the type of relaxation and repose he sought. With Eva at his side that first evening, he prowled through the house examining the medals and diplomas that Hoffmann had earned during his career. There was the gold medal awarded to him by the South German Photographic Association, the King Gustav of Sweden gold medal, the Great Silver Medal of Bugra and many others, all of which impressed young Eva. Since Hoffmann had once been determined to be a great painter, he had a large number of books dealing with art. Hitler, who had also wanted to be a painter, was fascinated by them.

'At one time I was a pupil of Professor Heinrich Knirr's Academy,' Hoffmann explained to both Eva and Hitler. 'Unfortunately my father had other ideas and insisted that I should adopt the profession of photography and prepare myself to take over the family business.'

Eva listened to the photographer and Hitler discuss art, and she who knew little or nothing about the subject was fascinated by their obvious knowledge. She was only seventeen but that night she learned a lesson many women do not acquire in a lifetime. She learned that if she was going to attract the interest of men she would have to study their likes and dislikes and cater to their obsessions, compliment them on their accomplishments and comfort them when they needed comforting . . . or whatever the particular moment demanded. She was at a loss during the conversation about Hoffmann's art books but she made up for it by telling Hitler about her examination of the file of photographs in the studio dealing with his political career. She emphasized how the women of Germany were attracted to him. To say that Hitler was pleased by her remarks is an understatement.

'My bride is Germany,' he told her. This was a statement that he was to make many times during his life. Eva was not exactly certain what he meant, but Hoffmann, who understood that Hitler was saying he would never marry because his country took the place of a wife in his heart, protested: 'Herr Hitler, you have but to make your choice. No woman, I'm sure, would turn you down.'

Hitler just smiled, took Eva by the arm and walked away.

The smile was meant to indicate to Hoffmann that while the photographer's appraisal of his appeal was obviously correct, Hitler had no intentions of making such a choice. What Hoffmann and many others who knew Hitler well at this time did not realize was that he had already selected a woman who pleased him more than any other – Geli Raubal, his niece, who was living at his Prinzregentenstrasse apartment.

Eva knew nothing about Geli Raubal. In fact, if anyone had

told her that night that Hitler had a young mistress she would have thought him completely crazy, although her impression of the man she had once thought comical had changed considerably. Talking and listening to him at Hoffmann's home that first night, she learned a great deal about him personally. Yet he certainly did not seem to be the type who would have a young mistress. She noticed that when her employer told one of his usual vulgar stories, Hitler blushed and tried to guide her out of the room before Hoffmann completed the joke. Eva was amused. She had heard most of the stories many times before at the studio and they didn't embarrass her in the least, but it was obvious they embarrassed Hitler. Later she was to learn that though he enjoyed obscene stories and pornography of all kinds, he didn't believe women should listen to such stories in public. Privately was another matter.

After their first meeting in Hoffmann's home, Hitler often requested the photographer to arrange other meetings with Eva. Hoffmann told Hitler's personal adjutant Julius Schaub that he thought Hitler was interested in the young girl.

'Often when he intends to stop at our house for an hour or so he suggests that I ask Eva to come over because she amuses him,' the photographer said. 'At other times when we are at the Café Heck, he will ask me to give her a ring at the studio and tell her that he is going to stop by and talk to her.'

Schaub just smiled and insisted that Eva meant very little to Hitler. The adjutant was well aware of Geli's presence in Hitler's apartment and what was going on between 'uncle and niece'.

Despite his affair with Geli, however, Hitler continued to see Eva and sent her flowers, candy and trinkets of modest value. Hoffmann had mixed emotions about the growing friendship between his employee and his idol. If the relationship developed into a permanent association, he knew that Hitler would remember who had introduced him to Eva and be grateful. On the other hand, he had hoped that Hitler would fall in love with his daughter Henriette. 'Henny', as she was known to her friends, had inherited many of her father's less desirable traits and by the time she was seventeen was spending a great deal of time among the male students at the University of Munich. According to reports that reached her father, she was teaching some of these boys gymnastics they had never heard of before but were delighted to learn. After Henny's mother died in 1928 Hoffmann's apartment had become a kind of gathering place for men and women who believed in hard drinking and sexual freedom. While neither had

46

been going on the night when Eva first visited the apartment, Hitler had attended some of the earlier gatherings, where he had met Henny. At first he had seemed attracted to her and Henny, urged on by her father, had been ready to reciprocate to the fullest extent. But after a short time Hitler had lost interest. When the despondent Hoffmann tried to discover what had gone wrong, Henny wasn't of much help. She vowed she had tried to please Hitler in every way possible but that he, after a platonic kiss or two, had turned away from her. The most affection he showed toward her was to call her *mein Sonnenschein*. Hoffmann then asked Ernst Hanfstängl why Hitler had rebuffed Henny.

Hanfstängl, who had watched Hitler's brief attempt to become friendly with his sister Erna, had definite ideas about Hitler's sexual ability, but in 1929, while he was still a member of the intimate circle, had no intention of making these ideas public. He merely shrugged his shoulders when questioned by Hoffmann and muttered, 'Perhaps he concentrates too much on politics to be interested in women.'

Privately, however, Hanfstängl called Hitler 'the barren hero'. Both he and his wife had observed Hitler squirm out of situations where women had literally invited him to go to bed with them. More than once this had happened in their own home, where privacy was assured, but Hitler would only cooperate to a certain point and then excuse himself. He seemed to fear that once he got his clothes off he would be useless. Yet Hanfstängl had heard some sordid stories from women who had slept with Hitler about how he had acted toward them when they were alone, heard them vow that the man was both a sadist and a masochist. He believed the stories but he did not repeat them to Hoffmann.

The photographer finally decided that Henny was not going to become Hitler's wife and concentrated on promoting Eva as the woman Hitler needed, hoping that if she did become his mistress he would get a justified reward from his idol.

4
The Affair

*Hitler had considerable cause for satisfaction during
1930 and 1931 despite various setbacks. Party
membership had reached 400,000 by the end of 1930.
Less than a year later, on October 17, 1931, the Nazis
held a rally at Brunswick and for six hours more than
100,000 of Hitler's SA and SS men passed the
reviewing stand and returned his salute. Forty special
trains and five hundred trucks brought party members
to the city. That same night a large torchlight parade
illuminated the countryside. President Paul von
Hindenburg knew that his supporters couldn't match
this show of strength.*

In his private life Hitler was not doing so well. His main problem was Angela Maria Raubal. Known to her friends as Geli, this blonde voluptuous daughter of Hitler's half-sister was both the source of his happiest hours and the cause of his deepest despair. Until he met Eva Braun at Hoffmann's photography studio Hitler had spent as much of his leisure time as possible with Geli. This wasn't difficult since he had made certain that she had personal quarters on both his Prinzregentenstrasse apartment in Munich and his house on the Obersalzberg.

The apartment in Munich was divided into two wings: Hitler lived in one, and Geli supposedly lived in the other. Actually she stayed near Hitler's bedroom in a room luxuriously furnished with antiques from Austria, several paintings (including one Hitler had painted during World War I), an expensive radio-phonograph with a huge supply of records, bedroom furniture with painted motifs, and embroidered sheets. Hitler's bedroom, down a long corridor from Geli's, was smaller, although it too was well appointed. Geli's mother slept in a room across from the anteroom to her daughter's chamber and the two shared a bath-room, while Hitler had his own bathroom adjoining his sleeping quarters. The apartment also included a reception room, a dining room and a library. Frau Annie Winter and her husband, who had formerly been valet to an army general, managed the servants, while Hitler's half-sister was in charge of the entire operation of the household.

In 1930, Geli was twenty-two years old, four years older than Eva, but she looked younger. When she first joined the Hitler household at Haus Wachenfeld with her mother, Geli was a skinny adolescent who attracted little attention from her uncle. Later she developed into a zestful young woman, pretty enough to stand out among the lovely women of Munich. And Hitler was not the last to notice. After acquiring the Prinzregentenstrasse apartment he made certain that she and her mother moved to Munich from the Obersalzberg. Her gaiety and beauty were exactly what he needed to rejuvenate him after the sober politics he spent most of his time on, and he was intelligent enough to understand this need in himself. He was also intelligent enough to understand that party members and others whose support he needed so badly during this period would frown on his living alone with a young girl, even if he did claim her as a relative. This was why he insisted his half-sister also move into the Munich apartment. Of course, he would much rather have left Geli's mother back on the Obersalzberg, but he was supremely conscious of his public image and wanted the citizens of Bavaria and Germany to believe that their welfare was always uppermost in his mind, that he had no time to waste on private love affairs.

Still there was grumbling among the party members about Geli, and Hitler was forced to invent a better rationale for her presence in his apartment than that he needed the housekeeping services of her mother. Geli was interested in a musical career, which Hitler had originally opposed. But now he decided that if he could convince the party members she had come to Munich to study music and that he only permitted her to live in his apartment because she didn't have money for lodgings elsewhere, it might quiet the rumors about their relationship. He arranged for her to start singing lessons with a party member named Adolf Vogel who had taught Bertha Morena, a well-known opera singer. Vogel did his best but he finally admitted to Hitler that Geli refused to take her voice studies seriously, seldom practiced what he told her to practice and lacked the talent to become an opera singer anyway. Hitler, furious, withdrew her from Vogel's studio and asked Hans Streck, another well known voice instructor, to take over Geli's training. Streck had formerly been an adjutant to General Ludendorff and knew Hitler well so he promised to do his best. Geli visited his studio in the Gedonstrasse, not far from the English Gardens, twelve times a month.

Hitler often visited the studio too and listened to her sing, but as the months passed it became obvious that she was not going to have an opera career. Streck took his money and kept his mouth shut concerning her ability, waiting for the day when Hitler would ask for a progress report. The request never came and it became apparent to him that Hitler knew Geli had no talent. Since he didn't know the real reason for the lessons in the first place, he was puzzled that Hitler continued to spend money on her training.

This subterfuge fooled few people besides Streck and the rumors about Hitler's real relationship with his attractive young niece continued. By the beginning of 1931 it was common knowledge in Munich that Hitler and Geli were having an affair that had the unpleasant suggestion of incest. They appeared together at social functions and Hitler made no attempt to hide his affection for her. Hanfstängl and his wife were at the Residenz Theatre one evening when they saw Hitler and Geli standing in one of the side galleries during intermission. When Frau Hanfstängl saw Hitler affectionately kiss the young girl on the cheek, she looked at her husband in surprise. 'A barren hero?' she asked mockingly.

There was little Hanfstängl could say in rebuttal. He had never seen Hitler act affectionately toward a woman before and he was puzzled. Had he underestimated Hitler's capabilities and desires? He wasn't the only one who was puzzled about Hitler's sex life.

One of Goebbels' greatest achievements during the years he was Hitler's propaganda expert was to project to the world an 'Ascetic Adolf'. Goebbels convinced the Bavarians, the Germans and the outside world that Hitler didn't smoke, that he despised alcohol and that he was not interested in women. Except for the smoking, Hitler was not an abstainer from any of these pleasures. His relationship with women, however, was the most misunderstood. In 1930 – and until his death – many party members and supporters believed that he had no interest in women except for their ability, financial or otherwise, to advance his political career. Goebbels studiously promoted this image. When he arranged for John Gunther, the celebrated journalist, to interview Hitler, he briefed Hitler so well prior to the meeting that Gunther went away with an altogether erroneous impression of Hitler's private life. It is easy to understand how both journalists and the German people were duped. The only sources of information about his private life were Hitler himself and his designated spokesman Goebbels. Those intimates who knew the public image was absurd had no desire to correct it, and even if they had, they would have been afraid to because they would have lost their 'favorite' status with Hitler and been banished. Consequently, Hitler's private life was a mystery during his lifetime and for a long time afterward. It was many years before the survivors of the Third Reich who knew the truth about the Führer's personal life overcame the fear that had been instilled in them during his reign of power and spoke out.

Gunther, along with many others, was completely misled by Hitler's public actions. Since he stated that Hitler was totally uninterested in women from a personal or sexual point of view, he obviously did not know about Hitler's relationship with either Geli or Eva. Gunther actually believed that Hitler never went beyond hand-kissing, that when he met women he screeched politics at the top of his voice until he was exhausted and then walked away. About the only correct statement he made in this area was that Hitler definitely was not a homosexual!

Hanfstängl, as already noted, considered Hitler unorthodox sexually, neither homosexual nor heterosexual. He firmly believed that Hitler was impotent, a repressed masturbating type who was incapable of a normal reaction with a woman. Several times he had arranged for Hitler to meet beautiful, willing women and on each occasion the results had been disappointing, both to Hanfstängl and the woman. After he saw how Hitler acted toward Geli at the theater that night, however, he did some additional investigating and changed his opinion to some degree. He remained convinced that Hitler was incapable of normal intercourse but decided that he was having an affair of some type with his niece. The only definite conclusion he came to at that time was that Hitler was a sadomasochist. He dared not become too inquisitive, knowing that if Hitler became suspicious of him it might cost him his life. The proof he sought, however, came to him one day when he happened to meet Franz Schwarz, the party treasurer, on the street in Munich and Schwarz invited him to his apartment for a cup of coffee. Hanfstängl was in a hurry and declined but the older man insisted. Seeing that Schwarz was upset about something, Hanfstängl decided to humor him.

As soon as Schwarz's wife had served them the coffee and left the room, the treasurer opened a desk drawer and pulled out a portfolio. 'Look at this.'

Hanfstängl opened the portfolio and was amazed to see several pornographic sketches. They had been drawn by Hitler and were of Geli, showing every detail of her body and revealing her in varied poses for which only a sadist would ask a girl to model. When he asked Schwarz where he had obtained the sketches, the treasurer explained that he had been forced to pay a large sum of money out of the party treasury to a man who had somehow stolen them and was threatening to blackmail Hitler. Hanfstängl took another look at the sketches and then returned them to Schwarz. His suspicion that Hitler was a sadomasochist was confirmed. Whether Geli was a willing or unwilling accomplice was debatable.

Later Hanfstängl, now more observant of Hitler's attitude toward women and sex than he had been before seeing the sketches, noticed that Hitler could hardly wait for the next edition of *Der Stürmer* to appear. He greatly enjoyed the obscene stories and cartoons that appeared in this sheet. In addition, Hitler insisted on more and more lewd films for his private projection room, many of which were provided by Hoffmann.

Next to Goebbels, Hoffmann was the man most instrumental in concealing the facts about Hitler's private life. Every photograph taken of Hitler was studied carefully, not only by the photographer and his assistants before it was shown to Hitler, but also by Hitler himself before he permitted it to be distributed. Only the image that Hitler wanted the public to have of him was depicted in these photographs. Naturally, pictures that would have revealed his love affairs were taboo. Hoffmann knew as much about the details of the Geli-Hitler affair as anyone, perhaps more, but, loyal subject that he was, he constantly tried to white-wash his idol and it wasn't until many years after Hitler's death that he told what he knew. Even then he tried to minimize the sordid affair and to place the blame for Geli's tragic ending on the events of history and everyone but Hitler. He did admit, however, that for a time Hitler was in love with his niece. Hoffmann learned this truth when he and Max Amann, the business manager of the party, escorted Geli to a Shrovetide Ball in Munich's Deutsches Theatre with Hitler's permission. When Geli asked if she could attend the ball, Hitler at first refused to permit her to go, saying that he was only trying to protect her from corruption. Finally he relented and ordered his two friends, Hoffmann and Amann, to take her. Even then, he ordered them to bring her home promptly at eleven o'clock. To the hard-drinking, woman-chasing Hoffmann eleven o'clock was more like the start of an evening than the quitting time, but he had no choice.

Hoffmann asked Ingo Schröder, a famous dress designer, to provide a gown for the young girl, but when Hitler saw the sketch of the proposed dress he was angry and refused to allow Geli to wear it because the front was much 'too low'. The ordinary evening gown she ended up wearing in no way inhibited the fun-loving Geli, and when it came time to leave the ball at eleven o'clock, Hoffmann and Amann had a difficult time convincing the champagne-filled girl to abide by her uncle's deadline. They finally managed to get her back to the apartment on Prinz-regentenstrasse without a public scene, but because Hoffmann sympathized with her he told Hitler the following day that he thought he was being overprotective and restricted the girl's actions too much.

Hitler promptly and sharply told Hoffmann that he intended to keep Geli under his personal supervision, that he considered her the personification of perfect young womanhood – unspoiled, gay, and clean – and he was going to make certain that no lecherous male destroyed 'her rare and lovely bloom'. He declared that in his own way he loved Geli and felt duty-bound to watch over her.

There is ample evidence that, contrary to general belief, Geli was as agreeable to the affair as Hitler. She was a sexually aggressive young girl who flirted with every man she met and went to bed with some of them if she thought her uncle would not catch her. The 'prisoner-in-the-room' theory that has existed through the years has no real basis. Frau Winter, Hitler's housekeeper, has verified that Geli had her own key to the room, that she was free to come and go as she pleased. Geli traveled back and forth alone between her voice instructor's studio and the apartment quite often, and if she had decided to take a train to Vienna, as many say she wanted to, there was really nothing to stop her. Hitler always provided her with ample money for the best clothes and jewelry and other things she wanted, so it would have been easy for her to buy a train ticket. The truth is she didn't want to leave Hitler, for she was delighted with the celebrity status of her uncle, which permitted her to bask in the limelight too. While Hitler was not nearly as famous as he would be in later years after he gained power in Berlin, even in 1930 and 1931 the public was noticing him and his companions. Geli loved this attention and was willing to put up with his demands, sexual or otherwise, to keep it.

Ada Dort, who became acquainted with Geli when they both took voice lessons from Adolf Vogel, remembers her as a devil-may-care girl who had no special interest in singing but talked continually about the men she knew.

'After we became better friends,' Frau Dort explained, 'Geli told me about her uncle and how he gave her expensive gifts whenever she was "nice" to him. When I learned that her uncle was Adolf Hitler, the radical politician, I warned her she was asking for trouble. Geli just laughed at me. She said she could wind him around her little finger when she was alone with him.'

A former SA officer who guarded Hitler's apartment, Wilhelm Stocker, agreed wholeheartedly with Frau Dort's comments. 'Many times when Hitler was away for several days at a political rally or tending to party matters in Berlin or elsewhere, Geli would associate with other men. I liked the girl myself so I never told anyone what she did or where she went on these free nights. Hitler would have been furious if he had known that she was out with such men as a violin player from Augsburg or a ski instructor from Innsbruck. After she was satisfied that I wouldn't tell her uncle – and I had a personal reason for not telling him – she often confided in me. She admitted to me that at times Hitler made her commit some acts in the privacy of her room that sickened her but when I asked her why she didn't refuse to do them she just shrugged and said that she didn't want to lose him to some woman that would do what he wanted.'

The 'personal reason' that Stocker had for keeping Geli's extracurricular activities secret from her uncle was that he also enjoyed her favors periodically. 'She was a girl that needed attention and needed it often,' he said. 'And she definitely wanted to remain Hitler's favorite girlfriend. She was willing to do anything he wanted to keep that status. At the beginning of 1931 I think she was worried that there might be another woman in Hitler's life because she mentioned to me several times that her uncle didn't seem to be as interested in her as he once was.'

Geli's concern was legitimate because by this time Hitler was spending quite a few evenings with Eva Braun. The difference in his treatment of the two girls added to the mystery of his personal life. He took Geli to plays, movies and restaurants, unconcerned about whether the public saw him with her or not. In fact, he seemed to enjoy the interest he aroused when he appeared with the blonde Geli on his arm. With Eva, however, everything was secretive. He never took her out in public and tried to keep his meetings with her concealed from even his closest friends. If he took Eva to Hoffmann's for the evening, he made certain that no one else except the photographer and his family was there. When he took her home, he would have Erich Kempka, the chauffeur, drop her off at her apartment where Hitler would bid her good night and leave, in case anyone was watching. Within the next hour he would meet her at a prearranged rendezvous and spend the rest of the evening with her alone.

Despite his growing interest in Eva, Hitler had no intention of allowing his niece to be unfaithful. When he caught her in the company of Emil Maurice, one of the most devoted party members and a personal friend of his, Hitler was furious. He was aware of Maurice's reputation for a roving eye and chased him from the apartment on Prinzregentenstrasse, forbidding him ever to return. It wasn't until many years later that he forgave the man, even though Maurice always vowed he was merely having an innocent visit with Geli that afternoon. Another party member who felt the wrath of Hitler because of Geli was Otto Strasser. Both Otto and Gregor Strasser, his brother, were early supporters and close friends of Hitler's. Therefore Otto Strasser thought nothing of agreeing to take Geli to one of the famous Munich masked balls. His brother warned him that Hitler might not like it, but Otto just smiled. That evening as he was getting dressed however the telephone rang. It was Hitler and he was furious. 'I won't allow Geli to go out with you,' he screamed over the telephone. 'I'm not going to have any of your filthy Berlin tricks in Munich.'

Otto tried to explain that he was merely taking Geli to a masked ball for some dancing and entertainment but Hitler wouldn't allow him to talk. Finally Otto admitted defeat and told Geli that it would be best if he didn't take her to the affair. The next day an angry Geli visited him and explained that her uncle didn't want her to go anyplace without him, yet he was so busy himself that he seldom took her out anymore. She was very upset. 'If I tell him I'm going out anyway,' she said, 'he goes into a tantrum. I don't know what to do.'

Strasser had no advice for the girl. He knew that she did not want to lose her favorite position with Hitler, but he also knew that to keep it she would have to pay the price demanded. Geli knew this, too, and returned to the apartment on Prinzregenten- strasse after unburdening herself, another sign that she was no prisoner despite her complaints.

By this time Eva knew about Geli and Hitler. As her interest in him increased and she spent more time with him, Eva learned a great deal about the niece-in-residence. She often talked about Geli with her mother, although Frau Braun was ignorant that Eva herself was now involved with Hitler. Just when Eva decided to do everything possible to establish herself as Hitler's love no one knows for certain. For several years it was thought by most people that she became his mistress only because of luck and circumstances, but a detailed study of the love affair reveals this is far from the truth. Eva pursued her plan to conquer Hitler so cleverly that no one, not even the jealous and greedy associates who surrounded him during the Third Reich era, ever realized what she had in mind or how she accomplished it. In 1930 Eva recognized Geli as the most formidable obstacle in her way and decided that somehow she had to be eliminated as a rival for Hitler's love.

Geli also knew about Eva. Just when she found out about her no one is certain but Frau Dort thinks it was in February, 1931.

'We were walking in the English Gardens one day in February after finishing our voice lessons with Herr Vogel,' she said, 'and I asked Geli how she was getting along with Hitler. She took several photographs from her handbag and gave them to me. All but one were of Hitler. The exception was a photograph of a very pretty girl. When I asked Geli who the girl was she blushed, grabbed the picture from my hand and put it in her pocket. It was obvious to me that she had given that picture to me by mistake. I remember that it was inscribed along the border in neat hand- writing: "To Adi with love, Eva".'

Later, when the two girls parted, Geli took Ada Dort's hand in hers and apologized for her rudeness. 'That girl is a friend of my uncle's. I don't like her.'

As Hitler's popularity and prestige increased during 1931, both Geli and Eva fought harder to win his sole affection. Even though the two girls never met formally, they had the opportunity to observe each other at various times. One occasion was when Heinrich Hoffmann took Eva to *Fasching* (the Munich Carnival) in March, 1931. As they entered one of the festive beer tents the photographer saw Hitler and Geli sitting at a table. He guided Eva to a table at the opposite side of the tent since he didn't want the two girls to confront each other. Hoffmann, tactless and crude as usual, introduced Eva to people in the tent as 'my niece', an obvious allusion to the relationship between Hitler and Geli. When this remark was passed on to Geli she was furious.

'I don't want to be put in the same class as that monkey-faced girl,' she muttered. She knew that Hoffmann's companion was Eva Braun. She had seen Eva's photograph in the window at Hoffmann's studio when she had accompanied the Schaubs there to have their wedding portrait taken.

Although Hitler managed to keep his budding affair with Eva concealed from nearly everyone else, Geli became more and more aware of it during the spring and summer of 1931. When his trips to Hoffmann's became more frequent, Geli was forced to spend most of her time in her room waiting for him. Occasionally she tried to get out of the apartment when he was with Eva but Hitler became furious if he found out she had left. Only when he was away from Munich was she able to enjoy herself, and as the summer wore on she became more and more frustrated. Frau Winter often heard Geli and Hitler arguing that summer but she thought little of it since they always 'kissed and made up' the following day. The causes of the arguments varied but most of them were occasioned by Hitler's possessiveness and jealousy, which Geli resented. In August, however, Frau Winter heard Geli bawling him out concerning a letter she had found in his pocket. At that time she didn't pay much attention to the incident. Later she realized that 'the letter' was an important factor in the tragedy.

Less than a month after the argument over the letter, Hitler began a campaign tour to the north of Germany. He invited Hoffmann to go along since he wanted maximum press and photo coverage. When Hoffmann arrived at the Prinzregentenstrasse apartment on September 17, 1931, Hitler was still packing, Geli was helping him, and as usual the two were arguing. The photographer was as accustomed to the frequent fights as Frau Winter, so he ignored the yelling and screaming as he drank a glass of wine. Suddenly he heard Hitler tell the girl to 'shut up' in a loud voice and a moment later he came down the steps and motioned to Hoffmann that he was ready to go. They joined the driver of the black Mercedes-Benz, Julius Schreck, and put their bags in the rear of the automobile. Hoffmann was just settling himself in the back seat of the Mercedes-Benz when Geli appeared on the second-floor balcony of the apartment. Hitler saw her and his face immediately turned red.

'For the last time, no!'

Then Hitler nodded to the driver and the Mercedes started down the street. Hoffmann looked back and saw that Geli was crying.

That evening Geli went to the Munich Playhouse with Frau Schaub to see Maria Bard. According to Frau Schaub's statement later, Geli was lost in thought during most of the performance and several times she thought the girl was going to cry. At the intermission, however, Geli bought a drink and a chocolate bar at the refreshment bar and seemed more cheerful. During the trip home she spoke only when Frau Schaub spoke to her. Before she went into the apartment she asked what Frau Schaub intended to do during the next few days, since she knew her husband was going to join Hitler on the trip. Frau Schaub explained that she had no definite plans.

'I will be in my apartment.'

Frau Schaub realized that Geli was upset but wasn't particularly concerned, thinking the girl was merely lonely. The next morning at 10 a.m., however, Frau Winter called to inquire whether Geli had stayed overnight with her, and if so, whether she was still at the Schaub apartment. When Frau Schaub said no, Frau Winter explained that when she had taken Geli the morning newspaper as usual there was no answer to her knock on the bedroom door. Frau Winter next called Geli's mother on the Obersalzberg and discovered that Geli was not there either. She then notified her husband and they forced the door open. Geli was lying on the floor of her bedroom. She was dead, shot through the heart. Hitler's Walther 6.35 pistol was in her hand.

Frau Winter, loyal to Hitler while he was alive and to his memory after his death, understood immediately what she had to do. She notified Rudolf Hess, at the time the second most powerful man in the Nazi organization, Gregor Strasser and Franz Schwarz about the tragedy — and *then* called the police and a doctor. Hess arrived at the scene within minutes, talked with Frau Winter and placed an emergency telephone call to the Deutscher Hof Hotel in Nuremberg.

Meanwhile, Hitler and Hoffmann had passed through the outskirts of Nuremberg and were on the highway to Bayreuth. A few miles out of Nuremberg Hitler saw a taxi gaining on them and was about to tell Schreck to speed up, since he didn't like other vehicles overtaking his Mercedes-Benz, when he noticed one of the occupants of the taxi was waving to him. It was a bellhop from the Deutscher Hof. At Hitler's order Schreck pulled to the side of the road and the bellhop notified Hitler that Hess was calling from Munich and the telephone line would be held open until Hitler returned to Nuremberg. Hitler knew that Hess would not make such a call unless there was an emergency so he returned to the hotel at full speed. When he got there he learned that Geli had committed suicide.

The mystery that surrounded the death of Geli allowed Hitler to appear a grief-stricken lover in the eyes of some, a murderer in the eyes of others. Yet no one has denied that he was shocked by her death – whatever their disagreement, he had not expected her to kill herself. But any emotion he felt about the loss of a beautiful girl who had given him many hours of pleasure was immediately subordinated to his concern about the impact of the suicide on his political career. Could the fact that she shot herself with *his* revolver in *his* apartment be kept secret? Hess and Schwarz made a strenuous effort to cover up the suicide that September morning, and while they were not completely successful, they did manage to obscure enough details so that Hitler escaped unscathed politically. Immediately after learning of Geli's death, Schwarz contacted Dr Franz Guertner, the Bavarian Minister of Justice and a Nazi sympathizer, and through the influence of Guertner's office the usual legal procedures followed in such cases were waived. Guertner termed the death an obvious suicide that required no inquest and burial arrangements were hastily made.

While no formal steps were taken to investigate Geli's death, the Munich newspapers, as yet unafraid of Adolf Hitler, gave the suicide extensive publicity. The *Münchener Neueste Nachrichten* reported the tragedy in the next morning's issue, stating:

According to a police communiqué, a twenty-three-year-old student fired a pistol aimed at the heart in a room of her apartment in the Bogenhausen District. The unfortunate young woman, Angela Raubal, was the daughter of Adolf Hitler's half-sister, and she and her uncle lived on the same floor of an apartment house on Prinzregentenplatz. Friday afternoon the owners of the apartment heard a cry, but it did not occur to them that it came from their tenant's room. When there was no sign of life from this room in the course of the evening, the door was forced. Angela Raubal was found lying face down on the floor, dead. Near her on the sofa was a small-caliber Walther pistol.

The motives for this action are not yet clear. Some say that Miss Raubal had met a singer in Vienna but that her uncle would not allow her to leave Munich. Others affirm that the poor girl killed herself because she was supposed to make her debut as a singer but did not believe herself capable of facing the public.

The errors in this news report were typical of the deliberately created confusion surrounding Geli's death. She was actually found in the morning, not during the evening; no one heard the shot that killed her; and there was no singing debut planned for her in the near future. As for the 'lover in Vienna' theory (some papers added the fanciful details that the 'lover' was a Jew and Geli was pregnant by him), there is no supporting evidence. Hitler himself could not have killed her, as some have proposed, because there is ample proof that he was not in Munich at the time. Besides, Hitler did not want Geli to die, for she was the one woman he trusted to satisfy his rumored unusual sexual demands, such as crouching over his face naked, urinating on him, kicking him as he lay on the floor and hitting him with the whip he usually carried.

Frau Winter said that when she heard Geli and Hitler arguing about a letter Geli had found in Hitler's coat pocket, she didn't pay much attention. But Maja Kempka, the attractive wife of Hitler's chauffeur, once saw a pile of letters that Christa Schröder, one of Hitler's secretaries, had cleared from his desk near the end of the war. One letter she remembered reading was from Hitler to Geli, telling her that he had to sacrifice her for his people, but that while he could not marry her, he wanted to keep her with him. Frau Kempka also recalled seeing several letters from Eva to Hitler and she thinks that Geli saw one or more of these secret love letters and became desperate. If her uncle had to sacrifice her for his people, why was he having an affair with Eva Braun? Depressed, frustrated at her virtual imprisonment in the apartment waiting for Hitler while he was seeing another woman, and angry because he flew into a rage when she mentioned Eva to him, Geli killed herself.

Her body was shipped back to Vienna in a sealed lead coffin after Dr Guertner and Senior Criminal Inspector Heinrich Müller closed the official investigation without further questions. She was buried in the Catholic Central Cemetery in Vienna even though she had committed suicide because Church officials decided that she 'was in a state of mental aberration and confusion and therefore not wholly responsible for her act'. Her funeral was attended by Ernst Röhm and Heinrich Himmler, head of the SS, representing Hitler, who was forbidden to enter the country by the Austrian government. His aides finally negotiated an agreement with the Austrian officials a week later that permitted Hitler to spend twenty-four hours in Vienna without risking arrest and he then visited Geli's burial plot for a few hours. It was seven years before he returned. On this second occasion he entered Austria as the country's conqueror.

Hitler kept Geli's room in the Prinzregentenstrasse apartment exactly as it was the day she killed herself. Only he and Frau Winter were permitted in the room and fresh flowers were placed on a table there daily by the housekeeper. Adolf Ziegler, the painter, was commissioned to do Geli's portrait from a photograph and this picture occupied a place of honor in the reception room of Hitler's home on the Obersalzberg. Professor Josef Thorack, a sculptor, made a bust of Geli at Hitler's request and it was prominently displayed in the Chancellery in Berlin. Thus every major building occupied by Hitler during the Third Reich had a remembrance of the girl. But just to make certain that all his associates were aware of his dramatic devotion to the dead Geli, Hitler always carried a photograph of her. He also carried a photograph of his mother.

Later events proved that his ostentatious devotion to Geli was more a theatrical ploy to gain sympathy than a true emotion. Though he was indeed shocked by her death, he thought more of his own career and his personal sexual desires than of Geli's suffering before her suicide. The stories of his desire to commit suicide at this time, his great depression, his lack of will to live after she died, and his temporary insanity because of guilt that Geli had shot herself on his account are greatly exaggerated – understandably so, because Hitler *wanted* others to believe these things and acted in such a way that they did believe them. But that is exactly what it was – an act. Within three weeks he was making political decisions again and plotting to overthrow the Berlin government. He was also seeing Eva Braun.

5
Eva's Overture

*In 1932 five Nazi Party members hacked to death a
Communist miner at Potempa, Silesia, and were
sentenced by the court to die for the crime. Hitler had
to decide whether to defend the SA killers or adhere to
his publicly professed aim of becoming Chancellor
through legal peaceful means rather than violence.
Finally, after a delay of several days, he made his choice.
He wired the five murderers: 'My comrades, in face of
this monstrous and bloody sentence I feel myself bound
to you in limitless loyalty. From this moment your
liberation is a question of honor. To fight against a
government which could allow this is our duty.' Hitler
had spelled out the key word for his future
reign – violence.*

Hitler was tender and quiet in his personal life during the months following Geli's death . . . especially with Eva. He took full advantage of his niece's suicide to project a 'sorrowful image' to the public, which he hoped might win him votes. He knew that many people considered him an eccentric radical with no real compassion or emotions and he seized this opportunity to convince the voting public otherwise. He spent many hours alone, seemed depressed and uninterested in political events, and continually talked about the great love he had had for his niece. At the same time he made certain that these actions were reported to the public through newspaper accounts, word of mouth and even radio broadcasts. Before many weeks had passed he was being referred to as 'poor Adolf' on the streets of Munich, testimony that his public relations program was succeeding.

A closer analysis reveals a much different Hitler. Within three weeks after Geli's death he met with Hindenburg, the President of Germany, to expound his views on the path the country should follow to recovery; took part in a great demonstration at Harzburg; published a scathing attack on the policy of the government; and, in general, intensified the political fight he had started years earlier. Geli's death had in no way slowed his climb to power.

Eva, meanwhile, realized that with Geli out of the way, she had an opportunity to ingratiate herself more deeply into Hitler's favor, and she took advantage of it. But, while Geli had been her greatest obstacle, Eva had other problems that interfered with her romantic plans. Her parents were extremely strict and she didn't dare stay away from home for an entire night. As it was, they often demanded to know where she had been and what she was doing when she stayed out later than they thought she should. Eva was twenty years old in February, 1932, but Fritz Braun believed that parents were in complete charge of their children until they married or left home for other reasons. Eva knew that if her father or mother learned that she was rendez-vousing with a man twenty-three years older than she, they would be furious – especially if that man was Adolf Hitler! Her father was still obsessed with the idea that Hitler was a radical who would most certainly destroy the country if he ever came to power. He was so uncompromising on this subject that Eva didn't dare mention the name of Hitler at home, let alone that she was meeting with him. Only her sister, Ilse, was aware of Eva's feelings toward Hitler but she kept Eva's secret.

By early 1932 Eva was certain that Hitler was the man she

wanted to spend her life with, and despite the anticipated opposition of her parents, she laid her plans to become his mistress. It must be remembered that in 1932 Hitler was not the all-powerful Führer he later became, that he was just one among several men vying for control of the nation. There is no question that he was obtaining a great deal of publicity and basking in the limelight of national affairs, but so were other politicians, government officials and generals. Eva's sincerity may be judged by the fact that it was during the confusing and often discouraging year of 1932, when Hitler's political failures outnumbered his victories, that she made up her mind she loved him. This refutes the later contention that she clung to him because he was the Führer. In 1932 Hitler was a struggling politician who believed he would gain control of Germany by legal or illegal means, but there certainly was no positive assurance that he could. Eva was aware of the gamble but disregarded it. She wanted Hitler for her lover and she set out to get him.

When Geli was living at the apartment on Prinzregentenstrasse, Eva was never invited there by Hitler, for obvious reasons. Nor did he take Eva to Haus Wachenfeld while Geli was alive because Angela Raubal spent much time there and would have been angry if he had brought another woman into the house. Even after Geli's death his half-sister continued to live on the Obersalzberg and made Eva's stays there miserable. Since it was politically dangerous for Hitler to take a woman to a public hotel for a rendezvous, the only place available to him and Eva while Geli lived was Hoffmann's home. Here they were assured of both secrecy and privacy. After Geli's suicide, however, Eva was invited to the apartment on Prinzregentenstrasse and she spent many evenings there with Hitler. These meetings were not approved of by many of Hitler's associates.

Some thought that he was asking for the same trouble he had had with Geli. They knew he had been fortunate to escape that incident without his political career being destroyed and didn't think that he could survive a second scandal. Most of his associates who thought along these lines considered Hitler a sexual deviate who indirectly caused Geli's death by his perverted demands on her coupled with his unfaithfulness. Others, who were taken in by Hitler's public role as a desolated mourner, were shocked by his quick switch to another girl. They couldn't understand how he could conduct a new affair in the same apartment where Geli had killed herself, all the while vowing his love for his dead niece. Since very few people understood Hitler during his lifetime, it is clear why this new love affair was disconcerting to so many.

There was also the group around Hitler who did not want him to fall in love with a woman because they feared her influence and their own loss of status. One such individual was Wilhelm Brückner, an adjutant on Hitler's personal staff, who often acted as an intermediary between Hitler and Eva. A jealous, crude character who wanted to have great influence on Hitler but didn't have the finesse to achieve his aim, Brückner did his best to break up the affair. Many of the notes and telephone calls that Eva directed to Hitler were 'misplaced' or never reported by Brückner, and he made no effort to conceal his hostility toward her when Hitler was not around. When Hitler was with Eva, Brückner would pretend he adored her, hoping to gain favor with his leader. In 1932 Brückner was more influential than Eva in the intimate circle that surrounded Hitler, but in later years he was to suffer for his rude and often cruel treatment of her. The 'quiet, stupid cow', as he often referred to her, made certain he paid dearly for his insults.

Eva fended off her enemies in a manner that showed her ability to handle difficult situations. Instead of running to Hitler with all her complaints, as those opposing her hoped she would do, she kept quiet and took the insults and rudeness in stride. Brückner, Goebbels, Göring, Frau Winter and others who frowned on the affair for their own personal reasons knew that Hitler quickly became disgusted with anyone who constantly complained to him about their troubles. They knew that if Eva started this practice Hitler would rid himself of her as soon as possible. He wanted to spend his time plotting and achieving his political aims, not tending to the minor troubles of a girlfriend. Eva was quick to grasp this fact. She concentrated on trying to relax him, to humor him, to make him forget his 'hard day on the political front' when he was with her, and for this Hitler was grateful. The result was that those who wanted to break up the affair fumed while Hitler spent more time with Eva.

During the early months of 1932 Hitler once again resumed his visits to Dr Krueger after an absence of half a year. Whether he wanted to consult the doctor because of Geli's suicide and his consequent guilty feelings, or because of his increasing sexual interest in Eva, Krueger never determined. It was obvious to him that Hitler was disturbed by the death of his niece, that he felt somehow betrayed, but Krueger was apprehensive about how to proceed with his questioning of Hitler in order to help him. He was aware of the rumors of secret police investigations and vague accusations against Hitler because Geli had shot herself with his gun and in his apartment. To add to Krueger's apprehension, Hitler, now affluent, summoned him to his own apartment on Prinzregentenstrasse instead of going to the doctor's office, and Krueger knew that the building swarmed with Nazi henchmen.

A security guard was waiting for Krueger when he arrived at the apartment and immediately took him to Hitler's study where he found Hitler pacing the room nervously. He couldn't determine immediately whether this was an act to impress him or whether Hitler really was overwrought. He decided to bide his time and listen. Since Hitler usually did most of the talking anyway, it was a simple tactic to follow.

'I had almost decided to let matters lapse between us,' Hitler said, 'but I needed someone with whom to talk freely.'

Krueger's recollection of this first visit after Geli's death was hazy but he did recall the overall tone and substance of the meeting. Most of the conversation dealt with Geli and Hitler's demands on her, which he felt might have indirectly caused her suicide. He told Krueger of a recurrent dream in which Geli would 'float' into his bedroom at night, kiss him, and, before he could grasp her, 'float' away again. He also explained that after he had caught her with Emil Maurice, a member of his staff, his attitude toward her had changed and his demands became more frequent and 'varied'. Would these demands have caused her to kill herself, he wanted to know?

Krueger knew the violent nature of his patient and was acutely conscious of where the session was taking place. He shook his head. 'From what you have told me, God, fate, nature – anything which represents the universe controls,' he said, 'but not you.'

This vague answer seemed to satisfy Hitler and relieve him of a great mental burden. But the session, and the information Hitler had previously given to Krueger about his sexual life, eventually sealed the doctor's fate in Germany. He was forced to flee the country within two years.

The earlier sessions with Krueger had enabled Hitler to overcome his impotence although as Albert Speer, a close associate who knew Hitler as well if not better than anyone, emphasized: 'He was never a passionate man and as he grew older and became more and more involved with political and military matters, his passion diminished even further, just as it would in any normal man.' Speer was one of those who knew Hitler intimately and insisted that Hitler's sexual life was normal despite the rumors hinting otherwise.

Frau Schaub, the wife of Hitler's adjutant, was another. 'These rumors that Hitler was supposed to be abnormal are false. As the wife of the man who was Hitler's adjutant for twenty years, I had numerous occasions to watch him in private and when in the company of ladies. I can assure you that he was definitely a very normal man. He loved women and loved to be in the presence of feminine beauty. I knew all about the relationship between him and Eva Braun from the beginning right up to the end. And I also knew about many other love affairs.'

Eva herself gave a hint that their love affair was progressing in a predictable manner in 1932 when she mentioned to a friend that a certain plush red couch in Hitler's apartment used to seat important visitors was also used for 'other' purposes. 'The couch has quite a history . . .'

From all indications Hitler engaged in various sexual practices with Eva and the other women he consorted with over the years. Dr Krueger, Speer, Frau Schaub, OSS reports and other statements pertaining to his sex life, if studied separately, gave first one answer and then another. Collectively, however, they provide evidence that Hitler was similar to thousands of other men who crave, demand and receive variety in their intimate relations with women, but since he was in the public eye, a world figure whose every word and action were scrutinized minutely, his relationships with women have been described as 'abnormal'.

Eva soon discovered that Hitler had other female companions who were just as interested in him as she was. One who especially caught his eye in 1932 was Winifred Wagner, the daughter-in-law of Richard Wagner. Hitler had made a cult of the music of the man he called 'His Excellency Baron Richard von Wagner, Privy Counsellor and Chief Conductor.' As early as 1923 Hitler began pilgrimages to the Bavarian town of Bayreuth, the shrine to Richard Wagner's music, and there he met Winifred Wagner, the English girl from Hastings who had married the composer's only son, Siegfried. His reception by the Wagner family during this initial visit encouraged him to return. He made certain that he attended the yearly Bayreuth Festival regardless of how busy he was at the time, usually staying at Haus Wahnfried, the family home. Winifred was an early Hitler supporter, but her husband was fond of neither the Nazi party nor its leader. During Hitler's visits to Haus Wahnfried, Siegfried was polite but not enthusiastic. His suspicion that Hitler was as interested in Winifred as he was in the festival proved to be correct. After Siegfried died in 1930, Hitler's visits to to Bayreuth became more frequent. By 1932 he and Winifred Wagner were very close – proof of Hitler's remarkable maneuverability considering that during those same years he was 'devoted' to Geli and also spending many hours with Eva. Winifred used the intimate form *du* and called him by his favorite nickname, 'Wolf', a privilege accorded few people outside his official circle. Her children called him 'uncle' and Hitler was very fond of them. After Geli's death many of Hitler's associates thought that a match between their leader and the daughter-in-law of Richard Wagner would be excellent for his political career and did everything they could to promote it. There seemed no comparison between Winifred Wagner, who was rich, influential and bore a name glorified throughout Germany, and a petty bourgeois clerk who worked in a photography studio. Eva was aware of their plans for Hitler. So was Hitler. Nor did Winifred Wagner oppose the idea. Yet nothing concrete developed, and though Winifred and Hitler remained friends for years, there was no marriage.

For a long time the reason the marriage never came off was a puzzle to Hitler's friends and associates. It seemed a perfect match, an excellent pairing between an upcoming politician and a beautiful woman with a great German name that would add legitimacy and style to Hitler's radicalism. Gradually the truth became known. Winifred Wagner had visited Dr Krueger in Munich, ostensibly to check on an examination her daughter had had earlier. During the conversation she began discussing her relationship with Hitler. It was apparent to Krueger that she had reservations about the way Hitler treated her when they were alone. She couldn't understand his occasional resistance to her advances, but more significantly, she was shocked by his unorthodox approaches to lovemaking. She sensed that Hitler had a soft, gentle side and a side 'like that of a beast' and she was doubtful that she could handle such a man. She was afraid to try. Later, when her daughter Friedelind (who had always opposed Hitler) sought refuge in England and was interviewed by Allied intelligence agents, she told them that her mother had misgivings about her affair with Hitler, especially after he had once asked her to whip him, and at other times when he treated her like his own mother, asking her to punish him. Winifred Wagner came to the conclusion that Hitler was completely beyond her control and she feared him. His tantrums, his fanatic determination to gain control of all of Germany, his tendency toward violence and his ruthlessness scared her. She wanted desperately to be the 'First Lady' of Germany, to be recognized as the one great love of Hitler's life, but she did not have the temperament and the skill to achieve this goal. Her indecision disappeared when Geli committed suicide. This incident convinced her that Hitler was too volatile a man for her to handle.

If Hitler ever intended to marry Winifred, as so many of his associates wished, he never gave any public indication of it. It was obvious that he enjoyed his time spent at Bayreuth with the Wagner family but there is no record that he ever mentioned marriage. After the two drifted apart as lovers, though, Hitler did not abandon Winifred or the music of Richard Wagner. Under the auspices of the Nazi Party during the Third Reich, Bayreuth once again became the music capital of the world and the proceeds of the yearly festival made Winifred wealthy. Some of Hitler's most pleasant hours during the late 1930s were spent at the Bayreuth Festival. He often invited visiting diplomats, celebrities and socialites to the festival as his guests. His final visit to Bayreuth was in 1940. After that he was too occupied with the war, and too conscious of his image to appear at a music festival while German soldiers were dying on the battlefield. Before he quit going to the affair, however, one guest accompanied him to Bayreuth several times: Eva Braun.

Frau Winter, the housekeeper at Hitler's apartment in Munich, often said that Eva 'was not very intelligent, just a pretty doll. She always talked about the parties she attended, the actresses and actors who were her favorites and other such trivial matters when she was with Hitler.' When she mentioned this shortcoming of Eva's to Hitler, however, his reply surprised her.

'Well, she keeps my mind off other things, which is a rest for me sometimes.'

The 'not very intelligent' Eva was much more perceptive than the other women who tried to attract Adolf Hitler. The photographs in her personal albums indicate that in 1932 she was spending much of her time with him and that he was happy when he was with her. Page after page of the albums is filled with pictures of Hitler, all dated 1932. One photograph is especially revealing. It shows Eva holding Hitler's hand during a visit to Hoffmann's home and underneath the picture Eva wrote: 'If people realized *how well* he knows me!' These photographs demonstrate that her campaign to win Hitler's affection was showing definite results in 1932 and that she was willing to walk where Winifred Wagner had feared to tread. If Eva had any reservations about Hitler's character or his actions, in public or in private, she gave no indication, nor did she exhibit any fear of him. She did give every indication that she was in love with him and, as Frau Winter said, 'chased Hitler all the time'.

So Eva was undoubtedly taking great strides toward her ultimate conquest of Hitler in 1932 but there was one lesson she had still to learn – that no woman had priority in Hitler's mind over his pursuit of power. His political activities took a large portion of his time and he had to travel constantly during his election campaigns, leaving Eva behind in Munich. Geli had learned about loneliness during her affair with Hitler, and in the end this loneliness coupled with jealousy had been too much for her. Eva, who had thought that other women were her main obstacle, soon discovered that loneliness and the waiting, waiting, waiting were a greater ordeal. These were factors she could not grapple with as easily as with another woman's designs on Hitler. Any attempt she might make to limit Hitler's trips would directly affect his political career and she was intelligent enough to know that Hitler's drive for the Chancellorship was much more important to him than the love of Eva Braun. Her upbringing had prepared her to recognize this, since in the Braun home the man was the breadwinner, the one member of the family whose vocation was important and whose ambition to advance subjugated all other family matters. Hitler's vocation was politics, and she knew that if she was going to win his love she had to be extremely careful not to interfere with this vocation. To avoid personal disaster she had to delicately balance her campaign for his affection with his campaign for power. This very nearly cost her life.

It was becoming increasingly clear to the German public that Hitler had enough support to wield considerable influence in the government even though he had not yet obtained an important official position. He was an expert in political intrigue and in-fighting, and as the year progressed he became involved in more and more complicated under-the-table deals. He helped indirectly to oust Heinrich Brüning as Chancellor in return for the promise that the temporary ban on the SA and SS would be removed and new elections for the Reichstag would be held. When Hindenburg learned that Hitler's Nazi Party would give tacit support to Franz von Papen if Papen were named Chancellor, he quickly agreed to the secret deal and asked for Brüning's resignation on May 30, 1932. While this political intrigue was in progress Hitler spent most of the month of May 'out of sight' in Mecklenburg and Oldenburg and saw little of Eva. When Goebbels notified him on

71

May 30 that Brüning was out of office, Hitler immediately drove to Berlin and spent time there attempting to strengthen his position with the new government. Once again Eva was left alone in Munich. She felt that Hitler was neglecting her, not knowing that he was preparing the final campaign in his battle to become Chancellor of Germany and that this campaign would take nearly all his time and energy for the next eight months.

Franz von Papen was personable, wealthy and self-confident, but as Chancellor he was no match for either Hitler or the clever General Kurt von Schleicher, who had great influence with Hindenburg and was pulling the strings behind the scenes. As the authoritative voice of the German Army and the liaison officer between the military and the various government ministries, Schleicher seized the opportunity in 1930–1932 to become one of the most powerful political figures in the country. He was the one who had proposed Brüning for Chancellor to Hindenburg and convinced a reluctant Brüning to accept the position after the President agreed to his appointment; it was Schleicher who ousted Brüning with Hitler's help; and it was this same general who proposed Papen as the new Chancellor and won the tacit support of the Nazi party and Hindenburg.

As the year 1932 progressed, it was these three men – Papen, Schleicher and Hitler – who held the future of the country in their hands. While they pretended to be allies, each was maneuvering for an advantageous personal position in a winner-take-all political battle – which left Hitler practically no time to visit Eva. Though she understood he was deeply involved in the new elections to be held that year, Eva could not reconcile herself to the loneliness and uncertainty. Perhaps if she could have discussed her problem with her mother it would have eased her mind, but Fanny Braun had no suspicion that her daughter was in love with Hitler and Eva didn't dare tell her. The lack of a confidante, the absence of some positive sign from Hitler such as a letter or a telephone call, and the conviction she had been discarded began to have their effect on Eva during the summer. She changed into a quiet, moody girl who seldom laughed, stayed at home and worried her parents and sisters. Only Ilse suspected the reason, but she was having her own difficulties and didn't want to get involved in a family argument over the merit or lack of merit in Adolf Hitler. Meanwhile, all Eva could do was read the newspaper accounts of Hitler's campaign and the reign of terror provoked by the lifting of the ban on the SA. From June 1, 1932, until July 20, 1932, there were over 450 political riots in the

72

country and nearly 100 persons were killed and 400 injured. Eva must have known that Hitler condoned the actions of his SA, but whatever she thought of the riots and killings, she was more worried about his personal safety. He was very likely in the vicinity of some of the riots. She silently hoped he wouldn't be killed . . . and waited for some word from him.

The elections for the Reichstag were held on July 30, 1932, and Eva didn't know whether to be delighted or disappointed when the Nazi Party outstripped all the other parties, winning 230 seats by accumulating 13,745,000 votes. She knew she should be happy because 'her man' now had the largest political party in Germany, which made *him* very happy. But then, she realized that the stronger the Nazi Party became, the busier its leader would be and the more he would be away from Munich. She was still in a quandary when she learned through Henny Hoffmann that Hitler was on the Obersalzberg, less than a hundred miles south of Munich. He had arrived there on August 5, 1932, after a meeting with Schleicher at Fürstenberg. Henny, who had never gotten over her rejection by Hitler, did everything possible to make Eva's life miserable once she found out that Hitler was interested in her. She took pleasure in showing Eva newspaper photographs of Hitler in Berlin, Hamburg and other cities in the company of beautiful women, always emphasizing that these women had wealth or position. As soon as her father told her to pack for a trip to Berchtesgaden where he was going to take photographs of Hitler and his visitors at Haus Wachenfeld, Henny hurried to the studio to gloat over Eva, to let her know that she and her father were going to the Obersalzberg, where Eva was not invited.

Eva was hurt that Hitler had come so close to Munich and not contacted her but she kept her feelings to herself, much to Henny's disappointment. She was amused and pleased when Hoffmann and his daughter returned to the studio from Berchtesgaden the following day because Hitler had already departed for Berlin.

Hitler had consulted with several party leaders at Haus Wachenfeld and had decided to meet with Papen and Schleicher. Now that his party was the strongest in Germany he intended to demand the Chancellorship. But he had underestimated the cleverness of his two erstwhile allies – all they would offer him was the Vice-Chancellorship, and without their support he knew that Hindenburg would not appoint him head of the government. He lost his temper, flew into a rage and stalked out of the meeting. Shortly after Hindenburg summoned him to the palace and gave him a verbal dressing down for demanding that the reins of government be turned over to him. The President also issued a communiqué that was very damaging to Hitler, explaining that the President 'had gravely exhorted Herr Hitler to conduct the opposition on the part of the Nazi Party in a chivalrous manner and to bear in mind his responsibility to the Fatherland and to the German people.' Hitler was humiliated and returned to Munich.

Eva thought he would turn to her for comfort, but though she saw him once or twice at Hoffmann's studio, he seemed distant, impersonal, almost in a daydream. Most of the time he was in Munich he stayed isolated in his apartment or at party head-quarters and Eva had little chance to visit with him. Not until later did she learn that he was in the midst of a serious crisis when one false move would have ended his political career. He was angry and frustrated, feeling that Schleicher, Papen and Hindenburg had treated him as an inferior and had tried to make a fool of him. But his main concern was what to do next. His bluff had been called. Now it was his move. Naturally he had little time to think of Eva, and since he never discussed political matters with her, she had no way of knowing about his inner turmoil. All she knew was that he did not call her, did not come to Hoffmann's to visit her and no longer even sent her notes or letters.

It was a miserable summer for both Eva and Hitler. Hitler felt that he had lost his battle for the Chancellorship and Eva felt that she had lost the man she wanted most in her life. Both headed for a new crisis which had its climax in November. On the night of November 1, 1932, Eva's loneliness and depression reached a level she could no longer control. She was alone in the Braun apart-ment. Ilse was working as a night receptionist and her parents had traveled to Geijelhoering to place flowers in the family vault. Her younger sister, Gretl, was in convent school. Sometime after midnight Eva opened the drawer of the night table beside her parents' bed, took out her father's 6.35-mm pistol, stretched out on the bed and shot herself. Her aim was not nearly as accurate as Geli's had been, however, and the bullet lodged near the neck artery. Lying there, still conscious but bleeding badly, Eva decided that she did not want to die after all, so she telephoned Dr Plate, Heinrich Hoffmann's brother-in-law. She knew that he was a good doctor and could help her; she also knew that he would notify Hoffmann immediately, who in turn would tell Hitler what had happened. And she wanted Hitler to know immediately. She didn't want to wait until the farewell letter she had mailed that evening reached him. Dr Plate was an excellent choice. He had her taken to a private clinic where he easily extracted the bullet from her neck.

Hitler, after receiving the news from Hoffmann, hurried to the clinic with flowers, and Eva, for the first time in months, had the full attention of the man she loved. He was properly solicitous of her condition and it was obvious that he was flattered she would do such a thing to prove she loved and missed him. The grand gesture strengthened his ego at a time when he needed it most. He was also extremely grateful that she had had enough common sense to call Dr Plate instead of another physician who would not have maintained the same discreet silence about the affair.

Her parents were upset but Eva's explanation satisfied them both. As Fritz Braun told inquiring neighbors: 'Eva got hold of my Browning and it accidentally went off. I asked her how it happened and she said that she had wanted to see what a gun like the one Geli had used looked like, and while she was looking at it, the gun went off. That's all there is to it. She is not serious.'

Eva was only in the clinic a few days and the wound healed completely, leaving no scar. Her desperate gamble was temporarily successful because Hitler now felt he had to watch over her. He told Hoffmann: 'She did it for the love of me. I must look after the girl.'

Before the end of that month Hitler encountered another crisis. During the November elections the Nazi Party lost two million votes. He had nearly lost Eva. Now it appeared he had actually lost his chance at the Chancellorship.

Part 2

THE
PRECARIOUS
YEARS

6
Mistress of a Chancellor

*Hitler became Chancellor of the Third Reich on
January 30, 1933, through a clever plan of backstairs
political intrigue supported by influential Germans who
thought they could control him. Their disillusionment
was swift and complete. The ruthlessness of Hitler soon
became obvious when he dissolved the Reichstag and
forced a new election during which candidates of parties
opposing the Nazis were assaulted and beaten. He
ordered Goering to purge the Prussian state service and
replace the officials with party members, and to establish
a powerful auxiliary police force. The day after the
Reichstag mysteriously burned down, Hitler issued a
decree suspending the guarantees of individual liberty
under the Weimar Constitution. It was upon this decree
that he established his dictatorship.*

Eva, who had worked late the night before, was still sleeping at noon on January 30, 1933, when Fanny Braun knocked on her bedroom door and called, 'Eva, wake up. I have news for you.'

Just then a nun who stopped at the Braun apartment once a month to collect money for the poor arrived. Eva and her mother joined her in the living room and the nun repeated the news that Fanny Braun had just heard over the radio.

'Herr Hitler has come to power!'

When Eva learned that Hitler had been named Chancellor that morning in Berlin, she was shocked. The last time Hitler had talked with her he had admitted that the future of his Nazi Party looked bleak. He was depressed by the elections of November, 1932, when his party had lost more than two million votes and thirty-four seats in the Reichstag. Both the Nationalists and the Communists had gained seats, making the defeat of the Nazis even more bitter. Consequently, Eva asked herself the question thousands of other Germans were asking that afternoon: 'What happened?' The answer was complicated.

Despite his frustration after the elections, Hitler realized that he still controlled the largest party in Germany and that Papen, whether he wanted to or not, would have to compromise with the Nazis on some issues. Indeed, Papen did make several conciliatory offers to Hitler in an effort to get the support of the Nazis so that he would have a ruling majority in the Reichstag, but Hitler refused them and sat tight. After Papen's failure, General von Schleicher decided it was time to take over. He feared that Papen wanted to become a dictator and that he was gaining so much influence with Hindenburg that Schleicher himself would lose all the power he had so carefully built up. He asked Papen to resign but Papen refused. On December 1, 1932, both Papen and Schleicher went to see Hindenburg. Papen proposed that since he could not get the support of a majority of the Reichstag, the President should proclaim a state of emergency so that he, as Chancellor, could rule by decree, using force to control the opposition, until he could obtain a majority. Schleicher opposed this move and suggested instead that *he* be named Chancellor, since he was confident he could obtain a majority in the Reichstag. He was uncertain of getting the support of Hitler himself but believed he could come to terms with Hitler's chief lieutenant Gregor Strasser and thereby draw a large number of Nazi deputies into the coalition. Hindenburg, who was still strongly opposed to Hitler, ignored Schleicher's proposal and remained loyal to Papen.

The following day, however, Schleicher made it clear to Papen that the German Army had no confidence in him, and that if he forced Hindenburg to declare a state of emergency so he could rule by decree, the army would not put down any rebellion by either the Nazis or the Communists. Papen had no choice but to tell the President of Schleicher's threat. Hindenburg, too, knew he had no choice.

'I am an old man and I cannot face a civil war of any sort in my country,' he explained to Papen. 'If Schleicher is of this opinion, then I must – as much as I regret it – withdraw the task which I charged you with last night.'

When it became public that Schleicher was the new Chancellor on December 2, 1932, Eva and Hitler were in his apartment on Prinzregentenstrasse. The wound in her neck was very nearly healed and Hitler, in another gesture of affection since her suicide attempt, had given her a necklace of pearls which concealed the remaining raw part of the scar. Eva had never been happier than in the past few weeks. Hitler had stopped many times to see her at the clinic, and after she was discharged, there was seldom a day that he didn't at least telephone her. Her 'accident' with her father's pistol had paid the dividends she had wanted. The despondency Hitler felt after the disastrous November elections made him more receptive to her condolences and encouragement and for the first time since she had known him Eva discovered she could indirectly influence him about certain matters.

When Hitler revealed that Hindenburg had no intentions of appointing him Chancellor, Eva constantly built up his ego. Paul Harns, a former waiter at the Carlton Hotel café in Munich, often heard her telling Hitler that 'it is always darkest before the dawn' and encouraging him in his political career during the month of December, 1932.

'I remember a few days before Christmas, 1932, Eva and I both tried to get Hitler to celebrate the holiday with us,' Harns said. 'He refused and when he said that he was going back to Berlin to see Schleicher instead, we both knew that he had decided to rejoin the political battle. We looked at each other, thinking that perhaps we had convinced him. That Eva could have convinced almost any man of anything. She was some woman!'

Another witness to Eva's exhortation about Hitler's great political future during December, 1932, was Maria Paith, a hostess and waitress at the Osteria Bavaria in Munich, a small café Hitler frequented. She knew Eva well since their families

6   81

lived only one block apart, but was unaware that Eva was Hitler's mistress. She thought that Eva accompanied Hitler to the café because she was employed by Hoffmann and Hoffmann was a close friend of Hitler's. Once, after she had heard Eva telling Hitler in the Osteria Bavaria that 'if he quit the political battle in Berlin he was a coward,' she warned her not to speak that way to him.

'If you make him angry,' she said, 'he will take his business away from Hoffmann and you may lose your job. I have seen Hitler very angry, so be careful.'

Eva just smiled and told Maria not to worry.

Just how much influence Eva exerted on Hitler at this low period in his political career cannot be estimated, but by early December he was back in the thick of the political fracas in Berlin. When Schleicher attempted to woo Gregor Strasser to his side so that he could gain control of some Nazi seats in the Reichstag, Hitler hurried to Berlin and confronted Strasser at the Kaiserhof Hotel. Intimidated by Hitler's angry accusation that he was trying to take over the leadership of the Nazi Party, Strasser resigned from the party and took a train to Italy. This desertion left Schleicher without the Nazi support he had confidently predicted he could obtain and he had nowhere to turn. Now Papen had his chance. On January 4, 1933, he invited Hitler to meet with him at the home of Cologne banker Kurt von Schröder. Papen had never forgiven Schleicher for ousting him as Chancellor and was willing to go to any length to get his revenge. He thought he saw a way to do just that early in January.

Hitler, aware of the part Papen had played in his humiliating meeting with Hindenburg in August, 1932, was careful to keep his journey to Cologne a strict secret so that if the meeting was a fiasco he would not be publicly embarrassed. He took a night train to Bonn, was driven to Godesberg in one car, then got into another to go to his rendezvous at Schröder's home. Only the banker was present in the study with the two political figures. Papen suggested that he and Hitler establish a coalition between the Nationalist and Nazi parties and become joint Chancellors. Hitler held fast and insisted that he would agree to a coalition only if he was appointed sole Chancellor, though he did promise that Papen's supporters could join his government as ministers. While no firm arrangement was made at this meeting, both Hitler and Papen concurred on one point: they both disliked Chancellor Kurt von Schleicher and wanted him out of office.

The remainder of January was a period of political intrigue

involving Papen, Hitler, wealthy industrialists, Schleicher and leaders of the right-wing Nationalist Party. The industrialists had decided that Hitler was the surest bet to keep the country out of Communist hands and were requesting Hindenburg to give him authority to form a presidential cabinet. Papen, who lived next door to the President and was very friendly with him, was trying to make up his mind whether he should convince Hindenburg to appoint Hitler Chancellor and himself Vice-Chancellor. He knew the president disliked 'that radical' Hitler very much, but he was confident that under this plan he could shortly overthrow Hitler and become Chancellor himself. Papen's alternative plan was to form a presidential cabinet with Hindenburg's approval, be appointed Chancellor, dissolve the Reichstag and request new elections in hopes of obtaining a majority. Meanwhile, Schleicher was desperately trying to obtain the support of either the Nazis or the Nationalists but he was not successful.

The climax came on the night of January 29, 1933. Eva was working late at the studio in Munich. As she sorted photographs of Hitler and other Nazi leaders, a different 'sorting' process was going on in and around Berlin. Schleicher, in a last-stand maneuver, sent a representative to Hitler at the home of Hélène Bechstein in Charlottenburg to warn him that Papen intended to ask for the Chancellorship himself and leave Hitler on the outside. The Chancellor suggested that he and Hitler form a coalition to rule with the combined support of the German Army and the Nazis. Hitler ignored the suggestion. A few hours later he was alarmed to hear that Schleicher was preparing a putsch with the support of the German Army and intended to kidnap the President and declare military law! Hitler alerted the SA and warned Papen and Hindenburg of the rumors. It was a long night for everyone concerned. Hindenburg, old and weary, finally agreed with Papen that he should name Hitler Chancellor – but on the condition that General Werner von Blomberg, his trusted friend, become Minister of Defense. The next morning Blomberg arrived in Berlin from Geneva, where he had been serving as chief military adviser to the German delegation at the Disarmament Conference. He accepted the offer and Hitler received the long-awaited summons from Hindenburg. Shortly after noon on January 30, 1933, Adolf Hitler was named Chancellor of Germany.

Eva congratulated herself on selecting a winner but there was no one to whom she could brag. Though her mother now admitted that perhaps she had underestimated Hitler, she still did not suspect how well her daughter knew him. She only knew that Eva was the caretaker of the Hitler photographic file at Hoffmann's and that she often met Hitler at the studio and several times had gone to lunch with him at a nearby café. But she was quick to tell the neighbors that 'Eva knows the Chancellor' and to garner any prestige this might bring the Braun family. At first Eva was amused, and then worried. Hitler was now Germany's man of the hour and all eyes were on him. His every move was followed religiously by newspaper reporters, supporters, enemies and plain citizens, and Eva knew that her presence at his side would be noted and duly reported. She was worried about how she would explain to her parents that she was more than just a keeper of Hitler's photograph file, that she was actually the new Chancellor's favorite feminine companion.

Eva needn't have worried about publicity concerning their affair, for Hitler had no intention of allowing the citizens of Germany to find out about her. As he told Heinrich Hoffmann, 'The *chère amie* of a politician must be quietly discreet.' But though Hitler wanted to impress on the German people that he was so dedicated to governing their country and leading it back to prewar eminence that he didn't have time for a serious love affair, he secretly planned to continue his relationship with Eva. Certainly he thought of Eva immediately after his ascension to power, for he placed a telephone call to her that night. The scene in Berlin was hectic. As the news spread throughout the city, a vast crowd of Hitler's supporters and the curious surrounded the Kaiserhof Hotel where he was meeting with his party officials. Later he went to the Chancellery and saluted the thousands of SA, SS and armed forces personnel who paraded past the building for hours carrying torches. Thousands of telephone calls jammed the Chancellery switchboard, calls from all over the world. Nearly one hundred requests for a telephone line to the Chancellery came from the United States alone that January night. Even for the new Chancellor it wasn't easy to obtain a telephone line, but in the midst of the wild celebrations, the conferences with Göring, Goebbels, Blomberg and others, and the multitude of calls and telegrams, Hitler spoke to his *chère amie* in Munich.

It soon became obvious to Eva that Hitler did not intend to allow their affair to become public knowledge, but this secrecy did not solve her personal problems. As soon as he returned to Munich after becoming Chancellor, Hitler invited Eva to his apartment, and with the assurance born of success, insisted that she stay all night. As Frau Winter said bitterly, 'He received many women but none of them ever stayed overnight. Eva Braun was the first.'

Such visits became frequent, as did his luncheon and dinner invitations to the Osteria Bavaria and the Carlton Hotel café. At these cafés Hitler was accompanied by party members so that the public never noticed Eva in particular. If her presence was questioned, it was quickly explained that she was a representative of the Hoffmann photography studio conferring with Hitler about pictures to be distributed. Though such explanations satisfied the public, at home Eva was becoming more and more entangled in her attempts to conceal her true relationship with Hitler. Her strict and uncompromising father could not understand her irregular hours and why she 'stayed overnight at a friend's house' so often – especially since she never explained who her 'friend' was or where she lived. Nor did he understand why Eva insisted on having her own telephone in her bedroom and allowed no one to answer it but herself. Ilse knew why Eva wanted the phone and often heard her sister having long conversations with Hitler while hiding under the blankets to muffle her voice. But she didn't want to get involved because she was working for a Jewish doctor and suspected Hitler wouldn't appreciate that fact. Ilse didn't like Hitler, but at the same time she didn't want to be the cause of his breaking off the affair with Eva. Eva's younger sister Gretl knew she was having 'quite an affair' with some man because of the secret telephone conversations and her overnight visits at a 'friend's house'. She didn't know who the man was, but being at a romantic age, she was in favor of her sister's adventure. Thus Eva was able temporarily to keep her affair secret from her parents even though all three Braun daughters shared a bedroom. Gradually, the web of deception became quite complicated, especially after Hitler began inviting Eva to Haus Wachenfeld on the Obersalzberg. On these occasions Eva had to be away from home for the entire weekend since the trip from Munich took several hours. At first she told her parents that Hoffmann insisted she attend to some business for him over the weekend and her father would reluctantly give her permission to go although he denounced Hoffmann as a very thoughtless boss. Eva would pack her small suitcase and walk to the intersection of Turkenstrasse where one of Hitler's black Mercedes-Benz limousines would be waiting to pick her up. When she returned on Sunday night from Haus Wachenfeld, the secret procedure was reversed. Hitler himself never came near the Braun apartment. Despite his acclaim as the new savior of Germany, he seemed to fear a confrontation with Fritz Braun as much as Eva did. Though the situation was agonizing to Eva she was determined not to relinquish Hitler regardless of the consequences.

In other ways the period immediately after Hitler's appointment as Chancellor was enjoyable for Eva. Now that he no longer had to spend so much time trying to become Chancellor, devising stratagems to beat out such men as Papen, Schleicher or Brüning, he had more time for her. He had the power to issue orders, and party members would take care of the details. Now the police of the country were trying to protect his privacy instead of invading it. He had a fleet of planes, several automobiles, special trains – any type of transportation he wanted was provided and Eva accompanied him on many trips. Once he became Chancellor all the special interest groups tried to win his favor, among them the rich industrialists. In their attempt to gain special advantages from Hitler, they provided the Nazi Party with more money than it had ever collected, and Hitler diverted much of it for his own personal use. When Eva celebrated her twenty-first birthday less than a week after his ascension to power, he bought her a complete set of tourmaline jewelry. Though it was not really expensive jewelry, it was the best she had ever owned. Before her death Eva had such a wide choice of precious jewelry that the tourmalines remained in her collection only because of their sentimental value.

As proud as she was of the birthday gift, she couldn't allow her parents to see it. This and the other nagging irritations surrounding her secret affair bothered Eva. She loved her parents. The obligation to obey them that her father had instilled in her during her younger years and the family closeness she remembered from her childhood made her feel guilty every time she lied to them. And during this period she lied quite often because she was seeing Hitler quite often. She finally decided that she had to bring Fritz and Fanny Braun face to face with Adolf Hitler! When she heard her father state at dinner one evening that while he didn't care much for Hitler's ideas or his political radicalism, 'the man must have something or Paul von Hindenburg would not have shaken hands with him,' Eva had her first glimmer of encouragement.

Every time Hitler made a speech Eva turned on the radio in the Braun apartment and despite his opposition, Fritz Braun listened. At first he criticized nearly everything Hitler proposed or did, but as unemployment was eased across the country and living conditions improved, he began to weaken. Once or twice within Eva's hearing he even made complimentary remarks about Hitler. Eva then decided the time had come to introduce her parents to Hitler and tell them the truth.

The Brauns often took automobile excursions on Sundays, and one day Eva heard her father suggest they drive south to Berchtesgaden and up into the mountains since they had not been in that area for a while. Fanny Braun agreed and early the next Sunday morning the Brauns and some of their friends headed toward the Obersalzberg. They had asked Eva and Gretl to go along but both refused, which hardly surprised them since neither girl traveled with them much anymore.

Eva had already planned to drive to Haus Wachenfeld with Hitler's entourage and this gave her the opportunity she had been waiting for. She knew her parents often stopped at the Lambacher Hof in the small town of Lambach between Munich and Berchtesgaden for tea and a snack. If she could get Hitler to stop there also, perhaps she could finally introduce him to her parents. Coincidentally, that Sunday while the Brauns were on the Obersalzberg, Fanny Braun suggested they go see Hitler's house in the mountains. It was their first visit. 'The people talk such a lot about it,' she said. 'I would like to see the place.'

They were both surprised at the size of the house – it was quite small. (They would see it many times in later years when it was much more elaborate and was called 'Berghof'.) A large crowd had gathered in front of it that Sunday, all shouting, 'We want to see our Führer! We want to see our Führer!' Frau Braun turned to her husband and said, 'Let's go. *I* don't want to see him.'

As Eva had predicted, the Brauns and their friends decided to stop in Lambach on the return trip to Munich. When they reached the town, however, they discovered that the road was guarded by SS troops who wanted to know where they were going. The troops explained that 'the Führer is on his way through Lambach' and strict security measures had been ordered. After Herr Braun said they were merely going to the Lambacher Hof for a snack, the SS officer in charge of the roadblock motioned them to pass. The number of SS troops and the excitement of the townspeople were the main topic of conversation among the Brauns and their companions as they sat in the café. They had just finished their coffee and were about to leave when a shiny Mercedes-Benz drove up to the main entrance and their daughter Eva stepped from the back seat. Fanny Braun could not believe her eyes for a moment but a second long look convinced her that the girl was Eva. She hurried over to her and said, 'Eva, you?'

Eva smiled at her mother but said nothing.

'Eva, what are you doing in this car?' her mother asked.

By this time Fritz Braun had recovered from his shock and had joined his wife near the Mercedes-Benz.

'Where have you come from? What does this mean?'

Very quietly Eva said, 'I have come from Haus Wachenfeld.' Without another word she brushed past her mother and father and disappeared into the Lambacher Hof. At that moment another Mercedes-Benz stopped at the café and Hitler got out. As the townspeople cheered and tried to crowd around his car in order to see him better, Fanny Braun edged away from the scene. Now that she knew Eva was more than just a casual friend of the Führer, she wanted time to think, to decide what she and her husband should do. Fritz Braun, however, did not move, and when Hitler stepped from the automobile, he extended his hand. 'I am Eva's father.'

He expected an explanation from Hitler but the Führer gave none.

'And where is your Frau Gemahlin?' Hitler asked.

Fritz Braun looked around in the crowd but he could not find his wife. Meanwhile Hitler and his entourage marched into the Lambacher Hof. When Herr Braun finally located his wife, she said, 'Let's go immediately.' She now understood why Eva had talked so much about 'our Führer', why she had always urged her parents to believe in him, and she wanted to get home quickly so she could analyze the situation by herself. Just as she and her husband reached their automobile, however, Hitler's adjutant came out onto the porch of the Lambacher Hof.

'Where are the Braun parents, please?'

Fanny Braun turned her back on the inquiring adjutant and murmured, 'I do not want to go in.'

Fritz Braun convinced her that it would be best if they did. They were ushered into the private dining room where Hitler and Eva were eating. Hitler immediately stood up and motioned for Frau Braun to take the vacant chair next to his. After he shook her hand, Fanny Braun sat down and Hitler immediately began talking. He never mentioned Eva. He spoke about the beautiful mountains, the cakes, the tea and other trivial subjects. Later Frau Braun came to realize the effort Hitler had put out that day, since he very rarely 'chatted'. In fact, as she deduced that Sunday afternoon, he was a very poor conversationalist unless he was giving a monologue on his political, racial or military ideas. Frau Braun was very attentive and waited for Hitler to speak some serious words about Eva, whom he called *du* several times at the table, but the words never came. When it came time to leave, Hitler took her hand and kept her in the dining room after the others had left. He squeezed her hand hard three times and, as Fanny Braun told her husband later, 'He looked straight through me as though he could look into my very soul.' Hitler never spoke a word while he squeezed her hand but she got the impression that he was trying to comfort and reassure her. The Brauns then left the café.

Eva got into her Mercedes-Benz and drove off with the Hitler column without saying goodbye.

The meeting between her parents and Hitler had come off just as she had desired but Eva didn't know what to expect from them when she got home. She was happy they now knew the truth, that she would no longer have to deceive them, but if it came to a showdown, Hitler was her choice. She was deeply in love with him, and now that he was the most acclaimed man in all of Germany, the Führer who was attracting attention all over the world, she had no intention of giving him up. She had fought too hard to reach her present position in his affections to allow parental objections to interfere. It was her life and she intended to live it as she pleased.

When she returned to the Braun apartment that night her father was waiting for her. 'Is it true that you are the Führer's mistress?'

Eva didn't answer the question directly. 'If you want, I'll leave.'

Fritz Braun turned and walked away.

7
Dangerous Love

Ernst Rohm, who more than any other person had helped Hitler establish the Third Reich, became a serious obstacle to Hitler's ambitions to succeed the dying Hindenburg as President in 1934. The German Army saw Rohm's SA as a threat, and as long as it existed the generals would not support Hitler as Hindenburg's successor. Hitler made his choice between friendship and ambition. On June 30, 1934, Ernst Rohm was shot to death at Stadelheim Prison on Hitler's orders. When President Hindenburg died on the morning of August 2, 1934, the officers and men of the German Army kept their part of the bargain by personally taking the oath of allegiance to Hitler. Hitler became both Head of State and Commander-in-Chief of the Armed Forces. He took complete control of Germany.

Eva understood Hitler's moods and knew he could be extremely irrational in dealing with others. Even men who had been close to him during the early years of his political career, who had befriended him when no one else would, found themselves outcasts if they opposed him. Worse, their lives became expendable. Kurt G. W. Ludecke, one of the early Nazis, was arrested by Göring and only avoided being shot by escaping into Czechoslovakia, then to Switzerland, France and finally the United States. His only crime was being caught in the middle of the interparty conflict of 1934. Dr Kurt Krueger, the medical expert whom Hitler had consulted over the years for his periodic impotency and other sexual problems, decided in 1934 that his life was in danger because he knew too many intimate details of Hitler's private life. After Hitler became Chancellor he visited Krueger a few times and on each of these visits the doctor sensed an increasing embarrassment in his patient. Hitler, he decided, didn't want anyone to know what Krueger knew, and there was only one possible solution – eliminate Krueger. The doctor didn't wait to find out when or where Hitler intended to achieve this aim. He bought a ticket to Switzerland in June, 1934, and he, too, eventually traveled to the United States. Later Ernst Hanfstängl, who handled the foreign press for Hitler, ran afoul of the Führer over the publishing of Hindenburg's last testament. Hanfstängl told Hitler that the only way he could satisfy the suspicious foreign correspondents about what the late President had actually written in his political testament was to have the text photographed.

'Let me have it for half an hour,' he told Hitler, 'and I can get the office of our firm in Berlin to copy it for you. Then the press will know that it has not been altered.'

Hitler, who fully intended to alter Hindenburg's testament to suit his ambition, shouted, 'I don't care what that pack of liars think.'

After this episode Hanfstängl was not welcome in the Führer's intimate circle and he knew that his life was in danger. Some months later he was summoned to Berlin and informed by Fritz Wiedemann that Hitler had need of his services in Spain.

'The Führer wishes you to fly immediately to Spain to handle the interests of our press correspondents there.'

He was hurried to the military airport at Staaken where he boarded the Luftwaffe plane assigned to him. Once in the air, however, he discovered that the pilot had orders to drop him over the Red lines between Barcelona and Madrid! He talked the pilot into making a fake forced landing at a small airfield near Waldpolentz, Germany, and Hanfstängl, too, escaped to the West.

Eva noticed these men were missing from the Nazi gatherings she attended with Hitler and accepted their absence as part of the game Hitler was forced to play in order to gain complete control of the country. Always she supported his actions against all critics – her parents, her friends, everyone. She gave the impression to all who knew her that Hitler could do no wrong. Yet while she had complete faith in his destiny to revive Germany's greatness, there were times when she wondered whether he intended to keep her with him. She could not forget the fate of Geli Raubal, or that Winifred Wagner suddenly became frightened of him after Geli's suicide. As Ludecke, Krueger, Hanfstängl and other close associates of the Führer disappeared one by one, Eva remembered the stories she had heard about those who had once been close to Hitler in his early political years and had either died or faded from sight. She began to wonder whether Hitler was directly responsible for their fate. She was intelligent enough to realize that if he tired of her, she, too, would be in danger because she knew intimate details about his private life, many of which she had learned on the famous red velvet couch in his apartment on Prinzregentenstrasse. She once confided her fears to Harns, the waiter at the Carlton Hotel.

'When he turns against a person, he can be very ruthless,' Eva told Harns. 'Very, very ruthless.'

Harns agreed but added, 'He would never turn against a beautiful woman like you, Eva.'

Whatever her fear, though, Eva responded to Hitler's every beck and call. Her father was still very angry with her but he did not force her to leave home. Whether he thought discretion was the better part of valor now that Hitler was Chancellor, or whether his love for his daughter was the overriding factor, he did not try to break up the romance. He still grumbled to his wife when Eva left for a weekend on the Obersalzberg or a late-night visit to Hitler's apartment, but he didn't carry the matter any further. Fanny Braun was torn between her pride that her daughter was an intimate 'friend' of the new Chancellor and her shame at what she knew was going on at Haus Wachenfeld and Hitler's apartment. Eva ignored both her father's remarks about the deteriorating morals of young German girls and her mother's subtle comments about the propriety of marriage between 'those who love each other'. She never missed a chance to spend time with Hitler when he wasn't busy with government affairs and she was overwhelmed by his sudden prestige. She often accompanied him to the palace in Berlin, where he stayed periodically (the only palace she had ever been in before was on a sightseeing tour outside of Munich). She was delighted when German soldiers presented arms to Hitler, when polite footmen opened and closed automobile doors for her, when people called Hitler 'Your Excellency' or '*Der Führer*' as they entered hotels or restaurants.

Still she did resent his extraordinary discretion about their affair. If he could go to the theater or the opera in the company of beautiful actresses like Olga Tschechowa and Lil Dagover and permit photographers to take their pictures (which would be in all the newspapers of Germany the next day), why couldn't he risk a little gossip and take her to a public restaurant alone? She was hesitant to demand an explanation for two reasons: Hitler might get angry and sever their relationship completely or he might become irrational and do her physical harm. She told Harns early in June, 1934, that she was 'nothing but a prisoner' and she was weary of it. She said she was going to give Hitler 'an ultimatum' that he either treat her as he treated his actress friends or . . .

When she didn't complete her threat, Harns asked, 'Or what?' Eva shrugged and shook her head. 'I can't leave him now.'

Harns' interpretation of the remark was that Eva was too deeply in love with Hitler to consider breaking off the affair.

Hitler was not Chancellor very long before a conflict arose within the Nazi organization that had to be resolved. General von Blomberg, who had been appointed Minister of Defense when Hitler became Chancellor, became closer and closer to the Führer during the final months of 1933 and the early months of 1934. This was deeply resented by Röhm, who was in charge of Hitler's 'private army'. Hitler, in the middle, tried to pacify both Röhm's SA, which demanded 'more revolutionary action', and the German Army, which demanded the disbanding of the ever-growing SA and expansion of its own forces. The imminent death of the ill President brought a showdown between the two opposing forces. Hitler had already made up his mind that when Hindenburg died he wanted to be named President, while retaining his title of Chancellor.

It was a delicate problem for Hitler. The SA was a collection of 'Old Fighters' who had been useful as street brawlers when he was trying to gain power, but now that he was Chancellor they were an embarrassment. Röhm and the other leaders of the SA sensed his attitude and resented it. In December, 1933, Hitler tried to smooth their ruffled feelings by making Röhm a member of the Reich Cabinet. This helped and so did a letter he wrote to Röhm early in 1934.

94

My dear Chief of Staff,

The fight of the National Socialist movement and the National Socialist Revolution were rendered possible for me by the consistent suppression of the Red Terror by the SA. If the Army has to guarantee the protection of the nation against the world beyond our frontiers, the task of the SA is to secure victory of the National Socialist Revolution and the existence of the National Socialist State and the community of our people in the domestic sphere. When I summoned you to your present position, my dear Chief of Staff, the SA was passing through a serious crisis. It is primarily due to your services if after a few years this political instrument could develop that force which enabled me to face the final struggle for power and to succeed in laying low the Marxist opponent.

At the close of the year of the National Socialist Revolution, therefore, I feel compelled to thank you, my dear Ernst Röhm, for the imperishable services which you have rendered to the National Socialist movement and the German people and to assure you how very grateful I am to Fate that I am able to call such men as you my friends and fellow combatants.

> *In true friendship and grateful regard,*
> *Your Adolf Hitler*

Eva Braun was to remember this friendly letter many times in light of what occurred in the months ahead.

Feeling more secure because of his appointment to the Reich Cabinet and the letter he had received from Hitler, Röhm moved to strengthen his position vis-à-vis the generals. While Hitler was visiting Eva in Munich in February, 1934, Röhm proposed to the Reich Cabinet that the SA be merged with the German Army in an expansion program and that a Minister be appointed to take charge of all Armed Forces of the State. Obviously, he intended to fill that post himself. But the German Army High Command was extremely angry at the proposal and appealed to Hindenburg for help. Hindenburg, who had insisted that Hitler accept General von Blomberg as Minister of Defense when he appointed him Chancellor, opposed the proposal, and for the moment Röhm was silenced.

Early in April, however, Hitler was secretly informed that President Hindenburg would not live much longer. He knew that if he was to gain absolute power in Germany, if he was to persuade the German Army to take the oath of allegiance to him as Commander-in-Chief of the Armed Forces, he had to resolve the conflict with the SA before the President died. There wasn't much time. On April 11, 1934, Hitler boarded the cruiser *Deutschland* at Kiel to observe naval maneuvers and Blomberg accompanied him. Exactly what they discussed concerning the SA-German Army problem was not recorded, but a few weeks later, at a senior officers' conference of the German Army, Blomberg's proposal that Hitler be named president and Commander-in-Chief of the Armed Forces when Hindenburg died was approved.

When this news was leaked to Röhm, he knew that he and his SA were in danger. Immediately he began to formulate plans to resist any takeover of the SA by the German Army or disbandment of his forces by Hitler. On June 4, 1934, Hitler sent for Röhm and during a five-hour conference warned him not to start an armed conflict within Germany. He assured his 'friend' that the matter could be resolved peacefully to the satisfaction of all concerned. Hitler knew, however, that time was running out, that Hindenburg could not last much longer and the SA had to be disposed of before he died. Röhm seems to have come out of the conference reassured because he announced that he intended to take a sick leave. Hitler immediately ordered the SA to go on leave for the month of July since their leader was 'ill'. Members were instructed not to wear their uniforms or take part in any exercises or gatherings during their leave. This was Hitler's way of indicating to the generals that the SA was going to be disbanded. His one hope was that Hindenburg would die while the SA was temporarily out of sight of both the public and the army.

Sometime during the month of June, 1934, probably on June 20 when he attended a funeral service for Göring's first wife, Hitler changed his mind. He went to the ceremony, taking Eva with him, because Frau Göring had been one of his favorite acquaintances during the early years of his career. Göring had met her while he was in Sweden as Flight Chief of the Svenska Lufttrafik in 1920, and although she was married to a Swedish officer, Nils von Kantzow, he immediately fell in love with her. Without the approval of her father, Swedish Army Colonel C. A. von Fock, Karin von Kantzow divorced her husband and married Göring. Hitler probably saw a parallel between Karin Göring's defiance of her parents to marry Göring and Eva's willingness to antagonize her parents for his sake. Karin Göring had died on October 17, 1931, but in 1934 her husband requested that her body be removed to his estate outside of Berlin, which he had named Karinhall for her, and that this second interment be accompanied by the full honors of a formal National Socialist funeral. Though Eva had never met the woman she was delighted to attend the ceremony with Hitler, ignorant that on that day plans for a blood purge were being formulated. While Eva was being shown through Karinhall and around the surrounding grounds, Hitler and Göring were having a long discussion about the SA and Ernst Röhm. This conference sealed the fate of hundreds of persons. Hitler decided that too much was at stake to gamble on the ill President's dying between July 1 and August 1, 1934, while the SA was on leave. The surest way to eliminate the SA threat once and for all was to get rid of Röhm and his contingent of leaders who commanded the loyalty of the old 'street brawlers'. If Eva noticed that Hitler was quiet and lost in thought on the ride back to Munich, she didn't think it unusual.

After June 20, 1934, Hitler conducted government business in a routine manner. Eva saw him only twice in Munich between June 20 and June 30, and to her, the person who knew him most intimately, his attitudes and actions appeared normal. On June 28 he told her that he was going to fly to Essen with Göring to attend the wedding of Staatsrat Terboven but that he expected to be back in Munich by June 30 at the latest. He didn't tell her he had a very good reason to make certain he was in the city at that time. From Essen Hitler and Goebbels, who had joined him there, announced a tour to the various labor camps in the area. Later Goebbels publicly confessed that this tour was made 'in order not to warn the traitors, so that the plan to carry out a thorough purge could be laid down in all details'. On June 29 Hitler and Goebbels stayed at the Hotel Dreesen in Godesberg, supposedly resting from their strenuous tour of the camps. During the evening messages of all types began arriving at the hotel for Hitler. Instead of the customary single telephone call he made every evening to Eva, he made and received a multitude of calls. Telegrams arrived periodically and Göring's special couriers delivered messages every half-hour from Berlin after having made the trip by plane to the Hangelar Airfield near Bonn and the remainder of the distance by motor-cycle. Hitler was obviously worried and became extremely depressed when the weather turned bad. He ordered his personal pilot, Hans Baur, to call Munich to check on the cloud cover and the possibility of flying to that city later in the evening or early the next morning. Baur reported a few minutes later that the skies should clear by 2 a.m. and Hitler was relieved.

At 2 a.m., while Eva Braun was sound asleep in the Braun apartment in Munich and Ernst Röhm was comfortably resting in his bed at the Pension Hanslbauer in Wiessee, a town south of Munich, Hitler left the Hotel Dreesen in Godesberg and was driven to Hangelar Airfield in a black Mercedes. Baur brought the aircraft down at the Munich-Oberwiesenfeld Airfield shortly after 4 a.m. where two armored cars and a detachment of Reichswehr troops were waiting for Hitler. Hitler got into one of the armored cars and was taken directly to the Ministry of Interior for a conference with Nazi leaders known for their strong-arm tactics. While he was in this building, many SA leaders who had been arrested during the night were brought in and he berated them in a loud voice and tore the insignias off their uniforms. Then, about the time Eva was eating her breakfast before going to Hoffmann's studio, Hitler, in his personal armored car with a convoy of six automobiles and five trucks of soldiers, passed within a few blocks of her apartment on the way to Wiessee where Ernst Röhm was still sleeping.

Well guarded, Hitler entered the Pension Hanslbauer and hurried directly to Röhm's room where he hammered on the door.

'Open the door!'

'Who is it?' Röhm asked, obviously still half-asleep.

'Hitler.'

Röhm, unaware that his death sentence had already been pronounced by his Führer, opened the door. Hitler stepped inside, still well guarded, and began screaming vile epithets at Röhm, who was momentarily taken by surprise. Once he regained his voice, however, the tough Röhm roared back at Hitler until he was overpowered by the soldiers. He was immediately hustled into one of the trucks and taken back to the Stadelheim Prison in Munich along with the other SA officers who had been in Wiessee. There, in the same prison where eleven years earlier he had been jailed for supporting Hitler in the Beer Hall Putsch, Röhm received his last token of 'friendship' from Hitler. The Führer ordered that a revolver be given him in his cell so that he could die 'heroically'. The angry and courageous Röhm spat at the gun.

'If Adolf wants me dead, let him do it.'

Hitler so ordered. Sepp Dietrich, leader of the SS Obergruppe Ost and commander of Hitler's Leibstandarte, entered Röhm's cell a few hours later and shot him.

During that final weekend of June, 1934, hundreds of Hitler's enemies died. Among them were General von Schleicher, the former Chancellor who had opposed Hitler's appointment by Hindenburg; Gustav von Kahr, the Bavarian politician who had helped block Hitler's abortive putsch in 1923; Edmund Heines, the SA Obergruppenführer for Silesia; General von Bredow, an ally of Schleicher's; Gregor Strasser; and Edgar Jung, Papen's adviser. Papen himself was held under arrest for four days and his office was wrecked, but he was not executed. Many of those massacred that Saturday had no connection with the SA but were victims of Hitler's hatred. Some had once been good friends of his, and by nightfall it was evident that being a friend of the new Führer was a dangerous relationship. He didn't just stop seeing people or talking to them when he became irritated. He killed them!

Eva, like most of the other citizens of Munich on June 30, 1934, became aware early in the day that certain individuals in the city were being hunted down and arrested. Hoffmann, who had married again in April, 1934, was in Paris on his honeymoon, so Eva could not ask him what was going on in Munich. All her attempts to contact Hitler were unsuccessful since the Führer was much too busy traveling between Munich and Wiessee and back and forth to the airport to talk to her. It wasn't until the next day – Sunday – that she heard from him. He was giving a tea party in the Chancellery garden in Berlin as if the grotesque events of the day before had never happened when he telephoned her. When she asked about the events in Munich, he avoided a direct answer, merely telling her that she would hear about it on the radio or read about it in the newspapers. When she did, she was horrified that so many men she knew had been killed, men who had sat at the same table with her and Hitler, eating and drinking and talking about old times or future plans. When Hitler spoke before the Reichstag and explained his reasons for the blood purge, however, she felt somewhat better.

'For fourteen years,' Hitler said, 'I have stated consistently that the fighting organizations of the party are political institutions and that they have nothing to do with the army. In the State there is only one bearer of arms and that is the army; there is only one bearer of the political will and that is the National Socialist Party. Röhm did not believe that so he was treated as a traitor.'

Eva's unasked question as she listened to the speech on the radio was the same one that was on the minds of thousands of German citizens. Why hadn't the men been tried in court before they were executed? Hitler answered the question toward the end of his speech.

'If anyone reproaches me and asks why I did not resort to the regular courts of justice, then all I can say to him is this: in this hour I was responsible for the fate of the German people, and thereby I became the supreme Justicar of the German people. . . . And everyone must know for all future time that if he raises his hand to strike the State, then certain death is his lot.'

And if, in anger, Eva should raise her hand to strike Hitler?

Later Hitler drew up a new set of regulations for the much diminished SA, which was put under the control of Viktor Lutze. The first rule on the list was also applicable to Eva Braun. All that was necessary was to change the 'SA' to 'Eva': '1. I demand blind obedience and unquestioning discipline from SA. . . . '

Throughout the twelve new regulations he stressed loyalty, obedience and comradeship. Eva knew that he expected these same qualities from her. She also knew that many of those who had died on the weekend of June 30 had been loyal, obedient supporters of Hitler. What had happened then? Had they all turned disloyal overnight? She didn't know but her faith in Hitler remained unshaken. When her father spoke against him at the dinner table after the Führer's speech, she upheld Hitler.

'The man is mad,' Fritz Braun exclaimed. 'Absolutely mad!' He was especially disgusted when he learned that an innocent music critic named Willi Schmidt had mistakenly been murdered by the SS who were looking for another man by the name of Willi Schmidt.

Eva was furious at her father's remarks. 'They were trying to betray him. They were not loyal friends as he thought they were,' she said. 'They would have killed him if he had not defended himself.'

The idea that Hitler was merely 'defending himself' was ridiculous. He was strictly on the offensive, but to Eva such facts were immaterial. After this argument she knew she would have to get out of the Braun apartment as soon as possible – she no longer wanted to live with a father who ridiculed and opposed Hitler – but for the moment she had no choice but to stay at home. Hitler was spending more time with her now that he was Chancellor, but she still was not certain of her position with him.

As she told Harns, 'It is hell to be twenty-two years old and in love with a man more than twice your age and still not know whether he is in love with you or not.'

She chose to continue her campaign to win Hitler's complete affection, even though she realized she was treading on dangerous ground. After the example of the SA purge, she knew that if she made one wrong move she could be eliminated by Hitler.

8
Isolation

Hitler's hatred for the Jews resulted in the Nuremberg Laws 'for the protection of German blood and German honor'. Promulgated on September 15, 1935, these laws deprived the Jews of German citizenship and forbade marriage between Germans and Jews. Many grocery stores and butcher shops refused to sell food to Jews. Jewish mothers found it nearly impossible to obtain milk for their children. Hotels turned Jews away. It was the beginning of Hitler's plan to massacre all Jews.

Eva was aware of Hitler's hatred for Jews long before he summoned the Reichstag to Nuremberg in 1935 for a special session to act on the proposals he had formulated. His hatred changed her own life style, and eventually she subjugated herself to his will. When she once asked him why he condemned *all* Jews, he gave her the answer that he was to give a great number of individuals throughout the remainder of his life: 'The Jew is the incarnation of egoism. His only gift is that of juggling with other people's property and swindling each and every one. The Jew has a talent for bringing confusion into the simplest matters, for getting everything muddled up. I've always said that the Jews are the most diabolic creatures in existence and at the same time the stupidest. We can live without Jews but they can't live without us.'

His usual tirade against the Jews was much longer and more detailed, but it was obvious Hitler was determined to rid Germany of all Jews though few people in 1935 realized the method he was going to use. Eva herself was surprised when she discovered that Martin Bormann, the Director of the Party Chancellery, was asking questions about her own ancestry. Despite his seemingly inconsequential title, Bormann was one of the most powerful and ruthless men in Hitler's inner circle, a palace guard type who slanted Hitler's thinking by controlling who saw the Führer and the topics and opinions such rare visitors could express when they did see him. Hitler appreciated Bormann's protective curtain and in return gave him absolute powers in many areas of administration and operation. Eva, her sisters, her parents and even her friends were investigated thoroughly by Bormann and his staff to make certain they had no Jewish blood. Eva was very angry when she first learned about the investigation, and not knowing that Hitler himself had ordered it, went to him with her complaint. He soothed her feelings and told her that he would immediately order a halt to such actions. Instead he told Bormann to continue the investigation but to be more discreet.

Heinrich Himmler, the Reichsführer of the SS who looked more like a schoolteacher than a Grand Inquisitor, was jealous of Bormann and especially resented the fact that Hitler had asked Bormann to conduct the Braun investigation rather than himself. Himmler felt that his office was responsible for such security measures and he didn't want Bormann to gather any laurels that would improve his status with the Führer. His own dossier on Eva Braun had proved a failure as far as his ambitions were concerned because it indicated that she definitely had no Jewish blood nor did any member of her family. Consequently, when he received a tip that Ilse Braun might be a spy for the Italians he decided to follow it up. His investigators discovered that Ilse had traveled through Italy, Austria and Yugoslavia within recent months, taking part in the European dancing championships, and had been very friendly with an Italian officer while staying at La Spezia. Himmler suspected the dancing championships were merely a 'front' for her spying activities.

When Ilse returned home she couldn't understand why her mail was always so late. The letters from the Italian naval officer in La Spezia took twice as long to reach her as they should have, but despite her complaints no one could explain the reason. When she told Eva about this mysterious delay, her sister laughed and said, 'You're just imagining that the letters take so long because you are in love!' One day, however, Brückner, Hitler's adjutant, asked Ilse to stop at his office. This was the same rude, arrogant staff officer who often 'misplaced' or 'forgot' the letters and telephone calls Eva made to Hitler during the early days of their romance. When Ilse Braun arrived at his office, Brückner asked her a long list of questions, most of which puzzled her. Finally, when the interrogation was completed and she demanded to know why he had summoned her to his office, Brückner admitted that Himmler had accused her of spying for the Italians. Ilse immediately told Eva, who relayed the information to Hitler. This time Hitler was genuinely surprised and asked Himmler to explain.

The clever Himmler had his answer ready. 'If you had kept me informed about Fraülein Braun's position, this misunderstanding would never have arisen.'

This was Himmler's subtle way of telling Hitler that if he had known, officially, that Eva Braun was the Führer's mistress, he would not have investigated Ilse. There was, of course, no substance to the spying charge. Ilse had become infatuated with the Italian naval officer and had had a vacation fling.

If Eva needed any evidence of Hitler's strong feelings against the Jews or Germans who associated with them she had only to remember what happened to the film actress Renate Müller. This beautiful and talented woman was one of the few actresses who was able to stay out of Goebbels' bed and still retain her star status. As Minister of Propaganda, Goebbels controlled the German film industry and was noted for his sexual demands on the actresses, but Renate Müller's resistance was firm. She didn't need to fear Goebbels or pay any attention to his threats because

Hitler also paid her special attention. They had first met at Goebbels' apartment in the Reichstagplatz when Frau Goebbels invited them both to dinner. Renate was entranced by Hitler's prestige, although he had not yet become Chancellor. He, in turn, was fascinated by her beauty. Frau Goebbels encouraged the attraction, calculating that if Hitler became enamoured of the actress, then her husband would have to forget her.

Renate soon discovered that Hitler was a strange lover. Once when they were alone in the Goebbels' home, and Renate fully expected him to make love to her, he raised his hand high and rigid in the Nazi salute. She eyed him curiously while he kept his arm in this position for several minutes. Finally she burst into laughter.

'You're funnier than Putzi,' she said.

She was referring to Ernst Hanfstängl, who often acted the clown, but Hitler didn't smile.

'This is no laughing matter,' he assured her. 'I can maintain this salute for two hours, longer than any of my associates. Do you know why?'

Renate stared at his trousers just below the belt. 'It must be some sort of compensation.'

Hitler dropped his arm and angrily hurried out of the room. But this insult to his virility only increased his interest in Renate. For the next few weeks he arranged to see her often and sent her flowers, jewelry and furs. At Hitler's insistence the German newspapers publicized her career and extolled her talents. Several times she visited him at the Reich Chancellery and once was seen leaving the building at 4 a.m. All the time Hitler was enjoying her company the usual security check on her background was going on. Himmler discovered she had a Jewish lover who had escaped from Germany and was living in Paris. A few weeks later she took a vacation in France and Himmler obtained photographs of her with her Jewish lover and gave them to Hitler. When she returned to Germany the Führer ordered Renate brought to him on the Obersalzberg, showed her the pictures and accused her of having extramarital relations with a Jew in violation of the Nuremberg Laws. She admitted her guilt and asked for forgiveness. Because of his fondness for the beautiful petite actress, Hitler did forgive her. For a while they were seen together again, but suddenly, without saying a word to Hitler, Renate disappeared. This time Himmler's investigators found her in Monte Carlo, again with her Jewish lover. When the word was relayed to Hitler, he was furious and vowed he would punish her.

Renate Müller returned to Germany of her own accord. She visited her director Zeissler, who knew of her affair with Hitler but was unaware of her Jewish lover. He jokingly asked her if she was having any more 'adventures' in the Reich Chancellery. He was referring to an episode she had told him about during the early stages of her affair with Hitler. She and the Führer had been in his apartment at the Reich Chancellery and she was certain that he was going to have intercourse with her. They had both undressed and were walking toward the bed when Hitler fell on the floor and beseeched her to kick him. When she hesitated, he begged her again, heaping all kinds of accusations on himself. Not knowing what else to do, Renate had kicked him hard in the side. The more she kicked him, the more excited he became. When she finally satisfied him and escaped from the room, she felt mortified and disgusted. Zeissler had thought the story exceptionally amusing, but when he mentioned it to Renate after her return from Monte Carlo it didn't evoke the usual laughter. She merely said, 'He is a very hard man to understand.'

The next day, while under surveillance by Himmler's men, she leaped to her death from her third-floor apartment. Hitler always blamed the Jews for her death, never admitting that his unmistakable intent to punish her drove her to commit suicide.

Eva, who did not know Renate Müller well, felt that it was to her advantage to have another of Hitler's feminine companions eliminated from the scene. The death of the actress did reinforce in her mind Hitler's deadly hatred of the Jews and those who associated with them. During a discussion with him about the suicide Eva unthinkingly referred to a German woman she knew who had married a Jew in 1930. This was several years prior to the Nuremberg Laws, and Eva didn't think Hitler would expect this woman to divorce her husband. She soon discovered she was wrong.

'I believe in a divine commandment such as "Thou shalt preserve the species." If she lives with this Jew and has children she is violating this commandment,' he shouted.

Hoffmann, overhearing the discussion between Eva and Hitler, later told her of an incident that had occurred in Munich during Hitler's early political campaigning. Hitler had picked up a street-walker and in the privacy of her room had subjected her to various degrading sexual acts after paying her the sum of money she asked. She then told him that she was Jewish and taunted him that he had had intimate relations with a Jew. He was so stunned that at the time he did nothing. A week later, however, he returned with several of his Nazi companions, broke into her room and compelled her to go through a routine of degradation with the others while he watched. He then hit her across the face and left.

Incidents such as these made Eva afraid to even speak to a Jew. She had many Jewish acquaintances and until she met Hitler she had never really given any thought to their religion. But now she decided that if Hitler believed the Jews were a dangerous cancer on the country, then she should believe the same. So, like Hitler, she proceeded to eliminate Jews from her life. Hitler had used the friendship of certain Jews to help him achieve political power, but once he no longer needed them, he set about destroying the entire race. Eva followed a similar pattern. Her Jewish friends were suitable when she was younger and lonely, but now that she was so close to the Chancellor of Germany, she deserted them.

Eva's new attitude toward the Jews caused considerable conflict between her and Ilse. They argued incessantly over 'the Jewish question' and Hitler's theories. Ilse was very fond of the Jewish laryngologist for whom she worked and constantly defended him during her discussions with Eva. Eventually, the Jewish doctor realized his life was in danger and also that he was jeopardizing Ilse Braun by permitting her to work for him. He dismissed her as his receptionist and later he escaped from Germany and went to live in New York. Ilse said very little to Eva about Jews after this incident because she was aware that Hitler's hatred knew no bounds. In turn, Eva seldom brought the subject up to Ilse, and according to Harns felt badly that she had been the cause of breaking up her sister's budding romance with the doctor.

Eva's emotional makeup prevented her from rigidly following Hitler's precepts about the Jews, even though she wanted to please him. She had once been good friends with Pearl Sklar, a Jewish woman who owned a small jewelry store in Munich not far from the Braun apartment. A widow with no children, Frau Sklar had taken a liking to young Eva. When Eva first started working for Hoffmann, Frau Sklar had sold her pins and earrings at a discount. Eva and the older woman ate dinner together quite often. As Eva's romance with Hitler developed, she was too busy to see Frau Sklar and had nearly forgotten about her until she heard Hoffmann mention her name one day. He was looking at a list of names on a sheet of paper, calling them off aloud, and one of them was Frau Sklar.

'What about Frau Sklar?' Eva asked.

Hoffmann looked at her. 'Do you know her?'

'I know a Frau Sklar who owns a small jewelry store here in Munich. Pearl Sklar.'

Hoffmann shook his head. 'She is a Jew.'

For a moment Eva was shocked. She told Hoffmann later that during their friendship she had never once given a thought to whether Frau Sklar was Jewish or not – at the time she did not care. But now, by the way Hoffmann said 'Jew', Eva knew immediately that her friend was in danger.

'So, she is a Jew.'

'Her store is on the list to be closed and the owner taken into "protective custody",' Hoffmann said.

While there is no evidence that in 1935 Eva had any knowledge of the concentration and labor camps where Jews were taken in 'protective custody' were herded, she did know that 'protective custody' meant arrest. When Hitler returned to Munich for a visit the following week, Frau Sklar's name was removed from the list of Jewish merchants in Munich to be arrested. Eva herself sent a note to the woman with a small sum of money and told her to leave Germany immediately. With the note and the bundle of marks was a pass signed by Heinrich Himmler ordering all Gestapo members to 'allow the bearer to cross the border of Germany unmolested.' Frau Sklar left for Italy within twenty-four hours.

It also seems Eva directly influenced Hitler's decision to permit the Jewish doctor who had treated him when he was a child in Linz to leave Austria unharmed. Dr Eduard Bloch had also treated Hitler's mother during her fatal battle against cancer. After Klara Hitler's funeral, the doctor seldom saw Hitler, although Hitler sent him postcards from Vienna, where he had gone after her death. Hitler was then making a meager living, painting postcards and drying them in front of a hot fire to give them an antique quality. One of the cards that Dr Bloch particularly liked showed a hooded Capuchin monk holding a glass of champagne. The painting was captioned *Prosit Neujahr* – a toast to the New Year'. On the back of the card Hitler had written a short greeting. 'The Hitler family sends you best wishes for a Happy New Year. In everlasting thankfulness, Adolf Hitler.'

Though Dr Bloch received these occasional messages from the boy he had treated in Linz, he did not follow Hitler's political career very closely. In fact, in Austria it was very difficult to do so since even the mention of Hitler's name was prohibited for a long time. By word of mouth he did hear rumors that Hitler was gathering a strong group of political supporters in Munich; that he hated all Jews; that he intended to gain control of Germany even if he had to do so by force. Until some Nazi supporters in the Linz underground party organization returned from a rally held by Hitler in Nuremberg after he became Chancellor, Dr Bloch had had no direct word from Hitler except the postcards. At the rally these Linz Nazis had talked with the new Chancellor and he had asked for news of Dr Bloch. Informed that the doctor was alive and still practicing medicine, Hitler said, 'Dr Bloch is an *edel Jude* [a noble Jew]. If all Jews were like him, there would be no "Jewish question".'

This was high personal praise but events proved that Hitler certainly didn't have a long memory. Shortly after he took over Austria in the *Anschluss*, the shops, homes and offices of the seven hundred Jews in Linz were marked with yellow paper banners indicating they were occupied by Jews. By decree Dr Bloch's medical practice was limited to Jewish patients only, a hint that he was expected to halt his work altogether. Gestapo agents appeared at the doctor's home while he was away and confiscated the postcards that Hitler had sent him years earlier from Vienna. As a final humiliation, Hitler ordered that all Jews were to leave Linz, his former hometown, within forty-eight hours. They were to go to Vienna, the first stop on the way to a concentration camp.

Former Gestapo officer Otto Beck, who was stationed in Austria during this period, was summoned to Vienna with several other German officers to confer with Himmler. During the meeting the name of Dr Bloch came up and Himmler gave orders that they were to give this man special attention. Himmler said that Hitler's 'stupid cow' had convinced the Führer that this Jewish doctor deserved 'favored treatment' because of his past association with the Hitler family. Himmler often called Eva Braun by this derogatory nickname because he was extremely jealous of her. His men, however, were not aware of the identity of the 'stupid cow' – in fact, Otto Beck didn't realize Himmler was referring to Eva Braun until he heard about the Führer's long-time romance after the war ended. He followed Himmler's instructions very closely, and when he returned to Linz he immediately told Dr Bloch to remove the yellow signs from his home and office. Nor did he permit the doctor's 'Aryan' landlord to evict him because he was a Jew. When the order came that all

Jews were to leave Linz within forty-eight hours, Dr Bloch was exempted.

Despite these 'favors', Bloch realized he was in danger and decided to leave Austria while he still could. He asked the Gestapo for one more favor: Could he take his savings with him? Not even Eva Braun could persuade Hitler to grant this wish. He was permitted to take sixteen marks instead of the usual ten, and even this small consideration from the Führer was exceptional. So Dr Bloch arrived in the United States penniless at the age of sixty-nine, but he considered himself fortunate.

After isolating herself from her Jewish friends, Eva found her position more lonely than ever. She still had a civil relationship with her sister Ilse, but they were not close. Many of her school friends had left Germany because of the man she loved, and Eva still had not achieved such status in the Führer's intimate circle that the wives of his associates made an effort to be friends with her. She found herself more and more alone, especially when Hitler was away from Munich. Her parents had still not come to terms with her affair. Though they seldom openly criticized her any longer, Eva could tell by their manner that they were both hurt and angry. Several times she had made up her mind to move out of the Braun apartment to a place of her own but had backed down because she didn't have enough money. While Hitler gave her many gifts and often took her with him to Berlin, Nuremberg and Haus Wachenfeld, he had not offered her any money or a place to live. Eva didn't feel secure enough with him yet to ask such a favor. She did hint to him several times that life with her parents was not very comfortable, that she often slept on a bench in Hoffmann's studio in order to receive his long-distance telephone calls rather than risk her father's wrath by taking them at home.

Her two closest friends at this time were her younger sister Gretl, a fun-loving girl who encouraged Eva's romance with Hitler, and Herta Schneider, a former schoolmate. Frau Schneider was married to the son of the authoress Schneider-Förstl from Pasing and was the one friend who was close to Eva both before and during her romance with Hitler. Except for these two, however, Eva had no one to discuss her problems with, as she once had with Frau Sklar, Ilse and her mother, before she became estranged from them because of Hitler. Yet despite the alienation of her parents and friends, her own confusion and doubt about many of Hitler's policies, and his patent neglect of her for weeks at a time, Eva's feelings toward Hitler never varied much. She loved him and she was determined that she could and would convince him that he loved her. Like the majority of Germans at that time, Eva thought Hitler was the greatest man alive.

9
Eva's Diary

Hitler believed that every woman was unreasonable. According to his theory, a woman in love lived only for the sake of her man and expected him to do likewise. When a man did not do this because of his devotion to his own ambitions or duties, then the woman usually became sullen and often bored to death. A couple in love, Hitler explained, create rights, and the woman sometimes feels that her rights are being violated. This could lead to disaster.

Eva Braun faced the year of 1935 with a great deal of uncertainty and disillusionment. She was very unhappy for several
reasons. Her romance with Hitler had progressed satisfactorily to
a certain point, but was now stalemated. She had no doubt that
Hitler was fonder of her now than when they had first met, but
she could not become accustomed to his long periods of neglect.
She had thought that once they became this close, he would keep
her at his side constantly, that he would grow attentive to her
needs and her feelings, but he seemed completely satisfied with
their rather casual arrangement.

Hitler's lack of ardor was emotionally painful to Eva; it was
also embarrassing. Ilse knew whenever Hitler failed to visit or
send for Eva for weeks at a time and she often remarked how rude
and thoughtless he was. Her mother and father usually wore an
I-told-you-so look on their faces during these periods of neglect.
The humiliation in front of her family, however, was something
Eva could endure. What she could not stand was the thought of
losing Hitler. Every time she read in the newspaper that the
Chancellor had attended the opera in Berlin or a musical concert
in Bayreuth, she wondered who had been with him. Often a
picture provided the answer – a beautiful actress – which only
made her more worried. She never ceased to hate her 'backstreet'
existence and in 1935, when she was not as sure of her position
with him as she was in later years, his public association with
other women made her extremely jealous – and angry.

To be angry and have no one to argue with was frustrating.
Her increasing isolation from her friends and family left her too
much time to imagine what was happening in Berlin while she
was 'stuck' in Munich. Gradually she became more and more
depressed about Hitler's indifference and expressed her growing
disillusionment in her diary:

FEBRUARY 6, 1935 – *I guess today is the right day to begin this
masterpiece. I have happily reached my twenty-third year, that
is whether or not I am happy is another question. At the moment
I certainly am not happy. That is because I have such expec-
tations of such an important day. If I only had a dog, then I
wouldn't be quite so alone, but I guess that is asking too much.*

*Frau Schaub [wife of Hitler's adjutant Julius Schaub] came
with flowers and a telegram as an 'ambassador'. My whole office
looks like a flower shop and smells like a mortuary. I really am un-
grateful but I hoped so much to get a little Dachshund, and now
again nothing. Perhaps next year or even after that. Then it will be*

112

better suited to an incipient spinster.

Let me not give up hope. I should have learned patience by now.

I bought two lottery tickets today because I was convinced now or never. They were blanks. It seems as though I'll never get rich. Can't do anything about it.

Today I would have gone to the Zugspitze with Herta [Schneider], Gretl, Ilse, and mother, and we would have lived like queens because one always has most fun when others share the happiness. But the trip didn't come off.

Today I'm going to eat with Herta. What else may a simple little woman of twenty-three do? Thus I'll bring my birthday to a close with gluttony. I believe I shall then have acted in accordance with his preferences.

Obviously Eva was feeling sorry for herself. She had hinted to Hitler many times that she wanted a dog to keep her company during the long hours she had to sit and wait for him, but on her twenty-third birthday she received 'again nothing'. The bouquet and telegram brought by his 'ambassador', Frau Schaub, were small comfort to a romantic young girl who desperately wanted to be with her lover. Frau Schaub had had experience in trying to comfort Hitler's girlfriends before. It was she who had taken Geli Raubal to the Munich Playhouse the night before Geli committed suicide. Eva had met Frau Schaub on May 5, 1931, when Julius Schaub brought his new bride to the Hoffmann studio for their wedding portrait. They had become good friends, though they didn't spend much time together because the wife of Hitler's adjutant had many duties. Whenever Hitler asked her to do something for Eva, however, Frau Schaub responded with tact and compassion because she liked Eva. When she brought the flowers Hitler had ordered her to take Eva on her birthday, she stayed and spoke to her about how busy the Chancellor was and how he had a multitude of problems to solve. Instead of feeling depressed, she pointed out, Eva should be proud and grateful that such a busy man, such a great man, had taken time to send her flowers and a telegram.

Hitler was indeed busy in February, 1935. The British and French governments had renewed their efforts to persuade Germany to come to an agreement on mutual assistance in case of war with Russia or another country or countries in Eastern Europe. Hitler was opposed to such an agreement (he was not afraid of any nation attacking Germany at that time, so why

8 113

should he take a pledge to help another country if it were attacked, he asked the Reichstag) but Germany's forbidden re-armament had reached such proportions that it could no longer be concealed. Hitler knew that if he agreed to the mutual assistance pact the Western Powers would overlook Germany's secret rearming. He was still trying to work out a solution on Eva's birthday, and it was impossible for him to take the time to fly to Munich to see her.

Five days later Hitler did go to Munich and he did see Eva.

FEBRUARY 11, 1935 – *He was just here but no dog and no clothes. He didn't even ask me whether I had a birthday wish. So now I bought myself some jewelry. A necklace, earrings, and a ring to match for fifty marks. Everything very pretty. I hope he likes it. If not he can buy me something himself.*

After this visit Eva was temporarily placated and happier than she had been for some time. According to the next entry in her diary, she was confident that she and an acquaintance named Charlotte (Charlie) would be invited to Berlin to stay with Hitler for a while:

FEBRUARY 15, 1935 – *It seems that the Berlin deal is really going to come off. I won't believe it until I am in the Reich Chancellery. I hope it'll be an agreeable affair. Too bad Herta can't come along instead of Charlie. She would be a guarantee for a few happy days. This way there will probably be a big ado because I don't think Brückner will show his more charming side for Charlie. I don't dare look forward to it yet but it might turn out to be wonderful if everything goes well. Let's hope so.*

Three days later Hitler stopped in Munich again and paid a visit to Eva. It is apparent from this date's entry in her diary that it was often difficult for him to contact her at the Braun apartment. Chancellor or not, he still had not been accepted by Fritz and Fanny Braun, so he never visited Eva at home. In 1935 the man whom much of the world was warily watching, who was feared by large numbers of Germans, shied away from a confrontation with Eva's parents. To Hitler's coarse, rigid mind it was best to avoid the parents of his mistress because they would make him feel uncomfortable. This was a quirk in his personality, a throwback to the Germanic parental disciplinary attitude of past years when the father of the girl decided whether the man she wanted to associate with was suitable. The fear he had of his own father in his youth made him hesitant to face Eva's father

114

in 1935. So Eva's suggestion that she should have a place of her own where she could meet him whenever he desired impressed Hitler as having some merit.

FEBRUARY 18, 1935 – *Yesterday he came quite unexpectedly and it was a delightful evening. The nicest thing was that he is thinking about taking me out of the studio and – I don't want to be too happy yet – buy me a little house. I don't dare think of it. It would be so wonderful. I wouldn't have to open the door for our 'honorable' customers and play salesgirl. Dear God, please make it come true within a reasonable period of time.*

Poor Charlie is sick and can't come to Berlin with us. She's really sick but maybe it is better that way. Maybe he would be very rude to her and then she would certainly be even more unhappy.

I am so infinitely happy. Happy that he loves me so and pray that it will always be like this. I should never want to be blamed if he should stop loving me.

Eva felt it was absurd that she had to 'play' the part of a sales-girl to cover up their romance. It was ironic that Hitler, who now had millions of marks at his disposal, controlled the German Army, was in complete charge of his country's political and domestic affairs and was making his presence felt in international politics, continued to slip in and out of Hoffmann's studio to see her and to arrange highly clandestine meetings at Hoffmann's home or at his own Prinzregentenstrasse apartment. This situa-tion depressed Eva for two important reasons. It made her status with Hitler ambiguous. As she often told Paul Harns, if he really loved her he would provide her with her own apartment and drop these elaborate subterfuges. Also she feared he was only using her and would eventually replace her with another woman. The fact that he didn't want the public or even the majority of his party members to know about their relationship emphasized its pre-cariousness. As her diary entry of February 18, 1935, indicates, she was overjoyed that he had finally mentioned the possibility of arranging for her to have her own 'little house'. Her fervent state-ment that 'I should never want to be blamed if he should stop loving me' expressed her firm intention to do everything within her power to keep Hitler's love.

Though she was happy when she wrote those few lines in her diary, the feeling didn't last long.

MARCH 4, 1935 – *I am again mortally unhappy. Since I can't*

*write him, this book must serve to assuage my pain. He came
Saturday when the town of Munich's ball took place. Frau
Schwarz [wife of the party treasurer] had given me a loge ticket
for it and so I was obliged to attend at all costs since I had
already accepted. Thus I spent a few wonderful hours with him
until 12.00 midnight and then went to the ball for two hours
with his permission.*

*He promised that I would see him on Sunday. In spite of the
fact that I called up from the Osteria and that I sent a message
that I am waiting for his news, he simply drove off to Feldafing.
He even refused Hoffmann's invitation to tea and supper. One
may look at everything from two sides: perhaps he wanted to be
alone with Dr Goebbels who was also here, but he could have
informed me. I was at Hoffmann's on pins and needles, thinking
that he might come at any minute.*

*We went to the train station because we learned that he had
suddenly decided to leave but only arrived in time to see the rear
lights of the departing train. Hoffmann had once again left home
with us too late so I couldn't even say goodbye. Probably I'm too
pessimistic again, I hope, but he hasn't been here now for
fourteen days and I am so unhappy that I have no peace of mind.
I don't know why he should be so mean to me. Perhaps on
account of the ball, but he gave me permission to go. I am use-
lessly wracking my brain as to why he should be driving away
without saying goodbye.*

Hoffmann gave me a ticket for tonight's performance of
Venetian Nights, *but I'm not going. I am much too unhappy.*

Whenever Hitler did not get his own way, he became very
angry. If he couldn't monopolize a conversation, he pouted. If
someone – personal associate or world leader – didn't agree with
him, he went into a rage. It seems he resented Eva's going to the
ball even though he gave his permission. The 'few wonderful
hours with him' prior to the affair had not satisfied his ego.
Probably he had been testing Eva by urging her to keep her
appointment with Frau Schwarz, thinking that she would choose
to stay with him instead. When the confused Eva went to the
ball because she did not want to disappoint Frau Schwarz, Hitler
decided to teach her a lesson. The diary remarks are evidence that
he completely ignored Eva for a period after this incident.

MARCH 11, 1935 – *I only wish one thing – to be seriously ill for
at least eight days. Why doesn't something happen to me? Why
do I have to suffer like this? I wish I had never seen him. I am*

116

*desperate. I am going to buy more sleeping tablets. At least then
I'll be half-dazed and won't think about him so much. Why
doesn't the devil come and get me? I'm sure it is nicer there than
here.*

*For three hours I stood outside the Carlton and had to watch
while he brought flowers for Ondra and invited her for supper.*

*He is only using me for very definite purposes. When he says
he loves me he takes it about as seriously as his promises, which
he never keeps. Why does he torture me so much instead of just
putting an end to the whole thing?*

It was bad enough not to see him, but when he visited Munich
and didn't even call her, Eva felt forsaken. It is evident from her
diary that she desperately tried to see him – she stood outside a
hotel for three hours while he dined with Anny Ondra, wife of
the onetime world boxing champion, Max Schmeling. Her statement, 'He is only using me for very definite purposes,' can only
mean that when they did meet they were having sexual relations
and that she now believed sex was his only interest in her. If this
was true, she realized, then her hold on him was tenuous since he
might meet another woman who was just as willing to meet his
sexual demands and she would lose him. This knowledge only
added to her depression.

MARCH 16, 1935 – *He went to Berlin today. If only I was not
beside myself when I see him less than usual. Actually it is quite
natural that he shows no great interest in me at present since
there is so much going on politically. I'm going to take a trip to
the Zugspitze with Gretl today and I think that will put my
craziness to rest. Everything has always turned out all right in
the end so far and it will be the same this time. One must have
patience, that's all.*

Most of her friends and associates thought that Eva knew
nothing of politics but this was not true. Rather she was perceptive enough not to discuss politics with Hitler. Hitler once stated,
'I detest women who dabble in politics. And if their dabbling
extends to the military, it is unendurable.' He often said that a
man who yells and screams during a political argument in the
Reichstag is 'not a handsome sight', but a woman in such a situation would be shocking. 'Her voice becomes strident, she is ready
to pull her hair out and her claws are showing.' Hitler felt that
everything that involved aggression was exclusively men's business, while women were best at training youth, decorating and

caring for homes and, of course, satisfying a man's sexual needs.

Eva may have been very careful to avoid the subject of politics when she was relaxing with Hitler, but privately she kept up to date. She knew, for instance, that while Hitler was trying to decide what to do about signing the mutual assistance pact being urged upon him by the Western Powers, Great Britain made a blunder. On March 4, 1935, the British government announced that it was going to increase its armaments because 'Germany was rearming openly on a large scale, despite the provisions of Part V of the Treaty of Versailles.' This announcement canceled any advantage Germany might have anticipated by signing the pact since the Western Powers were now openly acknowledging Germany's rearmament and reciprocating in kind. Five days after the British statement Hitler officially notified foreign governments that a German Air Force already existed. When neither Great Britain nor France reacted forcefully, the Chancellor made a more sensational announcement on March 16, 1935. (The entry in Eva's diary for this day states: 'There is so much going on politically.') He declared that the German government was reintroducing conscription in order to establish a peacetime army of thirty-six divisions consisting of 550,000 soldiers.

This time the British and French reaction was much more volatile. The British sent Sir John Simon, the Foreign Minister, to Berlin, accompanied by Anthony Eden, to protest the decision. France appealed to the League of Nations. In the end, however, both countries tried to conciliate Hitler, and he, gratified by the results of his announcement, went ahead with his military plans. He was unconcerned when France signed mutual assistance treaties with the Soviet Union and Czechoslovakia.

These political affairs kept Hitler busy, as Eva indicated in her diary, and it wasn't until April 1, 1935, that she saw him again. By this time his pique that she had left him to attend the Munich ball had faded somewhat but he was still cool toward her.

APRIL 1, 1935 – *Yesterday we were invited by him for supper at the Vierjahreszeite. I had to sit next to him for three hours and couldn't say a word to him. When taking leave he handed me an envelope containing money, as he had done once before. If only he had at least added a greeting or a kind word. I would have been so happy but he never thinks of anything like that.*

Why doesn't he go to Hoffmann's to eat? There at least I would have him to myself for a few minutes. I only wish he would not come anymore until his home is ready.

April was a very distressing month for Eva. Hitler's apartment was being remodeled by the architect Paul Ludwig Troost, and since Hitler did not like to stay in an hotel, his trips to Munich were few. He was also deeply involved in the delicate, dangerous maneuver of overseeing the rearmament plans while warding off any decisive moves by Great Britain or France in opposition. Eva, however, cared for only one fact – she was not able to see the man she loved and she missed him.

APRIL 29, 1935 – *Things are tough. Very much so in every respect. I keep humming to myself 'things will improve' but it doesn't help much. His apartment is ready but I am not allowed to go to him. Love does not seem to be on his program at present. Now that he is back in Berlin I feel a little better but there were days last week when I did my share of crying at night. Especially since I spent Easter at home by myself.*
I'm getting on everybody's nerves because I want to sell everything from my clothes down to my photo camera and even theater tickets. After all, my debts are not that big. He's kind – and equally tactless.

During the infrequent trips Hitler made to Munich during this period he did not invite Eva to his newly remodeled apartment nor did he arrange a meeting with her at Hoffmann's house. Usually, he had a set procedure for his visits. On the train or plane from Berlin he would talk to the associates he had invited to go with him to Munich about Troost's plans for altering his apartment. As soon as they arrived in Munich they would all hurry to Troost's studio just off Theresienstrasse. Everyone would study the architect's plans and Hitler would usually become very excited because architecture was one of his hobbies. After the studio conference they would all go to the Osteria Bavaria for lunch. The party at the café customarily consisted of Hitler, Hess, Bormann, Hoffmann and sometimes a painter or a sculptor. Until the Munich Ball incident Eva was also invited, but during March and April, 1935, she had to stand on the street with the several hundred other persons who had heard Hitler was coming and were waiting to see him arrive at the Osteria Bavaria. She loved him so much that she endured this mortification just to get a glimpse of him, hoping he would see her in the crowd and have one of his aides ask her to join him.

It was while being jostled in the crowd around the café one day that she first saw a new feminine face among Hitler's party. It

119

was Miss Unity Mitford, an Englishwoman who was obsessed by Hitler and the Nazis.

MAY 2, 1935 — *As Frau Hoffmann lovingly and tactlessly told me, he now has a substitute for me. Her name is Walküre and she looks it, including her legs. But these are the shapes that appeal to him. If that is true, he will soon have annoyed her until she gets slim unless she has Charlie's talent for thriving on worry. Worry seems to increase Charlie's appetite.*

If Frau Hoffmann's observations should turn out to be true, it is mean of him not to tell me. After all he should know me well enough to realize that I would never stand in his way if he should discover another romantic interest. Why should he worry about what happens to me? I'll wait until the third of June. By then it will be three months since our last meeting. Me, supposedly the mistress of Germany's and the world's greatest man, have to look at him through a window!

He has so little understanding. He still makes me appear distant even when we are among his friends. Well, one makes one's own bed. I guess it really is my fault but it is just one of those things which one likes to blame on someone else. This period of love fasting won't last forever and then it will be that much better. Too bad, though, that it just happens to be spring.

By this time Eva was becoming desperate. Hitler was her first and only lover and she felt she was losing him. Three months, a quarter of a year, without a personal, intimate visit with him must mean he was losing interest. Then she saw him several times at the Osteria Bavaria with Unity Mitford and had to listen to Frau Hoffmann's malicious chatter about Hitler's 'new love'. Despite the 'noble' remarks in her diary, Eva could not resign herself gracefully to the loss of her lover.

MAY 28, 1935 — *I have just sent him a letter, one that is decisive for me. Will he consider it as important as I do? Well, I'll see. If I don't get an answer by ten o'clock tonight I'll take my twenty-five pills and lie down peacefully. Is it a sign of the terrific love which he assures me that he hasn't spoken a kind word to me for three months? Agreed, he has been busy with political problems but haven't things eased off? And how about last year when he had lots of worries with Röhm and with Italy and still found time for me? True, I'm not in a position to judge whether the present situation isn't much worse but after all a few kind words at Hoffmann's would hardly have taken much time. I fear there is some other reason. It's not my fault. Certainly not. Perhaps it is another woman, although I doubt that it is the Walküre. But there are many others. What other reasons could there be?*

Lord, I'm afraid I won't get an answer today. If only someone would help me. Everything is so hopeless. Maybe my letter reached him at an inopportune time or maybe I shouldn't have written it at all. Whatever it is, the uncertainty is much worse than a sudden end would be.

Dear God, please make it possible that I speak to him today. Tomorrow will be too late. I have decided on thirty-five pills so as to make it dead certain this time. If he would at least have someone call up for him.

Immediately after mailing her ultimatum Eva began to have misgivings. At twenty-three years of age, involved in her first real love affair, she did not have much experience in handling men. There was no one she could consult – her mother or Ilse would have advised her to forget Adolf Hitler. But she did not want to forget him, she wanted to frighten him into realizing that he loved her. Once before this tactic had worked, but at that time Hitler was still immersed in his guilt over Geli Raubal's suicide and did not want another woman's death on his hands. Now he was engaged in what he considered his great political mission – the reconstruction of Germany – and he probably read Eva's letter with some irritation as the emotional blackmail of a designing woman. In any case, she received no messages from him by the deadline to which she had committed herself.

Early on the morning of May 29, 1935, Eva laid her diary beside her bed and swallowed two dozen Phanodorm tablets. Within a few minutes she was unconscious. Fortunately, Ilse decided to return an evening gown she had borrowed from Eva, and when she discovered her sister prostrate on the bed, she immediately called her employer, Dr Marx. Then, drawing on her medical experience, she gave Eva first aid. Within two hours the doctor had purged Eva of the drug and she was safe. Meanwhile, Ilse removed the pages from Eva's diary which referred to her plans to commit suicide and attempted to conceal the Jewish doctor's part in her recovery. The Nuremberg Laws had not yet been put into effect, but Hitler had already started his persecution of the Jews and Ilse was aware of it. She knew he would not hesitate to take action against Dr Marx in anger or guilt over Eva's attempted suicide, even though the doctor had saved her life. Ilse told their parents and Hitler that Eva was suffering from excessive fatigue and would have to stay in bed for several days. Hitler didn't question Ilse's version of the incident, but Himmler's men learned the truth within a matter of hours and the facts were relayed to the Chancellor.

Then life changed dramatically for Eva Braun.

10
Her Dream Villa at Last

*Suffering was good for mankind, according to Hitler.
He believed that people lost in a moment the memory of
the things that made them suffer; otherwise they would
live in constant anguish. As he often emphasized, a
woman forgets the terrible pains of childbirth shortly
after the child is born. Suffering was excellent for the
German woman, for the woman who adores a man.
'It's a fact,' Hitler stated, 'that women love real men.
It's their instinct that tells them they should seek the
protection of a hero.'*

Eva remade herself according to Hitler's conception of women. As his beloved, she had no wishes that did not please him. She slept with him as often as he desired. Yet until May, 1935, all she received in return were rebuffs, neglect and insults, interspersed with occasional visits and casual kindnesses.

After her second suicide attempt, however, Hitler's attitude changed. Eva's love baffled and flattered him. Once again he had come very close to losing it, and this time he realized it was irreplaceable. His first move was to arrange for Eva to move into a small apartment on Wiedermeyerstrasse in the Bogenhausen district. It consisted of only three rooms plus accommodations for a maid – certainly very spare for the 'mistress' of the Chancellor of Germany. Gretl Braun moved in with Eva, both because she wanted to and because Hitler insisted that one of her sisters live with Eva. Hitler, who was always a prude, did not want to be observed visiting Eva if she lived alone but seemed to think her sister was sufficient chaperon to preserve decorum.

Fritz and Fanny Braun were furious when Eva announced her plans to move away from home but there was little they could do about it. Ilse, who was also invited to live in Eva's apartment, refused. She knew why Eva was moving out, knew who was paying the rent and who would be visiting the apartment, and she preferred to have nothing to do with them. So on August 9, 1935, Eva and Gretl transferred their belongings to the apartment on Wiedermeyerstrasse and set up housekeeping. Lilian Mina, a young dancer who lived in the building, was delighted when the sisters moved in. She was the same age as Gretl and as adventurous, so before long they were good friends. The friendship became strained, however, when Lilian asked about the 'man who visited so late at night' at the Braun girls' apartment. Gretl, of course, refused to reveal Hitler's identity since he wanted his liaison kept secret and this made Lilian angry. Eventually the two girls became friends again but both Eva and Hitler realized it was impossible to keep their meetings secret if Eva lived in a public apartment building.

Hitler solved that problem by arranging for Eva and her sister to move into a thirty-thousand-dollar villa on the outskirts of Munich. It was a shrewd 'arrangement' that cost neither him nor the party a cent. Instead he convinced Heinrich Hoffmann to purchase the villa for Eva out of his own bank account in lieu of fees Hitler judged Hoffmann owed the Braun sisters. Eva and Gretl were photography buffs and often took pictures of Hitler, especially when they were on the Obersalzberg. Hitler always was more accommodating toward them than toward Hoffmann or other photographers and they obtained intimate photographs of the Führer in relaxed, smiling poses. Hoffmann had the exclusive rights to sell and distribute all photographs of Hitler, and this included the Braun sisters' albums. Since he was making millions of marks through these sales, Hitler decided that the photographer really owed Eva a villa.

The villa was across the Isar River from Hitler's Prinzregenten-strasse apartment in an exclusive part of Munich, near the Bogen-hausen Park. Eva now had her own private telephone and a three-litre Mercedes-Benz with a chauffeur, courtesy of the Nazi Party. Professor Porsche presented her with one of his first Volks-wagens. Finally, after hinting to Hitler for months that she wanted a dog, he gave her two Scottish terriers which she named Stasi and Negus.

For the first time since her romantic alliance with Hitler, Eva was truly happy. She no longer had to suffer the humiliation of constant bickering with her parents about her association with Hitler. Once her father had even locked her in her bedroom after she had announced that she was going to the Obersalzberg for the weekend (Eva managed to unlock the door with a key she had hidden in her closet). At other times he refused to speak to her for days on end and acted as though she were invisible. Ilse sided with her parents and often made abusive remarks about 'the old man Eva was chasing'. Eva's life at home was so miserable that she sometimes stayed at Herta Schneider's for days. Now she was free to come and go as she desired.

The house had been designed by a Munich architect named Roth and was built in 1925. Its six rooms were furnished largely with pieces from the United Workshops of Munich since Eva had no furniture of her own. On the ground floor were a small kitchen, a dining room and a sitting room with a lovely fireplace that Eva enjoyed on long winter nights. Several valuable oil paint-ings Hitler had obtained from various German art museums and the private collections of wealthy Jews hung on the walls. Up-stairs there were two bedrooms, with a blue-tiled bath between them. One was Eva's, the other Gretl's. Another room, so small it could barely accommodate a bed, was used by the maid who helped with the cooking and housework.

Eva was particularly delighted by the garden where she often spent the entire afternoon soaking up the sun or playing with her two dogs. A high wall surrounding the grounds hid it from view and she had the privacy she had craved so long. Later Hitler bought her another dog, a German shepherd named Basko, to keep away any curiosity seekers who were not discouraged by the high wall. Since very few Germans knew who Eva was, her privacy was seldom disturbed. Many of her neighbours did not know until after World War II that the young girl residing in their midst was Hitler's mistress.

Eva was never seen in Munich society even after she moved into the villa and her position with Hitler was more firmly established. She lived in complete retreat, amusing herself by reading, studying her paintings by Midgard, Gallegos, Popp, Fischbach and Rosl, sunbathing, caring for her beloved dogs and exercising. She was careful not to gain weight, much to Hitler's disgust because he preferred voluptuous women. But Eva's vanity and desire to look fashionable made her disregard Hitler's wishes in this one respect, and she watched her diet closely and did strenuous exercises in the garden or, if it was raining or too cold, in the villa daily. She also spent much time applying cosmetics, tinting her medium-blonde hair different shades and manicuring her nails. During this period she began buying more expensive clothes. She preferred casual clothes, tasteful and well made but never extravagant. The gift of the villa instilled a new confidence in the twenty-three-year-old Eva. She gradually changed from an immature shop girl to a poised lady who presided over the private circle around Hitler.

Just as encouraging to Eva as the villa was Hitler's treatment of her after her second suicide attempt. He could convince her that she was young and beautiful regardless of her features or her age by kissing her hand and calling her 'pretty one' or 'pretty child'. He always greeted women respectfully, let them go ahead of him and never sat down until they were seated (a procedure he seldom followed with the foreign dignitaries who visited him). Many a woman who thought she was going to meet a raving brute with no manners departed charmed and enthusiastic after talking with him. When he gave Eva this treatment after her recovery from the drug overdose in 1935, she was overwhelmed and more willing than ever to do and be anything he wished. Whenever he was in Munich, Hitler would have his chauffeur drive him to Eva's villa. Usually he arrived about 10 or 11 p.m. and would disappear through the gate in the wall. His bodyguards would take up positions just inside the wall, discreetly out of sight but prepared to stop anyone who tried to enter the villa. Usually Hitler was tired or depressed when he arrived, but as Hoffmann often remarked to other members of the Nazi Party, 'The Führer is always relaxed and smiling after a visit with Eva.'

The one note of discord was that Eva's parents were estranged from her. Once she moved to the villa they left her alone and she did not have the courage to go to see them. Eventually Fanny Braun accepted the situation and decided that if she was going to see her daughter at all, she would have to learn to tolerate Hitler. Her husband was more stubborn. When she first suggested they visit Eva, he flatly refused. But Fanny Braun kept up her arguments. 'It is better we go there occasionally and are on good terms with her,' she told him. 'Perhaps someday we can be of help to her. She might need us.'

It took a great deal of persuasion before Fritz Braun relented. Eva was delighted when her parents came to her villa for the first time and did everything possible to make them feel at ease but it was a trying time for all of them. Fritz Braun could not accept that his daughter was living in a house given to her by a man to whom she was not married and that this same man was buying her clothes, cars and jewels. Yet he loved his daughter and could not give her up. The first visit developed into a second and third, and before long Fritz and Fanny were having tea with Eva nearly every Saturday or Sunday. Fanny often visited with her two daughters during the week also, and while neither she nor her husband approved of the liaison between Hitler and Eva, they stopped opposing it.

After she made her peace with her parents, Eva began inviting a small circle of artists and friends to gay parties at the villa. One of these artists, Hans Kelter, came several times in 1935 and 1936. He had met Eva at an art exhibit in Munich and for a long time did not know she was Hitler's mistress. Only three years older than Eva, he was attracted to her and invited her to go dancing and skiing with him. Gretl always accompanied them on their dates even though she had not been invited. When Heinrich Hoffmann heard Kelter grumbling about the extra sister, he gave him an ambiguous and waggish warning. 'You are fortunate, Herr Kelter, that you have not had both arms broken. I would not complain about Gretl's company when you are with Eva. She may have saved your life.'

When the startled Kelter asked him what he was talking about, Hoffmann just smiled, shook his finger at Kelter as though he were a naughty boy and walked away. Later, when Kelter learned that Eva was Hitler's mistress, he understood what Hoffmann had been trying to tell him and it ended his bid for a romance immediately. Eva, who was amused by the artist's interest in her, never had any intention of permitting him to get serious.

Another man who professed to be interested in Eva Braun was the world-famous German film director Luis Trenker. According to Trenker, he and the sculptor Josef Thorak went to the villa on the Wasserburgerstrasse one evening because Thorak knew the owner. Trenker was introduced to Eva and Gretl Braun but he was so indifferent to them both at the time that he did not even recall their names. The sisters asked him a multitude of questions about various actors and actresses and details about movie-making. The arrogant director stayed all evening, talking mostly about his own film exploits, drinking, eating and dancing with Eva. When he and Thorak finally left, Thorak berated him for the way he had acted and for the small intimacies he had taken with Eva while they were dancing. He explained to the surprised film director that Eva was Hitler's favorite feminine companion and that it was through the Chancellor that she had obtained the villa. This information sobered Trenker but he insisted after her death that he saw Eva again several times, and wrote about their 'friendship', even going so far as to attempt to publish what he claimed was the diary of Eva Braun. The Braun family denied the diary was authentic and in a subsequent court action proved their case, and publication was halted.

At one time, from 1931 to 1933, Hitler was lavish in his praise of Luis Trenker. This was before Trenker knew that Eva Braun existed. Before he became Chancellor Hitler often went to the movies in Munich with old party comrades such as Schwarz, Schreck, and Hoffmann. In 1931 he saw the Trenker film *Mountain in Flames* which he enjoyed very much. In fact, he saw it several times and pronounced Trenker the best film director in Germany. Trenker's subsequent films – *The Lost Son* and *Condottieri* – were a disappointment to Hitler and he lost interest in him. Then, in 1939, Hitler decided that Southern Tyrol should remain a part of Italy instead of being annexed by Germany. The residents, however, were allowed to choose between German and Italian citizenship. Hitler expected Trenker, who owned a farm in Southern Tyrol, to apply immediately for German citizenship, but the film director abstained from making a decision as long as possible. Finally, because Goebbels pressured him, Trenker chose German citizenship. From this time on Hitler ignored him and made certain that he played no important part in the German film industry. Consequently the director's later claim that Eva was interested in him is not credible because Eva would never have jeopardized her alliance with Hitler by associating with a man he held in disdain.

It was fortunate that she was loyal to Hitler because a large file on Luis Trenker was later found in the Chief Reich Security Office (it contained the information that Trenker had been found guilty of plagiarism in one of his books by a Vienna court and that much of his film material was suspect), so Hitler had him under surveillance and if, as the director claimed, he had been having romantic trysts with Eva, the Führer would have known about it and taken swift action against them both. Since Eva once told her mother than Trenker was 'a disgusting fellow', it is hardly likely he was even a temptation she had to resist.

Eva, unlike the philandering Geli Raubal, was entirely faithful to Hitler during their association. Sometimes, when Hitler ignored her for long periods, she would try to make him jealous by mildly flirting with one of his bodyguards or associates but that was as far as she ever went. It was because of this loyalty on Eva's side and the frequent indifference on the Führer's that Fritz Braun decided to write to Hitler and express his personal views on the affair. The fact that Hitler was Führer didn't inhibit Eva's father, except that he used a polite tone in his letter:

> *Munich*
> *September 8, 1935*
>
> *Your Excellency the Chancellor:*
>
> *I find myself in the unhappy situation of having to contact you with a private problem. I know that you have a great many other problems and cares as Führer of the German nation. However, since the family is the smallest unit of the social structure, a unit that enables Germany to be strong, I think my letter is justified and I am asking your help.*
>
> *My family is now separated because two of my daughters, Eva and Gretl, have moved into an apartment that you have put at their disposal. I was not consulted on this matter. For a long time I have criticized Eva for coming home late, long after office hours, because I did not believe she was getting the proper rest needed for her health. Perhaps I am old-fashioned in this respect. However, the parents' supervision and the children's duty to live at home until they are married is an inviolable principle. This is my code of honor. Besides, I miss my daughters enormously.*
>
> *I would be very grateful if you would agree to help me. I ask that you not encourage Eva's desire for freedom from her home.*

Please advise her to return to her family.

> *Yours respectfully,*
> *Fritz Braun*

Fritz Braun sent the letter to Hoffmann and asked him to give it to Hitler at an appropriate time. Hoffmann was not stupid. He gave the letter to Eva, who read it and then destroyed it. Her father, however, kept a copy of the letter and presented it to the Allied investigators after the war in an effort to prove his opposition to Hitler and clear himself of any charges of Nazism. Fanny Braun, not knowing that her husband had written such a letter, seriously contemplated asking Hitler personally about his relationship with her daughter but never quite mustered the courage. Instead, she also wrote a letter to Hitler, asking as a mother what his intentions were toward her daughter. She gave her letter to Frau Winter, Hitler's housekeeper in Munich, and asked her to present it to the Führer. Later Frau Winter told Fanny Braun that she had forwarded the letter to Bormann. Frau Braun never received an answer and, as she said, 'We got so used to the affair that we did not even refer to it anymore after some years.'

Though Hitler never saw either letter he was quite aware of the feelings of Fritz and Fanny Braun. He ignored them as much as possible, rarely seeing them face-to-face, and if he was forced into an encounter, he was polite but distant. It was not only to her parents that Hitler refused to make a commitment about Eva Braun; he never admitted to anyone he was romantically interested in her. Before Dr Kurt Krueger fled from Germany he asked the Führer about Eva Braun during one of his consultations. Hitler had been discussing the age of actress Pola Negri and mentioned that 'she was over thirty'. Krueger asked if a woman in her thirties had no romantic interest for him and Hitler admitted that such a woman appealed to him as maternal but aroused no sexual excitement.

'How about Fräulein Braun?' Krueger asked without thinking. Later the doctor wondered how he had escaped with his life after inquiring about such a delicate matter.

Hitler parried the question by saying that Krueger had been listening to too many rumors.

Krueger shook his head. 'Not only rumors. She spent a week with you at Berchtesgaden and I put two and two together.'

Hitler told the doctor the same cover story he used on nearly everyone else. 'She photographs interiors, draperies, windows, vases and other objects, including me. The photographs are then stored in my archives.'

No matter how insistently Krueger questioned him about his relationship with Eva, Hitler refused to admit any romantic interest. It seemed to Krueger that Hitler was terrified of love, that he was afraid to acknowledge more than a casual acquaintance with Eva for fear it might destroy him. Krueger agreed with Kaiser Wilhelm II, who, when asked his opinion of Hitler, said, 'There is a man alone, without family, without children, without God. Why should he be human? He may be sincere but this very excessive sincerity keeps him apart, out of touch with men and realities. He builds legions but he does not build a nation. A nation is created by families, a religion, traditions. It is made up out of the hearts of mothers, the wisdom of fathers, the joy and exuberance of children.'

11
Leni Riefenstahl

The Olympics of 1936 entranced Adolf Hitler despite the fact that he was not a good athlete and did not participate in any sports. He believed that the triumphs of the German athletes at Berlin heralded a new German race of tough, well-formed men and graceful women. Hitler was convinced that the new Germans would rival the classical Greeks as innovators of beautiful forms and styles of life. He said that contestants in athletic meets were to be watched and admired 'not as sportsmen but rather as political troops who treat the sporting contests only as their particular branch of the great struggle as a whole.'

The 1936 Olympics fascinated Eva. She was very athletic and loved skiing, swimming, walking, diving and other sports. Whenever she went to the Obersalzberg with Hitler she spent a large part of her free time swimming in the Königssee or exercising along the shoreline. When she learned from Hitler that the world's greatest athletic event was going to be held in Berlin she was delighted – until she saw Leni Riefenstahl using the Olympics to try and usurp her.

Leni Riefenstahl was known as the 'priestess of the Nazi Olympics' and she deserved the title. Of all the women with whom Hitler associated during his lifetime, the most controversial is Leni Riefenstahl. Between 1933 and the beginning of World War II she played an important part in furthering the cause of the Nazi Party and bolstering Hitler's ego. Many Germans considered her Hitler's mistress during this period primarily because Eva was always hidden from public view. Leni Riefenstahl herself did nothing to refute this rumor at the time. In fact, she helped to spread it, and while she was not exactly Hitler's 'mistress', she was certainly his special 'friend'. Frau Christa Schröder, one of Hitler's secretaries, remarked to Eva that despite the rumors she did not think Leni Riefenstahl interested Hitler as a woman but only as a film director.

'It is to her advantage not to deny the rumor,' Frau Schröder said.

Eva, however, saw a dangerous rival in the beautiful Leni Riefenstahl. She knew that Hitler esteemed her because of her acting talent and her film-making ability, but she suspected there were other reasons as well.

Leni Riefenstahl went after what she wanted with a cleverness and perseverance that customarily resulted in success. She used her beautiful face, willowy body, love of life and brilliant mind to bend men's wills to her liking, and for a while she even succeeded with Hitler. She was born in Berlin in 1902 (although she changed her birth date in her biographical material quite often as many actresses do as they get older). Her parents had no involvement in show business – her father was a plumber – but when she showed talent as a child they saved enough money to give her ballet lessons. It was a good investment because by the time she was seventeen years old Leni Riefenstahl was starring in a production of the famous stage impresario Max Reinhardt. Three years later she was the featured feminine performer in a movie production of Dr Arnold Fanck, who specialized in films with Alpine backgrounds. His stories required an actress who was not only beautiful and talented, but athletic as well. Leni Riefenstahl met these requirements perfectly. She was an avid skier and mountain climber. She was also a passionate young woman who worked best when she was in love and Fanck was susceptible to her charms. The five films they made together established her acting reputation and she became one of the most popular actresses in Germany.

In 1933, the year Hitler came to power and Eva began to establish herself as his favorite feminine companion, Leni Riefenstahl decided that stardom, money and her choice of film roles were not enough – she wanted to produce and film her own movies. She quietly learned all she could from Fanck in preparation for the time when she could strike out on her own. When she believed she was ready, she left her Svengali, Dr Fanck, and established her own company to produce movies. The first film produced by the Leni Riefenstahl Studio Films of Berlin was *Das Blaue Licht* (The Blue Light) and it was an artistic success. The movie was filmed on location in the Italian Dolomites, using unusual camera angles and back-lit actors and actresses gamboling in the fog or at dusk. While *Das Blaue Licht* was not a moneymaker, as Riefenstahl's films with Fanck had been, its unconventional aspects caught the eye of influential men in the industry and of Goebbels, the Nazi Propaganda Minister. Her unusual beauty caught Goebbels' eye as well.

Though Goebbels' predilection for actresses was notorious, he decided to save the extraordinary Leni for his Führer. He had long desired to sponsor a new courtesan. Hitler was becoming habituated to Eva Braun but she owed nothing to Goebbels and ignored him. If he could insinuate a beautiful actress into the good graces of Hitler, he would be able to accomplish two objectives: one, a skilled bed partner might calm Hitler and make him easier to get along with; two, Goebbels himself would have more influence with the Führer through his actress-accomplice. It was a shrewd plan but Goebbels underestimated the toughness of the beautiful Leni Riefenstahl.

As the first step in his plan, Goebbels had his wife invite Leni Riefenstahl to their luxurious apartment for dinner on an evening when Hitler was going to be present. Hitler was familiar with Riefenstahl's films but this was the first time he had talked with her privately at any length. The actress was a brilliant conversationalist, exuberant and exciting, and Hitler was delighted. She knew when to listen, when to ask him questions, when to make remarks that bolstered his ego. After dinner, when she invited the

Goebbels, Hitler and Ernst Hanfstängl to her studio, the Führer was eager to go. Once they had been shown through the studio, the Goebbels and Hanfstängl, as prearranged among themselves, departed, leaving Hitler and the actress alone.

'If Riefenstahl can't manage this, no one can,' Hanfstängl told Goebbels. 'We might as well leave.'

When Hanfstängl met Leni Riefenstahl several days later, she merely raised her eyebrows when he asked how her evening with Hitler had turned out. Initially he thought she meant that Hitler had shown no sexual interest in her but later he changed his mind. According to Luis Trenker, Hanfstängl told him of a visit to the Riefenstahl apartment when the actress had danced nude for Hitler and him until the early morning hours. She was famous for her nude dances and it was said that once 'Leni shakes her navel in front of a man's nose, he never forgets her.' Hitler evidently didn't forget her, since he arranged to see her many times after this encounter, often in private so that not even his immediate staff knew what transpired between them. Naturally, reports of these meetings reached Eva's ears, sometimes purposely carried by the malicious Frau Hoffmann.

Hitler loved pageantry and used it effectively in his early Nazi rallies. He believed that such displays of showmanship brought him more converts than any other form of publicity. Therefore he was susceptible to anyone who possessed the art of showmanship and was willing to put that talent at the service of the Nazi Party. This was the key that opened the door for Leni Riefenstahl.

The yearly rally held at Nuremberg was a featured event for the Nazis and for Hitler personally. It usually opened on September 1 with the Consecration of Flags and lasted seven days. The crowd's excitement was carefully stimulated until, towards the end of the affair, the party members were lashed into a state of hallucination that enabled them to believe that Hitler outranked God. Albert Speer, Hitler's architect during the thirties, spent months planning each and every detail of a rally. Nearly 150 searchlight beams formed a curtain of light behind the Führer, church bells rang at the appropriate time, trumpets blared, army bands played and soldiers marched in perfect cadence. It was a show of shows and Hitler knew the value of such flamboyance. In 1934 he decided the Nuremberg rally should be filmed so that the heroic invincibility of the Nazi Party and its leader could be viewed in movie theaters throughout Germany by the unenlightened (such as Eva's father). In looking around for a film-maker, Hitler decided that Leni Riefenstahl was ideal for the assignment.

Eva was so busy with her own stratagems in 1934 that she scarcely noticed the announcement in the newspapers that Leni Riefenstahl was going to film the Nuremberg Party Congress. That summer the Röhm purge, the formal Nazi funeral at Karinhall for Göring's first wife, the death of Hindenburg and the assumption of the presidency by Hitler made her overlook this comparatively minor announcement.

Hitler summoned Leni Riefenstahl to his quarters in the Chancellery and told her of his decision. 'I want you to make a picture just for me, just about me and the movement. I want you to film the Nuremberg Party Congress this year.'

The ambitious actress-producer quickly accepted the assignment. By the time Eva learned about the Hitler-Riefenstahl collaboration, Leni was so secure in the favor of the Führer that their meetings were the talk of Germany. The actress was reported being seen leaving the Chancellery in the middle of the night and being driven home by one of Hitler's chauffeurs. Hitler's private plane ferried her around Germany and sometimes he was in the aircraft with her. She had access to his private quarters and to his headquarters when even Goebbels and Göring were denied an audience with Hitler. Goebbels, the originator of the plan to lure Hitler into her arms, was not happy, for once she got where she wanted to be, Leni became an independent agent. She shed her 'helpless beauty' manner and began to wear severe clothes instead of the fluff dresses she had often worn in her movies. Her attitude changed to match her clothes. She was extremely tough in her business dealings and did everything within her power, including negotiating behind bedroom doors, to win her argument. Goebbels soon discovered she had no intention of sleeping with him, a payoff he considered obligatory. When he threatened to blacklist her in the movies she just laughed at him. 'Perhaps you should check with the Führer first,' she said.

He did and promptly decided that he could do without Leni Riefenstahl in his bed.

Whatever Leni Riefenstahl's real relationship with Hitler (since the war she has denied she was his mistress), the movie she produced of the 1934 Nuremberg rally is a classic. *Triumph of the Will* is to Eva's snapshots of Hitler what Picasso's *Guernica* is to a news photo of the Spanish Civil War.

One week before the rally Leni Riefenstahl arrived in Nuremberg to begin her work. Under a blanket order from Hitler that she was to receive full cooperation in her filming efforts, the city's fire, police and public utility departments were put at her disposal. Aircraft, cranes, trains, automobiles and trucks were assembled near the stadium for Riefenstahl and her crew. She had sixteen cameramen and each cameraman had an assistant. Altogether the crew totaled 120 people. The budget for the film was unlimited. Hanfstängl shook his head and muttered, 'She really must have seduced Hitler that first night in her apartment to get all this from him.'

Eva arrived in Nuremberg with Frau Schaub for the rally and when she saw the elaborate setup arranged for Leni Riefenstahl she was furious. The sight of the actress-producer in her tight-fitting white suit that made every man stare at her didn't calm Eva any. Frau Schaub tried to convince Eva that Hitler was spending so much time with Leni Riefenstahl because he wanted the filming of the rally to be as perfect as possible, but Eva dismissed her rationalizations, knowing that both she and her husband were extremely loyal to Hitler. She suspected he had ordered them to mollify her. Though she kept her own counsel, Eva was determined to outwit the stunning Leni Riefenstahl in one way or another.

Meanwhile, placing her cameras in airplanes, on roller skates and in pits in the ground, Riefenstahl began filming the stirring events of the rally. She made Hitler the star (it was the only documentary he ever agreed to appear in). She directed the cameramen to caressingly pan his face again and again, often immediately after panning a group of young, extremely muscular and good-looking German soldiers. As Hitler later remarked, 'Everything was designed for seduction.'

Hitler's speeches, delivered in authoritarian and obsessive fashion, were highlighted in *Triumph of the Will*. Riefenstahl emphasized how he could hypnotize a huge audience with his plans for the rebirth of Germany, haranguing them into practically kneeling at his feet in awe and obedience. She understood the propaganda value of illustrating to those who were not at the rally how great crowds were ready to follow the Führer wherever he might choose to lead them. In one of the most memorable scenes Hitler, Himmler and an aide are shown walking slowly down a wide street to the rhythm of the march 'I Had a Comrade'. As the scene opens, only the three men can be seen, but the camera slowly lifts to show more than 100,000 soldiers flanking the trio on both sides. The three walk between these perfectly co-ordinated troops until they reach a monument dedicated to those who fell for the Nazi Party, where they salute, turn, and march away. This one scene, according to a movie critic, 'lured the observer into the thought that determined masses had power and historical grandeur and that the Nazi Party had a relentless destiny.'

The film premiered on March 28, 1935, and was acknowledged even by anti-Nazis to be a powerful and artful documentary. Leni Riefenstahl was acclaimed not only as a great film-maker but also as a genius in the field of political propaganda. Hitler was delighted with *Triumph of the Will* and with Leni Riefenstahl ... much to Eva's chagrin. In the Reich Propaganda Ministry they both admired and hated her, not certain whether her valuable contribution to the Nazi Party was worth having to put up with her arrogant attitude. Goebbels, whose opinion had once been eagerly sought by Hitler, now found himself running a poor second to Leni Riefenstahl. Hitler showered her with gifts and made certain that her talent was recognized throughout Germany by ordering an all-out publicity campaign in the newspapers and on the radio. She had been a well-known movie star prior to the release of *Triumph of the Will*; Leni Riefenstahl was now proclaimed a great director. When Mussolini visited Munich and was the guest of Hitler at a mass reception in the Brown House, of all the prominent musicians, architects, painters, directors, actors, writers and opera singers present only one was called from the audience for a personal introduction to the Italian dictator – Leni Riefenstahl!

Eva resented the exaltation of Leni Riefenstahl – especially since she herself seemed permanently consigned to the role of 'hidden love'. She began to intrigue.

Frau Schaub often stated, 'If one wants to expound a characteristic of Eva Braun, it is her extraordinary jealousy that leads her into various intrigues.' At the time neither Frau Schaub nor any other close associate of Hitler's gave the young ex-clerk much chance against the rich, famous and beautiful Leni Riefenstahl. Again, they underestimated Eva Braun.

Now that her reputation as a film director was established, Riefenstahl longed for bigger and better projects. Her chance came in 1936. Luis Trenker and other film directors were eager for the commission to film the Olympics, which were to be held in Berlin that year, but after Leni Riefenstahl's documentary and the publicity it brought the Nazi Party, she easily obtained the assignment.

'I have commissioned so many men to make a film,' Hitler said when he announced the assignment to film the Olympics. 'Now I'm trying it with a woman.'

Clothed all in white, Leni Riefenstahl at the Olympic site in 1936 reminded many of the priestess of Demeter, who was the only woman permitted at the ancient Greek games. But no priestess of Demeter ever handled a camera crew and captured the movement of an athletic contest in exciting images. Too many men concentrated on her ethereal beauty and her famous sexual magnetism and overlooked the fact that she was a genius behind and in front of a movie camera. She was indeed theatrical and never missed a chance to exhibit herself or point up her intimacy with the Führer. During daylight hours she wore a white, water-proof coat with large pockets and a large-brimmed matching white hat which emphasized her deep tan. She was always sur-rounded by muscular young men who wore black coats, and consequently she was the center of attention. In her chauffeur-driven car she speeded from one area to another, supposedly on important business, but she made certain that everyone on the route got a good glimpse of her. In the evening she donned a white gown and attended one or more parties in Berlin, often with Hitler. Within a short period of time she became one of the most popular and well-known figures at the Olympics, and this was no small feat since the Nazi Party was antifeminist. Thus while Eva sat at home in Munich reading about the preparations for the Olympics, Leni Riefenstahl appeared with the Führer in the capital in front of large crowds.

Yet she was the one person, male or female, who was then capable of combining sports and film into a work of art. In this respect Hitler was to be admired for his choice of director. By skillful editing she was able to condense a scene into a dramatic and unforgettable moment. She had the foresight, the patience and the courage to plan, shoot and edit footage that no other director even considered possible at that time.

'I had the whole thing in my head. I treated the whole thing like a vision,' she exclaimed. 'I was like an architect building a house.'

She had camouflaged tracks built for her cameras so that the film would depict the strain and agony on the faces of the runners; special cameras that operated so quietly that they did not distract the athletes were used for closeups; another special camera was designed to fit a saddle so that shutter movement could match the motion of a horse; and automatic cameras were placed in baskets attached to balloons flying high over the

140

stadium. When the filming was completed, Leni Riefenstahl began the difficult job of editing.

'For *Olympia*, I spent . . . I lived in the editing room for a year and a half, never getting home before five o'clock in the morning. My life was tied to the material and the film. In my editing rooms, I had glass partitions built, on each side of which I hung filmstrips that went down to the floor. I suspended them one next to the other, very regularly, and I went from one to the other, from one partition to the other, in order to look at them, compare them, so as to verify their harmony in the scale of frames and tones. Thus, in the long run, as a composer composes, I made everything work together in the rhythm.'

Olympia was released in 1938, and though it was generally acclaimed, it was not nearly as popular as *Triumph of the Will*. The intervening years had been time enough for the outside world to understand that the Nazis were not the noble group of leaders they had been portrayed as in 1934, and the swastikas, insignias and other trappings of the party in the film plus the closeups of Hitler himself were not well received. On the opposite side of the critical standard, devout Nazis were disappointed because there were not as many propaganda scenes as in the Nuremberg documentary. When Leni Riefenstahl took a trip to Hollywood, expecting to be received as a great artist, she was socially boycotted because of her friendship with Hitler and other Nazi leaders. She returned to Germany more subdued, but Hitler was quick to try and cheer her up. He commissioned her to make a film of Berchtesgaden and the surrounding mountains and for a while she was happy. Slowly, however, her influence with Hitler began to wane. No matter how hard she tried, she could not resume the intimate relationship she had had with him earlier. She was puzzled by this unexpected turn of events and so were many of Hitler's associates.

Eva was not. While Leni Riefenstahl had been basking in the glory of *Triumph of the Will* and her plans for filming the Berlin Olympics, Eva had been busy laying her own plans. She had discovered that Leni Riefenstahl was amorously linked with many men but her key discovery was the long-time arrangement she had with the famous pilot Ernst Udet. Here was an opportunity to put a wedge between the actress-producer and Hitler and Eva used it. She used it so cleverly that it wasn't until many years later that anyone really understood why the Führer had suddenly cooled toward Leni Riefenstahl.

Udet was popular with everyone, a fun-loving bachelor who

had shot down a record sixty-two enemy planes in World War I. After the war Udet became one of his country's top stunt pilots and traveled around the world displaying courage and skill in aerobatic maneuvers. He was feted in the United States, South America, Africa and Europe. His personal charm and warm personality endeared him to everyone he met. When he was hired in the early 1930s to make several films with Leni Riefenstahl, she, too, was attracted to him. A woman-lover of long repute, Udet wasted no time becoming better acquainted with the actress. Their relationship soon developed into an arrangement that satisfied them both. The first hint of trouble came when Leni began associating with Hitler. Udet was already a member of the newly formed Luftwaffe and in 1936, the year Leni Riefenstahl filmed the Olympics, he had risen to the position of Chief of the Technical Department of the Air Ministry. Hitler, recognizing his immense popularity with the German people, promoted Udet regularly until he directed the biggest armament concern on earth. The 'flying clown', as many dubbed the prankish Udet, did not subscribe to the double standard and accepted Leni's relationship with Hitler with equanimity. Hitler, Eva knew, had no such tolerance and would never put up with a woman who also slept with one of his underlings. So Eva leaked the information through Himmler's staff that Leni Riefenstahl and Ernst Udet had an 'interesting arrangement'. Within a matter of weeks, after Bormann investigated the rumor and verified it, Hitler was through with the actress. He wanted no part of an affair that could end with his associates laughing behind his back. Udet was the type of freewheeling individual who would delight in telling fellow officers how he and the Führer were coupling with the same woman. Hitler's love for Leni Riefenstahl was not deep enough for him to purge the famous flier so he turned away from her and went back to the open arms of Eva. Once again the 'little clerk' had defeated a rival who seemed destined to take her place.

While Hitler never mentioned the Udet-Riefenstahl affair publicly, he never forgave the famous pilot. He continuously blamed the inability of the Luftwaffe to stop the enemy bombers and fighters on Udet's failure to supply new types of aircraft in quantity. Udet's health began to fail and he lost his happy-go-lucky manner as the Führer's harassment continued. Finally, on November 17, 1941, when he could stand the criticism no longer, the brokenhearted, sick flier shot himself through the head. According to rumor, Leni Riefenstahl had been with him during his last days and after Udet's suicide she was threatened by

Göring with arrest if she revealed the reason for his death. Hitler told the nation that Udet had died in an aircraft accident. The Führer held an impressive, formal funeral with full military honors.

Eva didn't attend.

Part 3

THE
CONFIDENT
YEARS

12
Passion at the Berghof

When Hitler went to his home on the Obersalzberg, he went not only to enjoy the beauty of the mountains, but also to get away from the petty problems that plagued him at the Chancellery. The atmosphere at the Berghof also stimulated his imagination. He often stated that when he studied a problem in Berlin or at one of his field headquarters he could see it less clearly than when he lay in bed at night in the Berghof, with his eyes open, staring out the window at the moonlight-bathed mountains.

Quite often Eva lay at Hitler's side in the bed at the Berghof. She loved the mountains, where she escaped her own problems – the disapproval of her parents, her sister Ilse and others such as Frau Hoffmann who constantly tried to interfere with her affair with Hitler. Hitler's visit to Munich after he became Chancellor were usually hurried. At the Berghof he was relaxed and paid more attention to Eva. She was delighted every time she was asked to the mountain home in the early years of their romance. Later she was recognized by Hitler's inner circle as the hostess of the Berghof.

When Hitler was released from Landsberg Prison where he had been sentenced for the abortive putsch in 1923, he spent a great deal of time in the Bavarian Alps region. He had always liked the area around Berchtesgaden, and after his prison term when he had to regroup his party members and plan his future strategy, he returned to the mountains. At first he stayed at the Deutsche Haus in Berchtesgaden where he worked on a second book and newspaper articles. He also spent a great deal of time walking. One of his favorite strolling routes was from Berchtesgaden to Obersalzberg, a walk which took him approximately three hours. In 1928, after he had become familiar with the area, he decided to rent a small cottage, Haus Wachenfeld, which had originally been built for a German industrialist from Buxtehude. Later he purchased the cottage, remarking, 'I've spent up there the finest hours of my life.'

Frau Bechstein provided Hitler with the funds to purchase Haus Wachenfeld since his finances at the time were in bad shape. He called upon another woman, his sister Angela Raubal, to look after the house and cook his meals when he was there. Gradually Nazi Party members began visiting the area, too, in order to consult with Hitler or just to be near him in hopes of gaining his esteem. Kurt Ludecke and Dietrich Eckart often stayed at the Platterhof on the Obersalzberg, which was near Haus Wachenfeld. The Platterhof was an old farmstead which became a refuge for many Nazis while the party was being harassed prior to Hitler's coming to power in 1933.

After she began working for Hoffmann, Eva often heard him mention Haus Wachenfeld and the good times he and his friends had there. Hoffmann was more than just Hitler's photographer. He was the 'court jester' of Hitler's inner circle, rivaled only by Putzi Hanfstängl, who was an excellent piano player and singer of bawdy songs. Hoffmann could keep a roomful of people laughing since he was an excellent story-teller, mostly of the obscene variety. Arthur Kannenberg, a fat, witty cook from Berlin who was a favorite of Hitler's was a fine accordion player and Hoffmann often related to Eva how he and Kannenberg spent the entire weekend entertaining Hitler and his guests. It wasn't until Geli Raubal committed suicide, however, that Hitler began inviting Eva to the Obersalzberg, and even then the invitations were few because Geli's mother was still the housekeeper there, and she resented Hitler's bringing another woman to Haus Wachenfeld. Eva was aware of Frau Raubal's resentment since the older woman made no effort to hide her feelings. If Hitler noticed, he did nothing about the smoldering feud at the time. Eva, unsure of her position with him during these early years, accepted the insults without complaint, silently planning, as usual, how to eliminate one more obstacle to her romance with Hitler.

Martin Bormann, who, like Eva, was seldom noticed by the average German citizen but exerted a strong influence over Hitler, became the 'ruler' of the Obersalzberg area for the Nazi Party. He confiscated century-old farms, homes and churches in the vicinity and had the buildings torn down. These lands, plus the state forests he had already taken over, formed a Hitler estate that extended from the top of the 6,400-foot mountain to the valley below and encompassed nearly three square miles. Bormann had a network of roads built throughout this estate connecting the barracks, servants' quarters, guest houses and garages he had constructed. There were two fences surrounding the area. The outer fence was nine miles long and the inner fence two; guards were placed at strategic spots along both fences. Hitler's little 'cottage' was soon a well guarded elaborate enclave to which no one was admitted except by invitation.

In 1935 Hitler decided that Haus Wachenfeld was not suitable in size or luxury for the Chancellor of Germany and made plans to enlarge it. Albert Speer was Hitler's architect at this time and resided at the Obersalzberg complex at Hitler's insistence. In fact, the Führer had taken the home of his former friends, the Bechsteins, who had given him so much financial help before he came to power, had a studio built onto the house and gave it to Speer. Even with Speer in residence, Hitler decided to draw up the blueprints for the modification of Haus Wachenfeld himself. Using a borrowed T-square, drawing board and pen, he put on paper exactly what he wanted the contractors to accomplish. He was faithful to the old house and kept it nearly intact, building the new home around it. Speer thought Hitler's floor plan was impractical but didn't dare tell him because the Chancellor would be furious. When Hitler proudly showed Speer his plan for a huge window in the living room, Speer noted that the garages for Hitler's automobiles were to go directly underneath it, which meant that the living room would be filled with gas fumes every time the window was lowered. So this impressive window (always shown in photographs of the Berghof) was really a detriment.

The Berghof was not an architect's dream, but by the time Eva began to go there often, it was a luxurious place to stay in. She had her own apartment, consisting of a little living room and a bedroom, with access to a large marble bath (the Italian marble was a present from Mussolini). The door on the opposite side of this bath led to Hitler's bedroom. Eva had beautiful furniture in her bedroom, and the walls were hung with silk. On one side of the room there was a painting of a nude, for which, supposedly, Eva had posed. Opposite it hung a photograph of Hitler, in which he seemed to be staring at the painting.

Hitler's own bedroom was plainly furnished with a small side table, a larger table by the window, an easy chair and a desk neatly placed underneath shelves of books. He slept in a large iron-framed bed which was usually covered by a brown quilt embroidered with a huge swastika. The swastika also appeared on Hitler's brown satin pajamas, embroidered in black against a red background on the pocket. He had a matching brown silk robe.

Later an elaborate air raid shelter was built underneath the Berghof, accessible from Hitler's bedroom by elevator. The shelter had six luxuriously furnished rooms, its own water supply, an air-purifying plant, a kitchen and enough food for three months.

The main dining room at the Berghof, approximately sixty by forty feet, was dominated by a massive oak table standing in the center. The chairs were covered with red leather from Morocco, a rich contrast to the dark wood. On the wood-paneled walls, gleaming under the indirect lighting, hung several Dürer etchings. An expensive Persian carpet covered the floor. The white china used for the everyday table setting bore Hitler's monogram, as did the china he used in Berlin. For more formal dinners, usually when there were distinguished guests present, Hitler had the housekeeper use the solid silver place settings which Himmler's agents had stolen from a Jewish merchant in Nuremberg. When no outsiders were present, Eva was usually the hostess for dinner, especially in later years after she had established her right to reign over the other women at the Berghof.

Hitler received his guests in the large living room where the famous window overlooked the Untersberg peak. In front of this window was a twenty-foot-long table which was used for signing documents or, after the war began, for studying military maps. A huge clock embellished with a bronze eagle, a china closet, a phonograph, a long chest for phonograph records and several chairs were placed about the room. At the far end was a fireplace with several chairs grouped around it, one of Hitler's favorite sitting areas. Nearby was a second sitting area consisting of chairs placed about a glass-topped round table. Music, especially Wagner, and films were two of Hitler's favorite forms of entertainment and behind one of the sitting areas he had a movie projector hidden among the expensive tapestries. The speakers were on the opposite wall in a chest directly underneath a movie screen concealed by more tapestries. Hitler and Eva spent many hours sitting in this room listening to Wagner before going upstairs. As he listened to music, Hitler could look at a Bordone painting of a lady with an exceptionally large bosom or a Titian painting of a reclining nude to get himself in the mood for retiring to his bedroom. Eva teased him about the paintings several times when he was in a mellow mood, asking him if the models were friends of his. Hitler never answered, only smiled.

The Berghof had fourteen guest bedrooms. Each one had gray walls decorated with paintings from German mythology and a private bath of stone and marble quarried from different parts of Germany. Beside each bed was a bookcase containing a signed copy of *Mein Kampf* and several pornographic French books.

Guests at the Berghof were given a list of rules to follow when they arrived. They included:

1. *Smoking is prohibited in this bedroom.*
2. *The guest must not talk to servants or carry any parcel or message from the premise for any servant.*
3. *At all times the Führer must be addressed and spoken of as such and never as 'Herr Hitler' or other title.*
4. *Women guests are forbidden to use excessive cosmetics and must on no account use coloring material on their fingernails.*

This last regulation was often ignored by guests such as Henriette Hoffmann, Leni Riefenstahl, Emmy Göring and others. Eva herself always used cosmetics despite Hitler's irritation at such 'warpaint'. He never directly criticized her, however, even though he often tried to discourage her. Once, at dinner, when he noticed the print of her lipstick on a napkin, he asked Eva, 'Do you really know what a lipstick is made of?'

Frau Speer, who was at the table, said she had once heard it was made from plant lice. Eva, however, said that since she used a French lipstick, it was surely made of the best materials.

Hitler smiled sympathetically. 'If you knew that in Paris lipsticks were made of fat of sewage, surely you would color your lips no more.'

Eva knew his tactics. He didn't like lipstick and wanted to disgust her into not wearing it rather than directly forbid her. Eva and the other women at the Berghof (with the exception of Frau Gerda Bormann) continued to use lipstick.

The Berghof was managed by an SS man and his wife, who lived in a wing of the building. The waiters, who dressed in white vests and blacktrousers, were all SS bodyguards. These men, and the other men and women hired to serve at the Berghof, had to follow a certain procedure. Among the regulations were:

1. *Guests cannot discuss, even with other SS men, what they might see at the Berghof.*
2. *No discussion of politics is permitted.*
3. *Do not approach any part of the building or any other building you have not been ordered to approach.*
4. *No letter writing.*
5. *Guests are not permitted to keep a diary.*
6. *No whistling because Hitler dislikes whistling.*
7. *Never address Hitler unless he speaks first.*

Of course, the SS men stationed at the Berghof had certain advantages, too. The food was the best in all Germany, despite Hitler's eccentric eating habits; the scenery was exhilarating; they were exempt from fighting during the war; the work was comparatively easy although the hours were irregular; and they had the opportunity to do a lot of walking in the area since Hitler took a stroll every day. Perhaps the most important 'fringe' benefit of the year's stay at the Berghof (which was the mandatory length of assignment) were the fashionable streetwalkers brought from Berlin for the SS men. As Hitler explained, 'I understand the need for sex!'

Hitler's secretaries accompanied him to the mountain retreat and shared in the social life of his private circle. Eva got along well with all the secretaries except one, Gerda Daranowski, a slender girl with dimples, a flawless complexion and glistening white teeth. Fräulein Daranowski played a special role in the circle of secretaries. She was an aggressive woman with enormous vitality and a great desire to ingratiate herself with Hitler. She

152

always agreed with him during the long conversations the inner circle held in the late evening or early morning hours. Hitler was obviously attracted to her and she did everything to encourage him. Naturally, this made for tense relations between her and Eva, which did not escape Hitler, who was delighted to be the apex of a triangle.

The senior of his secretaries was Johanna Wolfe, who had been with Hitler since 1929. Eva liked this quiet, efficient older woman who wore her black hair short, used no makeup and dressed very conservatively. Whenever Hitler gave her any time off she would spend it with her eighty-year-old mother. She was especially tactful in settling the occasional disputes that arose among the women at the Berghof, especially the secretaries. Always a loyal assistant to Hitler, she worked hard though her poor health gave the others, especially Gerda Daranowski, an excuse to sometimes push her into the background. Hitler, however, liked Fräulein Wolfe and made certain that she obtained proper recognition for her loyalty and excellent work. He also took a personal interest in her medical treatments for heart trouble and a chronic gallbladder complaint.

A third secretary, Christa Schröder, had joined Hitler in 1933. Fräulein Schröder was a highly intelligent woman, skillful at handling people and strictly attentive to her duties most of the time. She did have one fault, though, and that was her habit of expressing her own views regardless of whether they coincided with Hitler's or not. At times she so exasperated him that she would stay away from the Berghof for a while, or Hitler would banish her temporarily. Eventually, the disagreement would be forgotten and she would be back. Eva never had to worry that Fräulein Schröder would supplant her with Hitler.

When a former servant of Hitler's named Junge married a secretary from the Chancellor's pool, she was assigned to aid Gerda Daranowski, Johanna Wolfe and Christa Schröder. Traudl Junge was only twenty-two years old when she went to work for Hitler. She was a very attractive girl with black hair, blue eyes and a round face that was always wreathed in smiles. When Junge, who had been an assistant valet to Hitler, was ordered into the army, Hitler urged him to marry Traudl.

'You had better marry her before you go away,' the Führer warned him, 'so that if anyone tries to molest her I can say, "Hands off; she's married." '

It was realistic advice because the SS men at the Berghof were constantly eyeing the girl. Frau Junge was very young to be in

Hitler's inner circle, but she soon overcame her shyness and her tact and charm made her one of Hitler's favorites (she was the sympathetic target of many of his long evening monologues). Her surface naïveté concealed sharp powers of observation and a quick mind.

On her first trip to the Berghof, Frau Junge was excited because she was finally going to meet Eva Braun. She had heard about Eva while working in the Chancellor's secretary pool and Junge had often described Hitler's mistress to her. After she unpacked her clothes in the small attic room she shared with Fräulein Schröder, she went down to the living room to meet the other guests. Later she described the scene for a friend.

'At this moment Eva Braun appeared, announced by the barking of her two dogs. Hitler went up to her and kissed her hand. Besides the fact that she was very well dressed and well groomed, her naturalness and openness struck me. She was not at all the ideal of a German girl that one saw depicted on the posters of the BDM propaganda [*Bund Deutscher Mädel*] or in the magazines. This day her well tended hair was tinted blonde and her pretty face was tastefully made up with cosmetics. She was not tall but had a decidedly good figure and was well poised. She understood excellently how to dress according to her own style. She was not overdressed but harmonically and tastefully dressed. She was wearing a Nile-green dress of heavy wool material whose upper part was close-fitting. The bell-shaped skirt was trimmed with a wide band of leopard fur. Her graceful walk brought the skirt into a soft, swinging movement. The dress was well fitted, had long sleeves and was low-cut in the front. She wore expensive jewelry including two gold clips which accented the cleavage of her bosom.'

Traudl Junge noticed that Hitler called Eva '*gnädiges Fräulein*' while the other ladies addressed her as 'Fräulein Braun'. The waiting time before the meal passed in informal conversation. Hitler teased Eva about her dogs, which he called 'hand lickers'. Eva replied that his dog Blondi was no dog but rather a calf. Frau Junge was amazed that Hitler, who had just arrived from a serious conference with his staff, could leave all his problems behind the heavy curtain that separated the hall from the living room. His face was that of a 'good-natured host who gives a party in his country home'.

Finally Heinz Linge, his manservant, came into the living room, stepped over to Frau Anni Brandt, the wife of the Chancellor's personal physician, and said, 'The Führer will escort you to the table.' An orderly instructed the other guests about the seating arrangement, then Linge approached Hitler and announced, 'Mein Führer, dinner is served.'

Hitler offered his arm to Frau Brandt. Eva took the arm of Reichleiter Bormann and they followed the other couple into the room. Hitler took his place at the middle of the table, facing the window. Eva sat on his left, and then Bormann. Across from Hitler and Eva sat the guest of honor or the highest service rank with his lady.

Fräulein Manzialy, who prepared Hitler's meals, was quite plain, the type of woman who would not attract notice, but Hitler considered her invaluable. She was a native of Innsbruck, Austria, where her Greek father and Tyrolean mother still lived. Prior to joining Hitler's household she had cooked at a school and then for a Professor Zabel in Berchtesgaden. Professor Zabel operated a clinic in this mountain town and Hitler, who constantly complained of stomach trouble, consulted him during one bad spell. The professor recommended a vegetarian diet and had Fräulein Manzialy send several meals from the clinic to the Berghof. Hitler was so elated with the meals that he hired Zabel's cook away from him. Fräulein Manzialy enjoyed cooking for the Führer, but she had one great worry. She was afraid Hitler might visit the kitchen some day and find her smoking. Eva told her not to worry. She herself smoked and would defend Fräulein Manzialy if Hitler caught her with a cigarette. This unobtrusive woman went to great trouble to make Hitler's meals nourishing and varied despite the fact that he insisted on a difficult diet. He wouldn't eat meat and usually delivered a sermon to any of his guests who did, and even his vegetables had to be from the special garden at the Berghof and cooked in a certain manner. He was fond of sweets, however, and Fräulein Manzialy tried to outdo herself in this area. Hitler appreciated her efforts and rarely a day passed that he did not mention to his guests or Eva that undoubtedly Fräulein Manzialy would have a surprise for him at mealtime. Occasionally Eva became annoyed at his solicitousness for the quiet Austrian cook but Hitler ignored her irritation. In fact, he began inviting Fräulein Manzialy to the teas and nightly gatherings at the Berghof and at times the cook surprised him by voicing an opinion on some matter under discussion. At first this only sharpened Eva's irritation, but eventually she became convinced that Fräulein Manzialy had no romantic designs on Hitler and the two became friendly. They sometimes even slipped out of the house together to have a smoke.

Eva didn't believe in Hitler's fetishes about food, so she did not have nearly as high opinion of Fräulein Manzialy's cooking as he did. She was very proud of her slim, dainty figure and went to great efforts not to gain weight. When she ate a very small amount Hitler would tease her.

'When I met you, you were so nice and plump, and frankly, now you're lean,' he complained. 'The women always say that they want to be beautiful for the man and then they do everything to work against his taste. They assert that they make all sacrifices to please him and, in doing so, subject themselves solely and completely to fashion. It is the strongest and only real power. The other members of her sex are the only authoritative public. All women only want to arouse the envy of their friends.'

Eva would protest strongly . . . but admitted she had a horror of getting fat.

There were a great many women in the Berghof – secretaries, the cook, staff wives – and some of them were quite attractive. Initially, Eva was quiet, unassuming, unobtrusive. But in time she changed. She never felt really secure enough with Hitler to relax; if she let down her guard for a second, she believed, he might discard her for another woman. Every woman who passed through the door of the Berghof was observed closely by Eva, and if she decided a woman was a rival, she immediately began planning how to handle her.

Being witness to the blatant way Hitler's associates conducted their extracurricular sex activities gave Eva a good education. Bormann, who was married and had several children, brought his movie-actress mistress to the Obersalzberg, where she stayed in the same house as his wife. Goebbels chased every movie actress in Europe despite his wife's objections. His affair with Lida Baarova caused his wife to demand that he live separately from her and the children. Göring's affair with the actress he finally married was nationwide gossip. Hitler was aware of these out-of-wedlock romances, and while he didn't approve of them, he took no action against them during the early years of his reign. His complaisance worried Eva. She often asked Paul Harns whether he thought Hitler was only using her to satisfy his physical needs or whether he was capable of real love. Was she, Eva wanted to know, just a 'plaything', like the movie-actresses Bormann, Goebbels and Göring went to bed with? Harns diplomatically tried to comfort her but he wondered about the answer himself. The one difference, he pointed out to her, was that while Hitler's associates soon tired of their mistresses, Hitler kept Eva at his side year in and year out.

Another woman Eva decided she had to defeat in her campaign to become the Führer's permanent mistress was Angela Raubal. Geli's mother was an irritating reminder of Hitler's earlier love affair, and worse, an insulting, hostile presence whenever Eva stayed at the Berghof. Eva bided her time and waited for an opportunity.

It came at the 1935 Nuremberg rally. Eva stayed at the Hotel Kaiserhof, as did Frau Raubal and the wives of high-ranking Nazi officers. While Eva was very careful how she acted and spoke in front of Hitler's sister, Frau Raubal knew no such discretion and was openly insulting to Eva. She called her 'the disgraceful blonde' who chased the Chancellor, and accused her of being worse than a common streetwalker. Eva took the insults without replying, remained calm and poised, and made a very good impression on the other women, some of whom had never met her and did not know her real status with Hitler. She didn't mention the matter to Hitler, confident that one or more of the other women would tell her husband about the incident, and that way it would be relayed to Hitler.

This is exactly what happened. When Hitler demanded to know what Frau Raubal had said to her, Eva at first refused to tell him. He insisted, she began to cry and then repeated the abusive insults Frau Raubal had directed at her in front of the other women. Hitler was so angry that his sister would dare meddle in his private affairs that as soon as the party rally ended he had his chauffeur drive him directly to the Berghof where he told his sister to pack her clothes and belongings and leave the Obersalzberg immediately. He then hired a Frau Endres from Munich to take care of the Obersalzberg.

Thus Eva's stays at the Berghof became much more enjoyable.

13
The 'New' Eva

Fritz Sauckel, Plenipotentiary General for the
Allocation of Labor, was in charge of the entire slave
labor program. A rude, pig-eyed little man who was
as tough as he looked, Sauckel delighted in having all
the foreign females medically examined. When he told
Hitler that 25 percent of them were still virgins,
Hitler was amazed. Hitler stated that virginity was not a
particularly desirable quality, and he suspected that
those who were still virgins had nothing particular to
offer.

Eva, in Hitler's opinion, had something particular to offer, and he had now made it clear that he would not stand for any maltreatment of her. The expulsion of Angela Raubal from the Berghof marked a sharp improvement in Eva's status. Those of the inner circle who had sided with Frau Raubal now found themselves at a distinct disadvantage and Eva delighted in their discomfiture. Julius Schaub, Hitler's long-time adjutant, was one of them. He was never fond of Eva but now his criticisms became much more discreet because his position depended upon Hitler's goodwill. Subtly, however, he did everything possible to discredit her in Hitler's eyes. When Angela Raubal was dismissed, Schaub was extremely unhappy. He decided to find out exactly how he should treat Eva now that she seemed to be the most important woman in the Führer's life. During one of their intimate conversations he mentioned to Hitler that the others at the Berghof thought he was going to marry Fräulein Braun.

Hitler stared at his adjutant for a few seconds before answering. 'I will never marry her,' he finally said. 'I haven't got the time. I am always away and cannot behave to a wife as a married man should.'

Schaub was secretly delighted at this reply – perhaps, then, Eva was less cherished than he thought – but his hopes abruptly faded when Hitler added, 'I am very fond of her.'

Others learned this, too. Ludwig Kreiger, an official stenographer from the Reichstag, was called to the Berghof to copy some official documents and on his way to a meeting with Hitler he saw two ladies walking their dogs. As was the custom, he saluted the women. When they didn't salute back, Kreiger was angry and only the fact that he was in a hurry prevented him from berating the women for their lack of respect to his uniform. Later, when he mentioned the incident to others at the meeting, they asked him what the two women looked like.

'Oh, those are the ladies of Führer. We do not talk about them.'

Before he left the Berghof Kreiger was informed by Bormann that he should not talk about anything that occurred or anyone who was at the mountain retreat. Kreiger knew that Bormann was especially referring to Eva and Gretl Braun, the two women he had encountered.

Others also learned about 'the Führer's lady' by accident. On a trip to Munich Eva stopped at the Sahn Studio to have her photograph taken. Hitler wanted a framed picture and he suggested that she go to this famed photographic salon since Hoffmann was busy. Although Eva told them she was a private secretary and

160

Hitler's favorite photo of Eva.

The Braun family: (left to right) Ilse, Fritz, Franziska, Gretl and Eva.

Eva posing in Hoffmann's photo shop in Munich.

Eva and Hitler leaving the Berghof.

Hitler and his secretary,
Johanna Wolfe.

Eva with Albert Speer.

Eva with Nazi officers at the Berghof.

Eva taking a picture of Hitler at the Berghof.

Eva (center) with Bormann (second from left) and friends. Dr. Karl Brandt (third from right) and Heinrich Hoffmann (right) are in the group.

Hitler teasing Eva during her birthday party in the Berghof, 1944.

Eva boating on the Königsee.

Eva cooling off at Berchtesgaden in the summer of 1939.

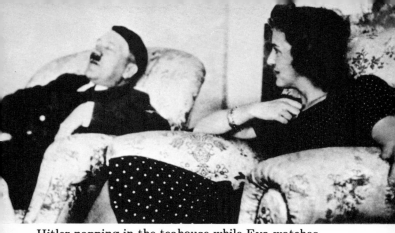

Hitler napping in the teahouse while Eva watches.
Eva with "Negus" and "Stasi"; Hitler with "Blondi."

Hitler and Eva (kneeling, right) at
wedding of Eva's friend Marion Schoenemann.

"First Lady of the World?"

Hitler kissing Herta
Schneider's daughter
while Eva watches.

worked at the Hoffmann studio, the Sahns became curious when she asked that a cabinet photograph be sent to the Berghof. When they mentioned this to some friends in Munich and showed them a copy of the photograph, the friends smiled. 'Don't you know that she is the Führer's girlfriend?'

Even Albert Speer's mountain guide suspected Eva's relationship with Hitler after she spent a vacation in the Alps with Speer and his wife. The guide's friends were soon privy to the knowledge.

Eva, of course, did not care if the public learned she was 'the Führer's lady', but Hitler did. So did her father. When a Czechoslovakian weekly published a photograph of her taken secretly in Berchtesgaden and described her as 'Hitler's Madame Pompadour', both Fritz Braun and Hitler were furious. Hitler gave strict orders to Hoffmann that he didn't want a single photograph of Eva put on the market, in Germany or anyplace else.

These bits and pieces of publicity influenced both those around her and Eva herself. Hitler's inner circle showed her more respect. As they did, Eva's self-confidence blossomed and she began to conduct herself as 'the Führer's lady'. She grew more serious and assumed more authority over domestic affairs at the Berghof and in the Führer's Munich apartment. She wanted to understand and share Hitler's thoughts, and to do so she switched from the love novels that had been her favorite reading material to history and general education books. Whenever Hitler discussed a subject unfamiliar to her during one of the early morning talk fests at the Berghof, she would immediately learn all she could about it so that she would be prepared the next time. Considering that Hitler discussed a great variety of subjects, Eva acquired a lot of superficial knowledge that made her appear much better educated than she was. It took her a long time to understand that her real value to Hitler was not her ability to relate facts of history to him.

Her real value was her ability to comfort him, to soothe his shattered nerves, to calm his anger and to divert his thoughts to pleasant subjects when he was upset over a political or military matter. She had accomplished this feat many times during the early years, before he came to power, but after Hitler became Chancellor, Eva concentrated on gaining a surface culture in an effort to impress him. But Hitler was not interested in a woman who would argue with him or one who disputed his statements all the time or corrected his facts if he made a mistake. He was interested in a woman who would listen to him, agree with him, bolster his ego, encourage him when he was depressed, congratulate him when he had achieved an objective. Eva finally learned her lesson by observing Hitler's reaction to Marion Schoenemann. Herr Schoenemann was an architect in Munich and only appeared at the Berghof on rare occasions. Frau Schoenemann, however, was a friend of the Hoffmanns and also of Eva's. She was of Austrian descent and was closely associated with the Vienna Opera circles through an aunt. She was a typical Viennese woman, with all the spirit and liveliness and charm that were characteristic of the women from that city. She was also an expert conversationalist who was able to make her point with a few well chosen words. Unfortunately for her, she quite often disagreed with Hitler and she never hesitated to say so. She often criticized the party leaders responsible for conditions prevailing in Munich and Vienna, which she thought deplorable. When these discussions with Hitler grew too serious, Eva tactfully would lead them into lighter channels. Finally, the relationship between Hitler and Frau Schoenemann deteriorated to such an extent that Eva suggested to her friend that it would be better if she didn't come to the Berghof. Hitler was delighted.

After the Frau Schoenemann episode Eva reverted to soft words and warm embraces. More and more often Hitler asked her to accompany him to the Berghof, until eventually he rarely went there without her. Before one of his periodic visits to Munich he made certain that Eva was notified so that she would be at her villa on the Wasserburgerstrasse waiting for him. (He usually kept his movements a strict secret – many times even the high-ranking party leaders who were traveling with him were unaware of the itinerary of the trip.) Hitler also arranged quarters for Eva in Berlin; she had an apartment in the so-called Führer-dwelling in the Wilhelmstrasse and one in the Chancellery. She never went to Berlin unless he was in the city on government business. Then she would fly there from Berchtesgaden or Munich in one of his official aircraft or, at times, go by sleeper train. It became obvious to the inner circle that Hitler's relationship with Eva was growing stronger with the years.

She also began to accompany him on his trips outside the Berlin-Berghof-Munich sphere. She stayed with him at Victoria Hostel in Stuttgart, the German House in Nuremberg and the Dreesen House in Godesberg. These were not the most luxurious hotels in these cities but they were the ones that had welcomed Hitler during his early days of political campaigning and he remained loyal to them after he became Chancellor. It was also much easier to stay out of the limelight in these lesser known hotels. Of course, if Hitler was in one of these cities on official business, Eva had to stay out of sight or pretend she was a secretary on his staff.

The only house she could enter socially was Heinrich Hoffmann's home in the Ebersbergerstrasse in Munich. Since Hoffmann had introduced Eva to Hitler and was well aware of their relationship, there was no need for secrecy in his home. Hoffmann was a man with a great deal of common sense who knew better than to interfere with or talk about Hitler's love affair since his livelihood depended upon Hitler's friendship. In fact, Hoffmann continually tried to hide the affair by explaining to anyone who broached the subject that there was nothing to the rumor, that Hitler had a large number of feminine friends and he certainly would not select one of Hoffmann's former clerks instead of the beautiful actresses or wealthy widows who were madly in love with him. The photographer had an open house – actresses, sculptors, painters, party members, businessmen and others met at his home day and night. Once a person was introduced to Hoffmann and invited to his home, he never had to wait for a second invitation to drop in for something to eat or drink. Hoffmann's hot liver sausage in loaf form, which was passed around so the guest could cut off as much as he desired, was famous. Henriette Hoffmann could, in Hitler's words, 'make the best spaghetti in the world'. Eva enjoyed her visits to Hoffmann's because she could relax and have fun with such film stars as Willy Birgel, Emil Jannings and Heinrich George, often dancing until the early hours of the morning while Hitler watched. He did not like dancing himself but didn't mind if Eva danced . . . as long as it was with someone he approved of and he was watching her.

Hitler now took care that Eva was recognized and respected within his inner circle. He personally gave orders that she should receive the salute reserved for the highest dignitaries and he stated, 'Make the salute snappy.' (This personal order was widely quoted in Nazi circles and 'Make it snappy' became a byword.) Worried about her safety, he told Eva that she had to stop driving around by herself in her car and he assigned bodyguards in black-and-silver uniforms to accompany her everywhere. He made certain that she had money enough to buy whatever she wanted, and since Eva had an obsession about clothes, she was soon the best-dressed woman in the inner circle. In fact, she seldom wore the same dress twice. The observant Frau Junge once noted during a stay of several weeks at the Berghof that Eva never appeared in the same outfit at noon, in the teahouse later in the day or at dinner. Eva's taste was for dark colors, especially black. Hitler's favorite dress was a heavy black silk with a bell skirt cinched in at the waist. Where the two pale pink shoulder straps ended at the bodice were two roses of the same color. Over it Eva often wore a short bolero jacket with long, narrow sleeves. While Hitler granted her the pleasure of buying all the new clothes she desired, he had a common male viewpoint on women's fashion.

'I don't understand why you women must always change. If I find a dress especially pretty, then I would prefer to see you always in this dress,' he explained. 'You should have to make all your dresses out of the same material and from the same pattern. But hardly have I gotten used to a beautiful dress, and you appear in something new.'

For years Eva had her clothes made to order in Munich at the firm of Auracher. On her trips to Berlin she wandered for hours on the Kurfürstendamm looking into one shop after another. Once, when she and Frau Schaub were strolling through Berlin, Eva spied a showcase with very fine lingerie. She immediately hunted up the store on the Kurfürstendamm and discovered a wonderful assortment of items, all extremely expensive. Eva bought to her heart's desire – nightgowns, dressing gowns with long trains, at least one of every item displayed. She was very happy with her purchases, not only because she liked the lingerie, but also because she was sure it was more glamorous than anything owned by a certain woman in Munich who always tried to surpass Eva in her dress. She made Frau Schaub promise not to disclose the location of the store to her rival!

On another occasion she and Gretl went to the famous leather store Lederer in Berlin. Eva wanted to buy a handbag but the arrogant clerk, judging her less than affluent, showed her only the cheapest ones. When Eva pointed out a bag she liked that was in the window, the clerk shook his head and told her it was much too expensive for her. This made Eva angry. She insisted the clerk summon the manager, and when he arrived she said, 'I want to buy everything that is in the display window. I want it delivered to the Chancellery this afternoon and the bill given to the Führer's private secretary.'

The frightened clerk and the stunned manager watched silently as Eva and Gretl walked out of the store and got into her Mercedes-Benz with its uniformed SS driver. Not only were the purchases delivered promptly that afternoon but the manager sent a large bouquet of flowers along with them.

Eva's hair was naturally medium blonde. First she had it bleached lighter, and then, in later years, had it tinted dark again. She constantly experimented with new hairstyles. Once when she had combed it into an upswept style, Hitler was disconsolate. 'You look completely strange, completely changed to me. You are a completely different woman.'

She immediately restored her hair to its old style.

Eva's new poise enabled her to cope with the difficult daily routine at the Berghof. As official hostess to the inner circle, she had the responsibility of entertaining guests during the long periods when Hitler was attending to business. His day was mostly taken up with one conference after another, lasting well into the evening. Only late at night did the small exclusive group of the Führer's associates meet for private conversation with Hitler. This left a great many hours for Eva to fill. Normally, Hitler would appear in the lower rooms of the Berghof around 11 a.m. after a few hours' sleep. He would usually check any incoming documents from Berlin or elsewhere, confer with Bormann and make any necessary decisions. He would then select the feminine guest he wanted to escort to the prolonged, ritualistic afternoon dinner. At the table Hitler would monopolize the conversation, which took the social pressure off Eva.

After the lengthy dinner Hitler invariably decided to walk to the 'teahouse'. This was a round building about twenty-five feet in diameter with a fireplace and a row of small windows overlooking the Berchtesgaden Valley. To the vexation of many of the guests, the walk from the Berghof to the teahouse took half an hour and was along a narrow path that was difficult to negotiate. Eva, who loved the outdoors and walking, enjoyed the daily trip. Bormann, on the other hand, hated it but Hitler made him go along.

Hitler again monopolized the conversation while he and his guests sat in the easy chairs and enjoyed the sweets and coffee, tea or chocolate laid out on the round table . . . until, as was his custom, he fell asleep. After that Eva would take charge of the conversation, talking in a whisper until he awoke. The affair usually lasted about two hours, and then Hitler would lead the procession to the parking area where a column of cars was waiting to take them all back to the Berghof. Usually Eva took her photography equipment along to the teahouse and tried to take pictures of Hitler. She was the only one he permitted to snap candid photographs of him, but even with his permission she had trouble. If the sun was shining he always wore his cap and the shadow from the brim put a dark streak across his face. Sometimes he wore sunglasses, which also obscured his face. Eva had great patience and a certain flair, however, and quite often got good pictures, much better than those of her former mentor and employer, Heinrich Hoffmann.

Eva often used the hours during which Hitler was in conference to show films she had taken with her 8-mm camera. She also had professional films to project. Between the walk to the teahouse and the evening meal she would have the list of films available brought to her and she, together with the other ladies and the men excluded from Hitler's conferences, would select one to be shown in the bowling alley of the Berghof. 'Please tell me when the conference is over,' she would instruct the orderly.

Then she would lead the group of eight or ten persons to the bowling alley. The 'Berghof Cinema' was open to everyone, even the kitchen staff, maids and soldiers when they were off-duty. If the audience was lucky, they got to see the entire film. More often, however, the shrill telephone bell would ring in the middle of the showing, signaling Eva that the Führer's conference was over and that he was waiting for the guests upstairs. Eva would shut off the projector and hurry to her room to repair her makeup and then join Hitler in the hall where he always awaited her.

After supper the group would move to the sitting area and gather around the large fireplace. Hitler usually sat on the right side of the fireplace, deep in the shadow ,and Eva would snuggle up in her deep chair close to him. The others found places on the sofas or easy chairs in either one of the sitting areas and braced themselves for a long, boring night. They sat so far apart that it was extremely difficult to hold a conversation. Hitler would spend a great deal of the evening whispering to Eva and holding her hand while the other guests murmured among themselves. Later Hitler would have the orderly play records and he would try to guess the names of the singers. The latest films would be discussed and Bormann always managed to get in some words of criticism about Goebbels or Göring or some other Nazi official he disliked. These discussions lasted until two or three o'clock in the morning, when Eva would finally stand up, have a few last words with Hitler and then go upstairs. A few minutes later Hitler would bid his guests good night and follow her. Those who remained then felt liberated and usually had a gay party where the champagne and liquor flowed freely.

The next day the same sequence of events would be repeated. The secretaries, who were expected to attend the talk sessions every evening, took turns resting during the day so that at least one or two of the four would be alert and wide awake that night. The guests, however, had to suffer the whole ordeal every day until they were so weary they couldn't think straight. They were always delighted when Hitler decided to leave the Berghof for a trip so they could get some rest.

In Berlin the routine was similar except that Eva had more time for shopping and other activities. She would spend part of each afternoon at the exclusive roof garden of the Hotel Eden. Sometimes she went to the theater in the evening and would be back in her apartment by the time Hitler completed his conferences. She had an overwhelming desire to attend the many night clubs in Berlin, but Hitler would not go himself and there was no escort of whom he approved.

The affair gradually developed into a contented alliance. Eva would never become a great woman but she did evolve into a good-humored and charming lady. To many of Hitler's associates it seemed astonishing at first glance that the gentle Eva could captivate such a strong-willed egotist, but captivate him she did. Even her strongest critic at the time, Bormann, admitted that Eva had a great deal of influence with Hitler – perhaps more than he had in certain areas. In a letter to his wife Gerda, written while he was away with Hitler, he warned her that if anything happened to him Eva would probably 'try to deprive you of this or that; for instance, stop you from getting things from the greenhouses or something of the sort.' He also advised her to have their children call Eva by her first name or *du* as she requested. Actually Eva treated the Bormann children very well, often taking them swimming or boating, though the antagonism between her and Bormann was no secret.

Eva had come a long way but Bormann knew that she had not yet completely conquered Adolf Hitler. In fact, he had already made detailed plans to use Eva's affair with Hitler for his own benefit.

14
Unity Mitford

'Women have a talent, which is unknown to us males, for giving a kiss to a woman-friend and at the same time piercing her heart with a well-sharpened stiletto.' Hitler had come to this conclusion while observing women struggling to gain his favor after he came to prominence in Germany. He believed that the most gentle woman was transformed into a wild beast when she thought that another woman was trying to steal her lover. 'The bigger the element of femininity in a woman, the further is this instinct developed.'

The 'new' Eva, as Bormann well knew, was not yet completely secure. Not only was she aware that the possibility of a war was increasing daily, a war that would take her man away from her for long periods, but she also knew that Hitler still had other feminine interests. The one woman who worried Eva most was Unity Valkyrie Mitford, the English girl she wrote about in her early diary.

Of all his romances, the long-lasting friendship between Unity Mitford and Adolf Hitler was the most surprising. It was also the affair that made Eva the most jealous, that turned her into the 'wild beast' Hitler predicted a woman could become when someone tried to steal her man. With Eva, however, the transformation was inward, not outward where others could observe it.

Unity Mitford was the exact opposite of the type of woman who usually attracted Hitler. She was tall and slender, flat-chested and had practically no hips. However, her shining gold hair, her smooth, flawless complexion and near-perfect features gave her a radiant beauty that immediately caught Hitler's attention when she first appeared in the Osteria Bavaria in Munich. He disregarded her lack of hips and bosom.

If her physical appearance was the antithesis of Hitler's customary desires, her family background was even more so. Her father was Lord Redesdale – David Bertram Ogilvy Freeman-Mitford – a member of the House of Lords and the British establishment. her mother, the former Sidney Bowles, was a reserved but determined Englishwoman who supported many causes she thought would aid the average British citizen. Both parents were initially strong opponents of the 'new' Germany and considered Hitler a radical who would destroy his country and probably envelop all of Europe in a war. Lord and Lady Redesdale, despite their noble name and reserved upper-class manners, were considered extremely liberal in England. They and their children (Unity had five sisters and one brother) were acquainted with Winston Churchill, Nevile Henderson, Anthony Eden, Lord Halifax and other British leaders and had been presented at Court. Sometimes the encounters between these Englishmen and the Mitfords were embarrassing since the daughters, as they grew older, espoused many causes and organizations that opposed the British government.

Unity's fascination was with Germany; Jessica married a Red who went to Spain to fight during the Spanish Civil War (unfortunately on the 'wrong' side according to the British establishment); Diana was convinced by Unity that Germany was the country of the future; and her brother Thomas became a well known playboy in London who concentrated on voluptuous women instead of politics and international affairs. Nancy, Pamela and Deborah, the remaining sisters, were the only conservative members of the family. The varied interests of Unity, Jessica and Diana caused a constant uproar in family circles as well as minor incidents in the English countryside. Especially disrupting were the battles between Jessica and Unity. Unity thought Hitler was the ideal man to save the world, while Jessica put her trust in Stalin. Swastikas and hammer-and-sickle symbols were in equal evidence at the Mitford estate and the fighting between the sisters only quieted down when Hitler and Stalin signed their short-lived agreement in 1939.

Unity's preoccupation with Hitler and the Nazis led directly to her first trip to Germany. She was determined that she would meet the leading Nazi officials in one way or another, and by nagging her parents she finally obtained their permission to go. They had tried to get her to attend a finishing school in Paris (traditional for upper-class British girls), but the headstrong and independent Unity refused. It was Germany, Germany, Germany. Lord Redesdale arranged for his daughter to meet wealthy, socially acceptable families such as the Bruckmanns, the Hanfstängls and the Bechsteins, thinking that her Hitler obsession would fade once she mingled with upper-class Germans. He had no idea that his class equals in Germany were supporting Hitler. Unity discovered, much to her joy, that the very individuals her father thought would dampen her enthusiasm for Hitler were the ones that made it possible to meet him. The first time she was invited to lunch with Hitler's then inner circle of associates was in 1932 and he was immediately attracted to her. Hanfstängl and Schaub filled him in on the background of the Mitford family. They never thought Hitler would become interested in a foreigner but they were wrong. He invited Unity again and again to the Osteria Bavaria and gradually she was included in the inner circle. Eva quickly heard about Hitler's 'English girlfriend' and saw photographs of them together in the newspapers.

The first time Eva saw Unity Mitford in person was at the Bayreuth Festival in 1932. At this time the eight-day visit to Bayreuth was an enjoyable interlude from politics that Hitler seldom missed. He and his guests usually stayed in an annex of Haus Wahnfried, but in 1932 he had a problem. He had invited both Eva and Unity Mitford and it would be unwise to put them up too close together. Unity, therefore, stayed in the main house as the guest of Winifred Wagner while Eva was quartered in the annex. During the first five days of the festival Hitler was successful in keeping Eva and Unity apart, helped by his adjutant Schaub, but eventually his plans went awry.

On the sixth night of the festival Hitler and Unity took a stroll in the gardens of Haus Wahnfried. During their walk the couple approached the veranda of the annex where he and Eva were staying. It was a lovely evening with a bright moon and apparently Hitler had a sudden attack of passion. Whether he thought Eva was at the concert nearby or whether he didn't care, he soon had Unity in a compromising position on the large couch on the veranda. At that moment Monita Garnier, Frau Wagner's French maid, appeared on the scene, but she quickly stepped back into the darkness when she observed the action on the couch. The maid had been sent to find Unity since Frau Wagner wanted her to meet some newly arrived guests. Monita was undecided what she should do. She couldn't very well interrupt the loving couple. Not only would it be embarrassing, but she was also afraid of Hitler. She had heard about his terrible rages and his habit of seeking revenge. Now, as she stood in the darkness watching the couple, she wondered just how much she had previously heard about Hitler was true. In front of her was proof that the rumors about his not being able to have normal sexual relations with a woman were false. While she was still pondering, she heard footsteps to her right and a moment later was shocked to see Eva Braun walking toward the veranda. Suddenly Eva stopped, stared at Hitler and Unity for a full minute, then turned and disappeared into the darkness. Monita, immediately sensing trouble that could cause her employer embarrassment, hurried back to Haus Wahnfried and reported to Frau Wagner what had happened. Frau Wagner only smiled knowingly, patted the French maid on the shoulder and said, 'We won't mention this to anyone, will we?'

There was no public scene by Eva over the matter. She probably decided it would be best to keep quiet rather than antagonize Hitler. It was a wise decision because Hitler never accepted criticism graciously, whether from a political associate, a general or a woman. Yet if Eva thought Unity Mitford was just a passing fancy with Hitler, she was mistaken. Unity returned to England, showed her parents and her sisters the photographs of herself with Hitler, Göring and other high-ranking Nazi leaders, and preached the salvation of Nazism to all who would listen. She wore the swastika emblem, raised her hand in the Nazi salute and, in general, tried to sell England on the invincibility of Hitler. She became a heroine to her adoring parents but barely escaped physical harm from Britishers who violently disagreed with her.

When she returned to Germany her sister Diana went with her, convinced by Unity that Hitler and his Nazis were the most exciting people in the world. Unity also arranged for her parents to visit Germany and meet Hitler and they, too, returned to England hypnotized by the charm and intelligence of the Führer and convinced that Great Britain should sign a treaty with him. Jessica thought that her sister was throwing herself away on a German radical who opposed Stalin, her hero, and tried to sway her parents' opinion but to no avail. Sister Nancy was so determined to 'save' Unity from Hitler that she forged a family tree that included a Jewish ancestor and sent the document to Himmler, who soon discovered it was faked.

Meanwhile Unity and Diana were having the time of their lives associating with the leaders of Germany and, in Unity's case, enjoying the favors of the Führer himself. She was a very personable young girl of approximately the same age as Eva and her conversation about England and the government officials she knew in Great Britain fascinated the Nazi inner circle. Hitler had a rule that no one could discuss politics during mealtime – Unity Mitford was the sole exception. The two Mitford sisters became so friendly with Hitler and his entourage that when they traveled around Europe in Unity's Austin the Führer made certain they were properly protected. The Austin was decorated with both the Nazi swastika, and the Union Jack, and wherever they traveled, one or the other of these symbols caused trouble. In Spain and Czechoslovakia Hitler's guards had to step in and save the sisters when protesters threatened to rush their car. During the Czechoslovakian melee Unity lost her camera and when they got back to Munich, Hitler gave her a new one. Later, when Diana returned to England and fell in love with Sir Oswald Mosley, head of the British Fascist 'Blackshirts', Hitler approved of Unity's plan for the couple to be married in Munich and later he invited them to dinner.

Eva was not oblivious to the ongoing intimacy between Hitler and Unity Mitford. She and her mother were sitting in a restaurant in 1938 when Eva pointed out Unity and Diana Mitford eating at another table. Turning to her mother, she said, 'Look, there are the two English girls the Führer is doing such a lot for.' She was calm, neither excited nor angry, but watchful.

Eva knew something that none of Hitler's other associates knew for certain, although they sometimes suspected it. Hitler was using Unity Mitford for his own purpose and this purpose had nothing to do with sex. Sex was only a fringe benefit. It was characteristic of Hitler that he could be charming, thoughtful and tender to anyone who could help him regardless of whether he liked the person or not. Though he was fond of Unity Mitford, he definitely was not in love with her. Unity was a direct pipeline to the British leaders and Hitler used her for propaganda purposes and for sounding out the British leaders about the approaching international conflict. At times he dropped remarks or hints about his own attitude toward England and how England and Germany should work together, knowing that Unity would repeat the remarks later to the right people in Great Britain. Often she told him facts about England that were important, facts that over a period of time, when they were gathered together and studied in context, gave Hitler an accurate picture of what was happening in England. So accurate that in 1942, long after the war had started, he told friends, 'Churchill and his friends decided on war years ago. I had this information from Lady Mitford; she and her sisters were very much in the know, thanks to their relationship with influential people.'

'Lady Mitford' (Hitler sometimes called her that although she had no claim to the title) had an obsession that Germany and Great Britain should be closely united. Heinrich Hoffmann, who was with her on many occasions in Bayreuth, Nuremberg, Munich and Berlin, was convinced that Unity intended to help effect an alliance between her country and Germany, and once that alliance was established, wanted to marry Hitler and become the 'First Lady of the Grand Alliance'. She told him: 'I dream of an impregnable and invincible alliance between the Ruler of the Seas and the Lord of the Earth.' She was convinced that together Germany and England could achieve a world dominion so strong that no other nation would dare oppose them, and with their great strength, wealth and influence they would be more just and benevolent toward their peoples than any civilization had ever been. Hitler would listen to her talk, nod his head and keep his own thoughts to himself. He didn't mention his personal plans for world dominion, his planned vendetta against all Jews, his scheme for a New European Order in which Germany would play the dominant role.

Unity was jubilant when Neville Chamberlain, England's Prime Minister, arrived in Germany in September, 1938, to confer with Hitler. Already her 'Lord of the Earth' had annexed Austria and was planning to move against Czechoslovakia unless the Sudetenland was transferred to Germany, which angered England and France and made the threat of war more imminent. After Hitler and Chamberlain met at the Berghof on September 15 and at Godesberg on September 22 an agreement between the two countries which was intended to avoid an armed conflict was signed in Munich on September 30, 1938. France and Italy also signed the pact. It gave Hitler a free hand to annex the Sudetenland. This conference was merely a formal session during which Chamberlain and Édouard Daladier, the French Premier, signed whatever document Hitler placed in front of them. They had no choice. Hitler had the military force to back up his threats and they knew it. The naïve Unity greeted this charade as a grand step forward in the alliance between Germany and England, her life's ambition.

Eva understood the circumstances under which the Munich Pact had been signed much better. On February 12, 1938, when Kurt von Schuschnigg, Chancellor of the Austrian Republic, arrived to meet with Hitler at the Berghof, she discovered how the Führer obtained his 'agreements'. The quiet, reserved, cultured Schuschnigg came to the mountain retreat thinking that he and Hitler were going to have a confidential discussion on the relations between Austria and Germany and lay down guidelines which would be beneficial in the future. He soon discovered how mistaken he was. Hitler, wearing a prominent swastika armband on his sleeve, had no intentions of discussing anything but meant to browbeat Schuschnigg into complete surrender before he left the Berghof. Several generals in full uniform roamed the halls of the house and went in and out of the conference room where Hitler was meeting with Schuschnigg. When the peace-loving Austrian stood by the famous picture window of the Berghof and remarked on the view, Hitler immediately interrupted him and began a tirade that lasted a full thirty minutes. Raving and throwing his arms about like a maniac, Hitler completely subjugated Schuschnigg. Every time he tried to interrupt Hitler with a quiet comment of his own, the Führer only screamed louder. He insisted that before Schuschnigg returned home he must sign an agreement that gave his government's three key offices to the Nazis – the ministries of war, finance and interior; join an economic union with Germany; and lift the ban on the Austrian Nazi Party. When the Austrian Chancellor refused, Hitler summoned his generals to his side.

175

'Chancellor, you will either sign it as it is and fulfill my demands within three days or I will order my generals to march into Austria,' Hitler yelled.

When Hitler left the shaken Schuschnigg alone to think over this threat, he gave instructions that no food or drink should be served him. When Eva learned of this, she was angry and ordered that Schuschnigg be given both. As she told Hitler later, 'All guests at the Berghof must be treated properly.'

Of course, the Austrian Chancellor signed Hitler's document before he returned home because he had no choice. Unity Mitford, who knew nothing of the Schuschnigg affair, believed Hitler and Chamberlain had truly and voluntarily reached an accord.

After the British Prime Minister flew home in September, 1938, Hitler ordered the German troops to march into the Sudetenland, confident that neither France nor England would interfere. Neither country did. However, instead of stopping his aggression there, as he had promised under the terms of the Munich Pact, Hitler decided that he wanted all of Czechoslovakia. Calling Emil Hácha, the President of Czechoslovakia, to Germany in March, 1939, and using the same 'negotiating' technique that Eva had observed him use against the Austrian Chancellor (Hácha fainted twice during the session after Hitler's tirades) Hitler obtained his signature on a document stating: 'The fate of the Czech people and the country are placed in the hands of the Führer of the German Reich.' England and France protested, but did nothing.

Within a month Hitler laid plans for the conquest of Poland, but when he summoned Colonel Józef Beck, the Polish Foreign Minister, to the Berghof for a browbeating session he discovered Beck was as tough as he was. He gave Hitler a blank refusal on Germany's demand for control of part or all of Poland.

This, of course, had no effect on Hitler's intentions to annex Poland. Throughout the summer of 1939, from the end of April until August, he stayed at the Berghof planning his military moves. Eva was with him during this last long stay at the Berghof prior to the beginning of World War II and knew of his plans for future action. While she understood his reason for seducing Unity Mitford, Eva was still unhappy and sided with the Foreign Minister, Joachim von Ribbentrop, when he vented his hatred against England. Whether or not her opinion had any influence on Hitler's final decisions during the summer of 1939 (and it is entirely possible, as Hoffmann said, 'since a woman can exert a great deal of influence on a man when she is in bed with him'),

176

on September 1 German troops attacked Poland. On September 3 England declared war on Germany and Unity Mitford's world fell apart.

The collapse of her grandiose ambitions for a British-German alliance and the hideous realization that Hitler had been using her were too much to bear for Unity Mitford. Gathering up her Nazi emblems – the swastikas that she had so proudly displayed in England and Europe, and the large framed autographed picture that Hitler had given her and that she had always carried with her – Unity stuffed them into a large envelope with a letter. She sealed the envelope and in a near hysterical state went to see Munich Gauleiter Adolf Wagner at his office. Wagner was extremely busy on September 3, the day England declared war on Germany, when the distraught Unity visited him, and he could only spare her a few minutes. He gave her what he considered kindly and well-meant advice: 'You should leave Germany at once and return to your own country.' She looked at him in stunned silence, got up and left the room. Wagner shoved the still sealed envelope aside and forgot about it.

The next afternoon the Munich police were notified that an unidentified young woman had entered a clinic on Nussbaumstrasse suffering from a head wound. She had shot herself in the English Gardens the day before and her condition was listed as serious. As soon as her identity was established, Hitler summoned the best doctors to treat her, including the famous Professor Magnus, and directed that all expenses be paid by the Third Reich. Eva, now that Unity was no longer a threat, could afford to feel sympathetic, and she sent flowers to the clinic and made certain that Unity had the toilet articles she required. Unity had to be watched closely all the time because she still wanted to commit suicide. When some of her Nazi friends visited her they brought along a framed autographed picture of Hitler similar to the one that she had always carried with her and a Nazi Party emblem like the one she had cherished. Before the visitors could stop her, Unity stuck the emblem in her mouth and swallowed it. Professor Magnus was summoned immediately and operated to remove the emblem, thus saving the English girl's life a second time.

Bedridden and technically an enemy subject, Unity Mitford was an embarrassment to Hitler. Finally Eva and Dr Theodor Morell, one of Hitler's physicians, convinced him that he should send Unity to neutral Switzerland on a special train where her parents could arrange to pick her up and take her back to

England. Unity arrived in Zurich early in 1940 with her nurse and doctor, and Lord Redesdale had her transported to England by way of Calais. Once she was home, she was arrested under Security Regulation 18B, which provided that seditious elements be interned for the duration of the war. She was charged with being 'a follower of Mosley and a friend of Hitler'. She was placed in a small cottage in the Cotswolds at Oxfordshire and was provided the best of nursing and medical care by her parents. She never recovered from her suicide wound and died shortly after the end of World War II, another casualty of the cruelty and duplicity of Adolf Hitler.

When Unity Mitford was finally sent to Switzerland, Eva went to the Munich railroad station to oversee the arrangements. Any pity she felt for the girl was submerged in relief that she was finally leaving Germany for good. While Eva had always known that Hitler was using Unity Mitford, this knowledge was cold comfort when she observed them together. Hitler understood Eva's feelings and in an attempt to show where his real loyalty and devotion lay, he revised his will in 1938, placing Eva first in the list of beneficiaries.

15
'Dictator of Love'

Hitler's morality was based on whether a belief benefited him personally or not. In one breath he would swear that the 'Ten Commandments are a code of living to which there is no refutation.' With the next breath he would state, 'I've much more respect for the woman who has an illegitimate child than for an old maid.' He maintained Eva Braun as his mistress for years but was extremely critical of the morals of others. Sometimes this criticism reached the highest levels of government and changed the course of history.

Eva had always wanted to marry Hitler but after a few years she accepted the fact that such a marriage was not probable. Consequently, she was shocked when Hitler, who believed that it was perfectly all right to live with her without benefit of clergy, became angry when one of his party leaders, army officers or personal staff members had love affairs that challenged social tradition. Erich Kempka, one of his chauffeurs, was a trusted staff member of Hitler's entourage, a man who knew many of the Führer's intimate secrets. Hitler trusted Kempka up to the day he died, when he asked the chauffeur to help the others dispose of his body. Yet, when he married, Hitler was furious. He berated him, saying that Maja Kempka was 'too little German', too modern, and too well associated with Italian and Hungarian embassy personnel to have good morals. Hitler even hinted that he had heard rumors that Kempka's new wife might have been a prostitute. Eva, who liked Maja, stood up for her and tried to defend Kempka's right to marry whomever he wished, but Hitler refused to budge.

'I'll give you good advice,' he told Kempka. 'Get a divorce. I, the leader of the great German Reich, am not sure anymore who is my friend and who is my foe.'

Kempka was afraid that if he didn't divorce Maja he would be sent to the front lines by Hitler, yet he didn't want to lose his new wife because he was deeply in love with her. Hitler gave him a twenty-four hour deadline to get Maja out of the Reich Chancellery, so Erich did the one thing possible. He divorced his wife, moved her to a home nearby and continued to live with her secretly when he was off-duty. Hitler never said another word about the matter; he was satisfied as long as Kempka was not legally married to Maja. To his warped mind, an illicit arrangement with a woman rumored to have 'loose morals' was preferable to marriage.

With Goebbels, Hitler reacted in just the opposite manner. His club-footed Minister of Propaganda was a devoted ladies' man who used his position as head of the German movie industry to crawl into bed with every beautiful actress who wanted to become a star. When he met the Czech film star Lida Baarova, however, he fell in love and entered into a long-term affair. Magda Goebbels was resigned to his dark-to-dawn 'romances', but this she refused to put up with. She demanded that he move out of their home on the Reichstagplatz. Albert Speer and his wife were planning a trip through Sicily and Italy, and when Speer heard about the Goebbels' breakup he invited Magda along, just as he had often invited Eva Braun to travel with him and his wife. Unfortunately, Karl Hanke, the young, personable State Secretary in the Ministry of Propaganda, was also along on the trip and fell madly in love with Magda. The sophisticated Magda decided that she preferred her younger, enthusiastic, and fun-loving lover to her humorless, selfish and unfaithful husband. A few weeks later the two announced their intentions of getting married as soon as she divorced Dr Goebbels. This was more than Hitler could tolerate. He told Hanke that he would not permit Magda Goebbels to divorce her husband under any circumstances. He then summoned his Minister of Propaganda and informed him that he wanted him to return to his wife and treat her as a high Nazi official should treat his wife. He forbade Goebbels to attend any public affair until he and his wife had reconciled and could appear together and, at least in public, give the impression they loved each other.

This decree did not please Eva. Magda Goebbels had once loved Hitler and always gave the impression that she would forget her husband in a minute and go to Hitler if he beckoned. Hitler never beckoned but Eva, still wary of losing her position to another woman, had hoped that Hitler would permit Magda her divorce since this would have eliminated her from the inner circle. Once again she was taken by surprise when Hitler decided that public image meant more than love or morality.

Hitler actually spent a lot of time trying to be the 'dictator of love' among his close associates. The Nazi Party leadership was exceptionally prone to sordid affairs, and Hitler was kept informed of them all. Wilhelm Brückner, an early Nazi Party member and one of Hitler's adjutants, spent many of his leisure hours being unfaithful to his wife. Hitler was well aware of Brückner's infidelity but paid little attention to it since it wasn't interfering with his work. Nor was Brückner high enough in the party hierarchy for his adulterous escapades to hurt the Nazi image. Eva, however, had never forgotten how the crude Brückner had treated her during the early years of her association with Hitler, refusing to relay her calls to Hitler, destroying her letters to him and, in general, making her life miserable. When she learned that Brückner's divorced wife tried to kill herself, Eva was tempted to tell Hitler about Brückner's sordid affair with his current mistress, but she kept quiet. Not until the gloating but unsuspecting Brückner had married his mistress did Eva go to Hitler and give him the complete details. Hitler was furious. For a long while he would have nothing to do with Brückner, and even when he finally relented and permitted his adjutant back into the inner circle, he refused to allow Brückner's second wife in the Berghof or the Reich Chancellery. Eva had eliminated another of her enemies and Hitler had once again ruled on a Nazi love affair.

One of Hitler's rulings on love probably changed the course of history because it eliminated Werner von Blomberg, Minister of War and Commander-in-Chief of the Armed Forces of the Third Reich. It is entirely possible that had Blomberg remained in control of the military forces of Germany during World War II the outcome of the conflict would have been different. Blomberg was a handsome, broad-shouldered man with a warm personality – just the opposite of the usual stiff-backed Prussian military man who seldom condescended to speak to everyday mortals. Sometimes the extroverted Blomberg gave the impression that he was a public relations director for the German military forces. Yet it was his brilliant mind and organizational skills that remade the defeated German Army into the most powerful and effective military force in the West by 1939. His reward for this feat was appointment as the Commander-in-Chief of the German Armed Forces, the first man in German history ever to hold such a rank.

Hitler owed Blomberg a debt of gratitude because if it had not been for him, Hitler might not have been appointed Chancellor by Hindenburg in 1933. Hindenburg agreed to turn over the reins of government to Hitler only on the condition that Blomberg be included in the government as Minister of Defense. Blomberg was an old, trusted friend of the President's and Hindenburg believed he was the one military officer who could hold the eccentric Hitler in check. Shortly after Blomberg accepted the post Hitler renamed him Minister of War and promoted him to Field Marshal.

As the years passed, Hitler forgot how essential Blomberg's cooperation had been to his own ascension to power. The top Nazis, especially Göring (who coveted Blomberg's ministry), cooled toward the stiff-backed General Staff. In the tug-of-war between the Nazis and the army officers Blomberg was caught in the middle. While he was a loyal military officer who had been trained to lead men in battle and to administer the armed forces in the best interests of his country and his troops, Blomberg was also a firm supporter of Hitler. The officer cadre who opposed Hitler began to turn against Blomberg. On the other side, Hitler, who was both Chancellor and President of Germany, needed only the command of the armed forces to be in complete control of the country. Only Blomberg stood in his path.

On November 5, 1937, Hitler called a meeting at the Reich Chancellery of the six most important men concerned with his future plans: Erich Raeder, Commander of the German Navy; Hermann Göring, Commander of the Luftwaffe; Werner von Blomberg, Minister of War; Constantin von Neurath, the Foreign Minister; Werner von Fritsch, Chief of the Army Command; and Friedrich Hossbach, Hitler's military adjutant, who took the minutes of the meeting. At the meeting he detailed his plans to annex Austria and Czechoslovakia, by force if necessary. For nearly five hours he expounded on Germany's need for *Lebensraum*, living space, and his willingness to use force to obtain it. Since, except for Neurath, all the men he had summoned to the meeeting were military officers, Hitler had anticipated that they would be delighted with his plans. He was badly mistaken. The officers were violently opposed to war at that time and didn't hesitate to tell the Führer so. They argued that the German forces were not yet properly prepared and that a military attempt to take over Austria and Czechoslovakia was too great a gamble. There was a distinct possibility, they told him, that England, France and perhaps Russia might oppose such a move and that would be fatal for Germany.

This verbal revolt by the military men, especially Blomberg and Fritsch, whom Hitler considered the two most powerful, made Hitler extremely angry. He decided that night that both men would have to be eliminated from their influential positions – but in such a way that neither the armed forces nor the German citizenry, who idolized them, would be antagonized. It was Eva who gave him the idea of how this could be accomplished. After the widowed Blomberg married again in 1938, she asked one question.

Eva had heard rumors about the new Frau Blomberg from Göring when the Luftwaffe commander was half-drunk. The Field Marshal had made the mistake of asking Göring for advice prior to his marriage. Blomberg had met twenty-three-year-old Erna Grühn when she was hired as a secretary in his office at the War Ministry. He was nearly sixty years old at the time, widowed and lonely. His children were grown and had their own families and friends, so when Fräulein Grühn became interested in him, he quickly succumbed. It was an ego-restoring experience for the Field Marshal to have a young, pretty girl less than half his age in love with him. But he was a product of the German General Staff system, the most precise and powerful military organization in the world. He well understood that to marry his secretary might damage his prestige and status as Germany's number one soldier, that the Nazi leaders, especially Hitler, might disapprove and resent his action. For that reason he consulted with Göring, who was second in power in the Nazi hierarchy. He told Göring that Erna Grühn was his secretary, that she was less than half his age and that she had associated with 'other officers and men earlier'.

'Would the Führer approve of such a marriage?' Blomberg asked.

The bombastic Göring assured the Field Marshal that there was nothing to be concerned about. 'The Nazi Party has abolished the priggish customs of the past,' he said. 'The Führer will be delighted to know that our greatest soldier is going to marry a common German girl. It will be an indication to the German citizens that prejudice has been eliminated under the Third Reich.'

Göring even agreed to send a young German officer who was also romancing Erna to South America so that he could not hamper Blomberg's marriage plans.

Alfred Jodl, a military officer who was to distinguish himself during World War II, noted in his diary shortly after he heard about Blomberg's marriage plans:

What an influence a woman can exert on the history of a country, without even knowing it! One has the feeling of witnessing a decisive hour for the German people.

It was an excellent prediction! On January 12, 1938, Blomberg and Erna Grühn were married in a civil ceremony which Hitler witnessed and the pair went to the Mediterranean area for a honeymoon. Shortly after they returned to Germany Eva asked her vital question, 'Have you ever checked on the background of Frau Blomberg?'

Hitler, now eager to get rid of Blomberg, immediately ordered a secret investigation of Erna Grühn. One of Himmler's officers went to the Berlin police headquarters and checked the files at the morals squad office. He found a file marked 'Erna Grühn' and it was a thick one. The secretary had been arrested and convicted for prostitution, and had posed for pornographic photographs which showed her in a wide variety of poses and involved in sexual acts. Further investigation revealed that her mother had operated a massage parlor in Berlin that sold 'love' instead of rubdowns. As Hitler told Eva after he read the police file on Erna Grühn, 'Blomberg is finished!'

184

Once it became publicly known that Blomberg, the Field Marshal of Germany, had married a common whore, he was assailed from all sides . . . just as Hitler had planned. The Nazis insisted that they had been betrayed by the highest-ranking German military officer, that his marriage embarrassed the party and the country, and that he had put the Führer in a very distressing situation. Officers who were angry with Blomberg because of his pro-Nazi sentiments and jealous of his influential position in the country attacked from the opposite side, saying that he had betrayed the German Army, seriously damaged the reputation of the officer corps and destroyed the morale of the soldiers. Jodl, more knowledgeable now, made a second entry in his diary:

The marriage of the Field Marshal affects the entire officer corps of the Wehrmacht. We cannot tolerate his marrying a whore. He should be forced to divorce his new wife or be removed from the officer corps. He should no longer be the commander of even a regiment.

The military leaders sent a naval adjutant to Blomberg's residence to persuade the Field Marshal to either divorce his wife or use the gun the adjutant had brought with him to commit suicide. To their chagrin Blomberg refused both their proposals. He had no intention of giving up his young wife for the honor of the military corps, and he told the young adjutant to so inform his fellow officers. Blomberg realized, of course, that his career was destroyed, that his usefulness as War Minister and Commander-in-Chief of the German Armed Forces was at an end. He resigned and went with his wife to a small Bavarian village south of Munich to live as a civilian.

Hitler was pleased to be rid of Blomberg, but his problems were not over. The position of Commander-in-Chief of the German Armed Forces was coveted by both Hermann Göring and Blomberg's deputy, Werner von Fritsch, the Chief of Army Command. Many Nazi Party leaders insisted that Göring was the logical choice, but the powerful officer corps demanded the post be given to Fritsch, an arrogant, humorless man who wore a monocle in his left eye and who despised the 'low-class Nazi hoodlums', who ruled the country. Fritsch was by far the more qualified, and Hitler knew it. He had both the military experience and the seniority of rank, and if he was passed over for Göring, Hitler would have to have an excellent reason or the German Army would turn against him. He decided to find a reason.

Once again Himmler was ordered to check the files at the Berlin police headquarters, a task Himmler found delightful because he hated Fritsch. Fritsch thought that the Gestapo and the SS were unnecessary and accused the Nazis of trying to build an independent army with these two organizations to challenge the traditional German military forces. He privately criticized Himmler, who was the commander of both the Gestapo and the SS, and the Führer for permitting these organizations to flourish. Consequently, Himmler was determined that his men would not leave the Berlin police headquarters until they found something on Fritsch. While studying the dossier of a pimp named Hans Schmidt, they learned that he had once observed a homosexual by the name of 'Fritsch' and another man called 'Bavarian Joe' committing a homosexual act on a dark street in the outskirts of Berlin. Later he approached Fritsch and threatened to expose him. According to Schmidt, Fritsch had been paying him blackmail ever since the incident. Himmler immediately tracked down Hans Schmidt and questioned him about the appearance of the man named Fritsch. The frightened man nodded every time Himmler described a physical feature of the Commander-in-Chief of the Army, even down to the monocle in the left eye. When this information was relayed to Hitler, he smiled. 'It is Fritsch all right. Summon him to the Reich Chancellery!'

In the library of the Reich Chancellery Hitler read off Hans Schmidt's charges to Fritsch. Fritsch denied the charges categorically and stated, without emotion, that Hans Schmidt had made a serious error. Hitler was prepared for the denial. Schmidt, who had been waiting in an anteroom off the library, was shoved into the room. The Führer pointed to Fritsch and asked, 'Have you ever seen this man before, Schmidt?'

The man stared at the rigid army officer and nodded. 'That is the man I blackmailed.'

Fritsch didn't flick an eyelid at the accusation. He merely said to Hitler, 'The man is mistaken. Are you going to take the word of a convicted pervert or the word of a Prussian army officer?'

Hitler didn't hesitate a minute in affirming whose word he would take, 'Fritsch, I must ask for your resignation.'

A few hours earlier Fritsch believed he would be the next Commander-in-Chief of the German Armed Forces. Now he faced disgrace. He refused to resign and demanded that the facts be presented to a military Court of Honor. Hitler agreed, knowing that once the charges became known Fritsch's career would be ruined whether the Court of Honor found him guilty or not. The Führer, with the help of his Nazi associates, had the rumors of

Fritsch's homosexuality spread throughout Berlin, although no official news account was published. Fritsch's indefinite suspension made his fellow officers and acquaintances curious. Once they heard the gossip about his homosexual activities, many of them believed it and in their minds Fritsch was convicted before the trial began. This was a tragedy because the German Army investigators working in behalf of the Commander-in-Chief of the Army soon discovered that Fritsch was completely innocent of the charges. The 'Fritsch' whom Schmidt had blackmailed was a 'Captain Frisch' of the cavalry who was retired from military service. Himmler had been aware of the error all the time and intentionally used it; whether Hitler also knew before the Court of Honor convened was immaterial because the damage to the Prussian officer's career had already been done. Göring, Fritsch's competitor for the coveted post of Commander-in-Chief of the German Armed Forces, presided over the Court of Honor and listened to the evidence pile up which proved that Fritsch was innocent. After Hans Schmidt admitted that he had lied, Göring voted with the other members of the Court of Honor to acquit Fritsch. He also voted for the execution of Hans Schmidt, which occurred shortly after the trial.

Fritsch was proved innocent in the Court of Honor but neither the verdict nor any other facts of the case were made public. Only the rumors were available to the curious, and they were detrimental to Fritsch. He never recovered from the accusation. Hitler did not give him back his post as Chief of the Army Command. Instead he was demoted to a minor command which, added to the rumors, made him appear guilty in the eyes of all who knew about the affair. Fritsch understood that Hitler had destroyed him but he was not of the same mold as Blomberg. He was not content to retire in disgrace to a small village. Instead he sought a military death and he found it in the suburbs of Warsaw when he accompanied his old regiment into battle. He was shot in the thigh and bled to death before help arrived. Hitler ordered a full military funeral for Fritsch and Göring presided at the ceremonies.

As soon as Fritsch had been discredited, Hitler made a move that surprised both his Nazi associates and the German military. He personally assumed the post of Commander-in-Chief of the German Armed Forces. He had finally taken the last step in his grand objective – complete control of Germany – through intrigues based on the exposure and slander of other men's sexual lives.

16
Eva's Happy Interlude

After the success of the Anschluss *in 1938 Hitler
immediately turned his eyes toward Czechoslovakia.
On October 1, 1938, German troops marched into
that country. Hitler still was not satisfied. After
stunning the Western leaders by signing a non-
aggression pact with Stalin on August 23, 1939, Hitler
ordered the invasion of Poland on September 1. Two
days later both England and France declared war
on Germany. From the German invasion of Poland in
1939 until the autumn of 1942, Hitler's plans of
conquest were most successful: Poland, Denmark,
Norway, the Netherlands, Belgium, Luxembourg,
France, Rumania, Hungary, Bulgaria, North Africa,
Crete and Turkey all came under his control.*

The period of Nazi conquest, 1938–1942, was the happiest time of Eva's life. Hitler was so involved in political intrigue and military plans that he had no time to pursue other women. Eva was also relieved that her family had finally become fully reconciled to the fact that she was neither going to leave Hitler nor marry him. Perhaps her greatest joy, though, was that she finally felt needed, almost indispensable. Hitler was under intense strain during the long months prior to the start of World War II, when he was playing a game of international bluff with France and England, and during the initial months of the war, when he was still uncertain just how well his plans would succeed. He required Eva's comforting arms, soothing conversation and constancy as never before. And he became more thoughtfully appreciative: he noticed and complimented her appearance, gave her most expensive gifts, treated her mother and father with greater respect and even arranged for her sister Ilse, of whom he was not very fond, to work with Albert Speer in an excellent position.

Eva traveled a great deal during this period, not always with Hitler's approval. Shortly after he had forced the appointment of Nazi puppet Arthur Seyss-Inquart as Chancellor of Austria German troops marched into the country and less than eight hours later Hitler personally crossed the frontier and drove through cheering crowds to his former hometown of Linz. The public square was a turmoil. All afternoon Nazi supporters sang the Horst Wessel song and '*Deutschland über Alles*' while Luftwaffe planes crisscrossed the sky. Late in the afternoon Hitler, riding in a six-wheeled Mercedes flanked by SS men on motorcycles, slowly drove through the town. Dr Bloch, Hitler's former family physician, watched the procession from his window. Since he was a Jew, he was not among those invited to talk with Hitler. After a short speech from the balcony of the town hall, Hitler rested in the Weinzinger Hotel for the night. The next day, a Sunday, he visited his mother's grave, and shortly afterward departed for Vienna. Not, however, before he gave the order to begin the arrest of all those who had opposed the Nazi Party and all Jews.

The Führer was expected to arrive in Vienna on March 13 but Himmler warned him to stay away until the 14th since the SS still did not have the proper security arrangements completed. Hitler, though furious at the delay, abided by the decision of his SS chief, because he knew many Austrians opposed the *Anschluss* and that his life might be in danger. He had scheduled the trip to display publicly his confidence in the German military might and to show the world, especially France and England, that the Austrians welcomed the annexation. To do this, the triumphant entry into Vienna had to be staged and Himmler was twenty-four hours late with his arrangements. Eva decided she wanted to share in Hitler's triumph. She didn't realize that Hitler's excursion into Austria so soon after the *Anschluss* was dangerous, and if she had, she probably would have insisted on going anyway. She telephoned her mother and asked her to come. 'I want to see what is going on,' Eva explained.

Fanny Braun quickly agreed. Eva sent her car for her mother and a short time later they were headed for Salzburg. Since Eva did not intend to stay overnight, she had not taken any extra clothing or her toilet articles. She wasn't even carrying a handbag so she had no money either. She fully expected to catch up with Hitler and his entourage at the border, visit with him and share his victory, and then return to Munich. However, when Eva and Frau Braun reached Salzburg, they discovered that Hitler had already gone on to Linz where he intended to visit his mother's grave. After a short consultation with her mother Eva decided that they would go to Linz also. Once again they were too late – Hitler was on his way to Vienna. Now they were in a predicament because if they continued on to Vienna they definitely would have to stay overnight, perhaps two nights, and they had no money or clothes. Checking with their driver, Junge, they discovered that he had a small amount of money so once again the two women had a short conference.

'How about it, *Mutti*, shall we go to Vienna?'

Fanny Braun was willing but she was worried about the driver. Eva just laughed.

'Junge can go anywhere as long as he has lots of food to eat.' Eva sent him into a restaurant, where he had a big meal, while they waited in the Mercedes and then headed for Vienna. They arrived in Vienna at 4.30 a.m. on the morning of March 15, 1938. When their large black Mercedes stopped, the Viennese opened the car door, pulled Eva and her mother out, and hugged and kissed them both. They didn't know who they were, but knew anyone driving such a car had to be from Germany and the on-lookers, fortunately for Eva and her mother, were Nazi supporters.

Eva learned that Hitler was staying at the Hotel Imperial, and knowing that he might be angry that she and her mother had come to Vienna without his knowledge, she went to another hotel. The manager, recognizing them as Germans, gave them one of the best suites. When he asked for their luggage Eva just smiled and said, 'Oh, that's following in another car.'

Late that morning Eva rang the Hotel Imperial and asked for Hitler. Schaub, the adjutant who had accompanied the Führer, was shocked when he learned that Eva was in Vienna. 'There will be a row over this escapade,' he warned her.

He was correct. Hitler was furious that she had made the trip with only Junge to guard her. After he had berated her for a few minutes she became 'very red in the face and stamped her foot'.

'Don't go on scolding me so much,' she said. 'It was not dangerous at all and anyhow, *Mutti* is with me. She is standing right here beside me.'

Hitler became even more angry. 'Your mother should have more sense than you.'

After he calmed down, he sent for Eva and she went over to his hotel. Later her mother joined her in the hotel dining room for lunch. As they sat down, Schaub brought Eva a check from the Führer since he knew she had no money to pay for the meal. Both women were half-starved because they had not eaten for so long, but before Eva could finish her salad, Schaub came to the table again.

'The Führer is flying back to Berlin and if you wish to come you must hurry. There is a vacant seat,' he explained.

Eva put down her fork and got to her feet. 'Of course, I'll come with him.'

As she hurried away from the table, not even bidding her mother farewell, Frau Braun called after her, 'Eva, I have no money. What shall I do?'

'You'll manage,' Eva said as she disappeared out the door.

Frau Braun was still staring after her daughter when Schaub reappeared and handed her another check. It was large enough so that Frau Braun could stay over in Vienna for several days. She had a lovely time.

In May, 1938, Hitler visited Rome for a formal meeting with Mussolini. Every Nazi official tried to get an invitation to accompany him in one of the four special trains headed for Italy but there wasn't room for everyone. Donna Eleanora Attolico, the beautiful wife of the Italian Ambassador to Berlin, suggested that some of the leading ladies of the Third Reich should also be invited. Frau Ribbentrop, Frau Hess, Frau Frank, Frau Keitel and the others were delighted but there was one small factor that no one had taken into consideration – or at least considered seriously enough to obtain the advice of experts. That was the proper protocol and clothing for a formal state meeting. Eva had also been invited, but she was not consulted on either clothing or protocol, which was unfortunate because she probably had a better idea of what would be needed than any of the other women. Frau Ribbentrop decided that she was the proper person to take over the planning of the trip since her husband was the Foreign Minister. She promptly decreed that the regular military uniforms the Nazi leaders wore were not suitable for the Italian state visit and she helped design a new 'special uniform' for formal occasions (she allowed the normal uniforms were good enough for more casual affairs). By the time the four trains pulled away from Berlin the private compartments looked like actors' dressing rooms. The 'special uniforms', several regular uniforms, mufti, tails, swords, daggers, shoes, riding boots and belts filled every inch of space.

Eva, meanwhile, traveling as an unofficial guest of Hitler's took her most beautiful dresses and coats and lingerie and was completely unburdened by the special clothing Frau Ribbentrop thought the other women needed for the official affairs.

The Germans were unaccustomed to formal state visits and their *chef de protocol* (who was fired by Hitler before the trip ended) was just about as confused as the rest of the Nazi entourage. Frau Ribbentrop thought that she was 'Germany's First Lady' and Hitler had a difficult time convincing her that Frau Mackensen, wife of the German Ambassador to Italy, Hans Georg von Mackensen, was entitled to that honor during the state visit. While this internal bickering was going on, the remainder of the women demanded to be presented to Her Majesty the Queen Empress of Italy, though none of them knew the court etiquette required for such a presentation. At the last minute Donna Eleanora Attolico and Edda Ciano, the daughter of Mussolini and wife of Count Galeazzo Ciano, tried to teach the German women to curtsy but the rehearsal was more comic than instructive. The wives of the Nazi leaders either fell down, stepped on their own dresses or looked like barmaids leaning too far over the bar. Eva, who observed the practice from a hidden alcove, laughed so heartily that she was nearly sick by the time she returned to her hotel room. She could curtsy very gracefully, but because of her unofficial capacity in Italy she was not presented to the Queen.

The formal dinner at the Royal Palace didn't improve the humor of the Queen of Italy, who did not like Hitler in the first place. By the time the ladies of the Third Reich had completed their farce before her, giving the onlookers the best entertainment they had had in years, the Queen had to face another problem – what to do with Frau Ribbentrop and Frau Mackensen, who both considered themselves 'Germany's First Lady'. Her solution was to seat Frau Mackensen on her right and Frau Ribbentrop on her left. Throughout dinner she addressed herself almost exclusively to Frau Mackensen in Italian, which Frau Ribbentrop did not understand.

Eva created more excitement in Italy than any of the other ladies of the Nazi entourage. She was more beautiful than any of them and much more carefree. She ignored the petty bickering about status that the others engaged in and enjoyed every minute of the trip despite her unofficial position. Hitler found time to visit her occasionally but she spent much of her time with the handsome virile SS men and the Italian officers assigned to watch over her while she was in Italy. Many of the Italian officials were curious about 'the blonde with Hitler' but few learned her real identity. One who did was Don Arturo Bochini, the suave Chief of Police of Rome. When he was finally introduced to Eva he was delighted. Later he told Eugen Dollman, Hitler's interpreter, that he would 'never have given Hitler credit for such good taste'.

Eva did a lot of shopping during the trip. She loved handbags, shoes and other articles made from alligator hide and after one shopping trip in Rome she returned to her hotel looking as if she had been on a hunting trip to the Congo. She also purchased some expensive jewelry. Between shopping trips she was squired around the city's night spots by various Italian officers, who were completely unaware of her intimate association with Hitler but were delighted to spend the evenings with her. Eva loved to dance and on two occasions she returned to her hotel shortly before daybreak. When Hitler was told about this by Schaub, who had learned of her escapades from an Italian aide to Mussolini, he was angry and told Eva that he 'wanted her back at her hotel at a decent hour'.

'I will be back at a decent hour,' she told him, 'when you quit holding hands with the Italian Madonnas at the Grand Hotel.'

Despite this mild rebuke, Eva had a wonderful time on the Italian trip. When Hitler reviewed the host country's naval fleet at Naples aboard the battleship *Cavour* with the King and Mussolini, Eva was on board a smaller ship cruising nearby and observed all the ceremonies. Later she teased Hitler about not wearing braid and medals as did the King and Mussolini. Actually, she was very proud of him that day.

Eva returned to Germany a much more respected lady by those

who had been on the trip. The wives of the Nazi officials had exhibited their coarseness, their lack of sensitivity and their complete ignorance of the style and manners needed at important formal state affairs. Eva's actions, in contrast, were those of a lady, and a lady who could handle herself in all situations with grace and poise. Hitler appreciated the manner with which she had conducted herself in Italy (except for the dancing episodes) and was proud that so many Italian officers and officials had inquired about the 'blonde beauty'. While he still did not allow her to attend any official state dinners or other formal functions at the Reich Chancellery or the Berghof, he did permit her much more exposure at both places than he had previously.

Eva was present but not conspicuous, for instance, when Hitler invited the French Ambassador to the Obersalzberg. With the threat of war increasing, the Führer decided to talk with the one foreign diplomat for whom he had a marked liking – André François-Poncet. At the time of the invitation François-Poncet was the Ambassador to Rome, but earlier he had been the ambassador in Berlin. Instead of receiving him at the Berghof, Hitler told Eva to arrange for the meeting to be held in Eagle's Nest, the pavilion he had constructed a mile up in the mountains. The report François-Poncet made to Georges Bonnet, French Minister for Foreign Affairs, described this fantastic abode:

In inviting me on the evening of October 17 to go to see him as soon as possible, Chancellor Hitler had placed at my disposal one of his private planes. I, therefore, left for the Obersalzberg by air the next day. After landing, however Hitler's chauffeur drove me not to the Berghof where I had met him previously but to the 'Eagle's Nest', an extraordinary spot where, when the weather is good, he loves to spend his days.

Seen from afar, this place appears to be sort of an observation point or hermitage perched 1,900 meters high on a crest of a rocky ridge. One arrives by a winding road about 15 kilometers long, hewn from stone, its daring construction paying tribute to the talent of the engineer Fritz Todt who completed this gigantic task in three years.

The road ends at the entrance to a long tunnel which thrusts into the earth. Heavy, double brass doors guard the entrance. At the further end of this tunnel a large elevator with copper walls waited. Rising up a vertical shaft of 119 meters cut out of rock, the elevator ascends to the level of the Chancellor's abode.

Here I was greatly surprised. I saw a squat and massive con-

struction, consisting of a gallery of Roman pillars; a huge glassed-in circular chamber with a vast chimney in which was burning large logs of wood; and a table surrounded by about thirty chairs, as well as several side rooms furnished elegantly with comfortable arm chairs.

On every side, looking through the bay windows, I could see, as from a high speeding plane, passes leading into the panorama of mountains. In the distance I could see Salzburg and its neighboring villages above which rises, as far as the eye can see, a horizon of mountains and peaks and of pastures and forests which cling to their slopes. Close to the house, which appears to be suspended in the void, and almost hanging over it, an abrupt wall of naked rock rears itself. The whole, bathed in the glow of an autumn evening, is glamorous, wild, almost eerie.

By the time of François-Poncet's visit in October, 1938, there was no doubt in the minds of those in Hitler's inner circle who was 'Germany's First Lady'. Even Eva's parents understood her changed status, although this realization came very slowly. When Fritz Braun was under consideration for a promotion to assistant master of the school where he taught, the director of the school discovered he still was not a member of the Nazi Party. Since the director was aware of Eva's friendship with the Führer (though not the details of the romance), he considered it ridiculous that her father was not a party member. When the director questioned Herr Braun on this, he discovered Herr Braun was still not convinced that Hitler was the right man to govern Germany. He therefore did not get the promotion. Later, when Hitler's policies decreased unemployment and appeared to be helping the average German citizen, Fritz Braun quietly applied for party membership. As soon as he was accepted, he was promoted to assistant master of the school. However, Fritz Braun didn't tell Eva that he had joined the Nazi Party. She didn't find that out until the night of November 8, 1939, when an attempt was made on Hitler's life at the Bürgerbräukeller in Munich. On this date each year Hitler appeared in Munich for a reunion with the 'Old Fighters', the veteran Nazi Party members who had taken part in the ill-fated putsch of 1923. It was customary for him to give a long speech to his comrades in the Bürgerbräukeller, but in 1939, for reasons never explained, he made a very short speech and hurried back to his special train, which was waiting to take him to the Berghof. Shortly after he left, a bomb inside one of the pillars near where Hitler had been standing was set off electrically.

Several party members were killed and a large number were injured. One of the injured, much to Eva's amazement, was her father. Not only had he joined the Nazi Party, but Hitler had awarded him a 'green membership card' which entitled him to meet with the 'Old Fighters' in the Bürgerbräukeller. Unfortunately, this favor backfired and Fritz Braun was seriously injured by the bomb blast. Eva was frightened when she first heard the news, but later, after her father fully recovered, she was so proud of his participation in the meeting and of his being 'wounded for the Führer's sake' that she bored everyone by repeating the story over and over, until Hitler reminded her that many others had also been wounded in behalf of the party.

Both Fritz and Fanny Braun were invited to the Berghof often after they reconciled with their daughter. Gretl spent nearly as much time there as Eva. Only Ilse remained an 'outsider', although occasionally she stopped on the Obersalzberg for a day or two. In fact, the family spent so much time at the Berghof that Göring told his friends that 'there are as many Brauns on the Obersalzberg as there were Brown Shirts in Munich and that Hitler should change the name of the Berghof to Braun Haus'. The Führer seemed fond of Fanny Braun though he would never talk to her about Eva. One day in the teahouse he offered her the cake and cookies. When she took only a small cookie he personally piled her plate high with all the cookies and cakes that he liked, saying, 'Now, Madam, you must eat this. It is good for you.' On another occasion he insisted that she drink a cup of his special tea which was made of apple peels. Later, when Fanny Braun told Frau Mittelstrasser, a kitchen helper, that the tea was not bad, the older lady laughed.

'Don't tell the Führer,' Frau Mittelstrasser said, 'but it is not made of apple peels. It is regular tea with a little apple wine in it. It is Eva's idea.'

While the German forces were winning victory after victory during 1939, 1940, 1941 and 1942 Eva and her mother made regular trips to Italy, usually to Rome and Florence. Sometimes Gretl went along. On these carefree jaunts the women had a great deal of fun. Eva could smoke as much as she wanted, drink if she so desired and dance all night without being berated by Hitler. And she did. While Hitler was occupied by the invasion of Norway, the defeat of France and the Low Countries, the Dunkirk affair and his plans to double-cross Stalin and pull a sneak attack on Russia, Eva and Fanny Braun were seeing the world first class. On one trip to Italy Eva took six suitcases full of clothes, including thirty-seven pairs of shoes. During her stay she bought nearly as many dresses and pairs of shoes as she had brought with her. At the German customs the inspector told her she owed a large amount of duty on her purchases. He, of course, had no idea who she was. Eva asked to use a telephone. When the customs officer heard her request the Reich Chancellery in Berlin he laughed, thinking that she was bluffing, but a few seconds later he found himself listening to Hitler telling him to pass 'the young lady' across the border immediately without any further luggage checks or payment of duty.

The customs inspector had his reply ready, 'Heil, Hitler!'

Eva and her mother often took cruises. On one cruise aboard the Milwaukee Frau Braun became so seasick for three days that she thought she was going to die. While ministering to her Eva made a comment that expressed the pride and security she now felt in Hitler's love: 'If I would get seasick, I would not stay on this ship for one day. I would immediately telephone the Führer and he would send his seaplane for me and take me home.'

Hitler telephoned her every day she was away from him. When he called, Eva would always tell him her plans for the next day and he would outline his own plans to her. Whether he was at one of his military field headquarters such as the Wolfsschanze (the infamous Wolf's Lair buried deep in the evergreen forest of East Prussia) or the Adlerhorst (his headquarters in the Taunus Mountains) or at one of his command posts in the west, Hitler called Eva every night, usually around 10 p.m. Though he never discussed military matters with her over the telephone, he did tell her about the interesting things that had happened at headquarters that day, especially any humorous incidents, and he listened to her problems, no matter how insignificant. Once when she complained that Goebbels was demanding that all women forgo cosmetics and permanent waves because the materials were needed for more essential products, Hitler said that he would take care of the matter. Eva continued to get her cosmetics and hairwaving materials. Another time Goebbels decided that no more American movies could be shown in Germany. Eva pouted, Hitler relented and she saw all the American movies that were available, screening them for herself and her friends while Goebbels fumed helplessly. Sometimes when Eva was at her villa in Munich Hitler would unexpectedly arrive at the Berghof for a few days' rest. As soon as he discovered that she had not yet arrived or had not yet received his message outlining his change of plans, he would immediately send his special train for her. He did not like to have her make the trip in her car or fly for fear she would get hurt.

These were the years Hitler and Eva enjoyed themselves in the luxurious surroundings of the Berghof or the Reich Chancellery or Eva's villa or Hitler's Munich apartment – talking, laughing, eating, drinking and loving while all around them others were dying on the battlefield or in the concentration camps.

17
Eva's Nemesis

During the successful era of the Third Reich various party leaders maneuvered in every manner possible to gain more power, to become second in command under Hitler. At the outset Hermann Göring was the favorite, but as the war progressed and his Luftwaffe failed to keep the skies over Germany free of Allied aircraft, others began to push him aside. Goebbels, with his flair for publicizing Hitler and his gutter tactics, became very influential. Himmler, who had the backing of the powerful SS and the Gestapo, became a man to be reckoned with. Eventually, Albert Speer, the man who, as head of war production, controlled the hardware necessary for the Third Reich to wage war, stood out from most of the others. Yet the man who became the most important Nazi leader after Hitler was barely known to any except Hitler's closest associates. That man was Martin Bormann.

The two most obscure members of the Third Reich inner circle were the two most powerful as far as personal influence on Hitler was concerned, and they despised each other.

Eva Braun influenced Hitler much more than was believed immediately after the end of World War II. Subsequent studies indicate that in her subtle manner Eva was able to guide Hitler's thoughts along the channels she desired. She often prevailed upon him to take time from his busy day to see certain individuals she wanted him to talk with; and since she directed Hitler's leisure life, she was able to use this time to promote causes of her own. When, late in the war, Hitler decided to use thirty-five thousand prisoners-of-war as hostages, it was Eva who saved them. Hitler had instructed General Gottlob Berger of the Waffen-SS to take the hostages to the mountains south of Munich and hold them there until he could obtain a satisfactory truce from the Allies. If he was unsuccessful, the prisoners were to be executed. Eva learned that Berger opposed the plan, that even if ordered he would not kill the prisoners. She decided that it would be best if Hitler gave the signed orders to Berger rather than to some other officer who would carry out the Führer's command. She and Berger, both convinced that such executions were morally wrong, entered into an agreement. She arranged for him to have an appointment with Hitler, and while Hitler was discussing the matter with the general, Eva brought the typed orders pertaining to the executions into the room and handed them to the Führer. He immediately and automatically signed them and Berger left the room with the documents in his possession. Both he and Eva knew that he could stall off Hitler until the war ended without carrying out a single execution, and that is exactly what happened. As General Berger stated later: 'Eva Braun made it possible for me to handle the prisoner-of-war matter as it should have been handled.' No one except Berger knew about Eva's influence in this matter.

The other person in Hitler's inner circle who was able to influence the Führer greatly was Martin Bormann, variously called 'Hitler's Evil Spirit' and 'the Smart Fox'. The 'master' and the 'mistress' of the Führer, as they were secretly referred to by Hitler's entourage, fought an internal battle that lasted for years and only ended when Eva died and Bormann disappeared. Eva was charming, likeable and respected by most of the Nazi leaders and their wives. Bormann was coarse, rude, despised and feared by the same people. Gradually, the inner circle split into two divisions: the Bormann supporters and the Eva Braun supporters.

Bormann operated on fear. He had done so since his days as a member of the Freikorps, the illegal paramilitary organization that terrorized Germany in the early 1920s. While active in the Freikorps he was accused of murdering another member of the group who had been suspected of spying for the government and he spent a year in Leipzig Prison. As soon as he was released, Bormann joined the Nazi Party. No member was more suited to the party program. From 1925 until Hitler became Chancellor in 1933 Bormann schemed and wormed his way through the maze of intrigue prevalent in the organization until he had reached the position of secretary and chief-of-staff to Rudolf Hess, Hitler's deputy. Seizing a wonderful chance to advance himself even faster, he married Gerda Buch, daughter of Walter Buch, the chairman of the party's disciplinary court. This combination of good connections and his own ruthlessness made Bormann a powerful man in Hitler's cadre by the fateful year of 1941. All the while Bormann was scheming his way into Hitler's favor, Eva was gaining equal status with the Führer by use of her feminine charms. It took the strange action of Rudolf Hess in 1941 to bring the blonde beauty and the stocky Nazi thug into a personal confrontation that ended only when the Third Reich ended.

On May 10, 1941, Rudolf Hess drove to the airport at Augsburg, climbed into a Messerschmitt fighter plane and took off. Heading west in a strong crosswind, Hess reached Scotland a few hours later and parachuted from the aircraft. His avowed purpose was to prevail on his 'friend' the Duke of Hamilton (a Britisher he had met at the Berlin Olympic Games in 1936) to arrange for him to meet with the Prime Minister so that he could negotiate a peace settlement between Germany and England! The mission was doomed from the beginning . . . if that really was Hess's plan. Albert Speer, however, thought that Bormann, by ingratiating himself with Hitler and excluding Hess more and more from Hitler's favor, finally drove Hess to the foolhardy flight in hopes that he could regain his lost status in the Nazi hierarchy by a grandstand maneuver. Bormann, Speer and Eva were all with Hitler at the Berghof when he opened the letter brought to him by Hess's two adjutants, a letter in which Hess explained to the Führer what he was planning to do.

While Speer and Eva stood by idly and watched the activity, Hitler ordered Bormann to put through a call to Ernst Udet to ask whether the Messerschmitt fighter had the necessary range to reach England. Informed that Hess had used a Messerschmitt-110 which could easily fly that distance, Hitler became furious.

Later, after Churchill reported that Hess was in custody, Bormann urged the Führer to avenge himself on Hess's wife Ilse and his staff officers. Naturally, Bormann didn't mean that he, Hess's deputy for seven years, should be punished. Far from it! He had already decided he should have Hess's Chancellery post and Hitler agreed. At Bormann's suggestion, however, Hitler had Captain Karlheinz Pintsch, Hess's young adjutant who had the thankless task of delivering Hess's final letter to the Führer, sent to the Russian front. Hitler also ordered that Frau Hess be evicted from her Berlin quarters on the Wilhelmstrasse and that the Hess house in Harthauserstrasse be confiscated. Eva, hearing about Bormann's actions against Ilse Hess, promptly intervened. She convinced Hitler that Frau Hess was an innocent victim, that she did not know about her husband's plans, and finally the Führer relented and permitted Frau Hess to remain in the house. This was the first direct clash between Eva and Bormann after he assumed Hess's post, but victory in the initial battle by no means decided the personal war.

Martin Bormann was by far the cleverest of all the rivals for Hitler's attention that Eva had yet encountered. Compared to Leni Riefenstahl, Unity Mitford, Luis Trenker, Julius Schaub and other schemers with whom she had competed in the past, Bormann was a genius. He was adaptable, a person who could take a defeat such as the one involving Frau Hess, keep quiet and then suddenly take the offensive with a devastating maneuver. He was completely ruthless and disloyal to everyone but Hitler. His treatment of Frau Hess was an example of both his ruthlessness and his disloyalty. Ilse Hess's four-year-old son resembled Bormann a great deal, which created quite a lot of gossip. Hess had homosexual tendencies and Bormann had a reputation for seducing many women, so it was natural for people to think there had once been something between Bormann and Ilse Hess. If so, this did not stop Bormann from turning on her when he thought it would make him look good in Hitler's eyes. After Eva stepped in and prevented him from throwing Frau Hess out of her home, Bormann changed tactics again and spent a great deal of time with the boy. There was no way to predict Bormann's next action and Eva soon understood this important fact.

She learned another important fact early in her war with Bormann. It was of no use to complain to Hitler about Bormann's actions unless she could sustain her charges, which was difficult because everyone was afraid of Bormann. Once when she complained that Bormann was harassing the churches in Munich,

Hitler immediately summoned him to his study and asked if this was true. (It was.) When Bormann denied it and Eva could find no one with enough courage to back her up, Hitler told her she had been misinformed and not to bother him again with accusations based on gossip. Bormann used this incident to remind Eva time and again that she had better keep quiet – unless she could find someone to corroborate her accusations. Eva learned to her dismay that Bormann controlled most of the inner circle and they were afraid to speak out against him even though they disliked him. Eva didn't give up the battle, though. She just retreated long enough to plan the better strategy.

While Bormann was making himself indispensable to Hitler, Eva used both her charm and the friendship of Albert Speer to overcome Bormann's growing influence. Speer did not like Bormann, nor did he ever compromise with him as did so many of the others. Hitler liked Speer and considered him the 'artistic' member of the inner circle, the best educated and most cultured. After Hitler conceived the grandiose idea of building a 'new Berlin' after World War II, he spent many hours with Speer going over the blueprints. In his sentimental moments the Führer regarded himself as an *artiste manqué* and thus felt a special rapport with Speer. When Dr Fritz Todt, the Minister of Armaments and Munitions, was killed in a plane crash, Hitler promptly appointed his young architect to the post, and with this increased power and prestige Speer became one of the most powerful Nazi leaders.

Speer had always been friendly with Eva. During the early years of the Hitler–Eva affair he had sympathized with her because of Hitler's neglect and her loneliness and he and his wife Margarete had often invited her to their home and had taken her on trips with them, including some mountain-climbing excursions, which Eva loved. By the time Bormann succeeded Hess and tightened his grip on the inner circle, Speer and Eva were close friends. The stage was set for the high-stake battle between Eva and Bormann.

After his setback in the Frau Hess incident Bormann moved very carefully against Eva. He was aware that Hitler was in love with her so in front of the Führer he treated her with grace and respect. Each evening he offered her his arm as they went to dinner (a custom that Hitler insisted be followed at the Berghof), smiled at her in as charming a manner as was possible for him, and tried to keep up an animated conversation with her until Hitler took over. This consummate acting didn't fool Eva. She knew that Bormann hated every minute of the walk to the table and the forced conversation, that he wished he could eliminate her from the Berghof, of Reich Chancellery, Munich and Germany. But she played back to him, smiling and holding up her end of the conversation. So skillfully did the two enact their charade that Hitler actually thought they got along very well.

Bormann, through a series of maneuvers, became the legal owner of all of Hitler's properties. The Berghof, the surrounding acreage, the Eagle's Nest, the Munich apartment – all were in Bormann's name because he handled Hitler's private business as well as Nazi Party business. Hitler thought it best not to own property in his own name in order to avoid any charges that he was 'raiding the party treasure'. He knew that Bormann was loyal to him and that the man was completely trustworthy as far as Nazi Party business was concerned. By 1943 Bormann had reached the status of personal secretary to the Führer. This meant that he selected the people who met with Hitler personally. Using this power to advantage, Bormann soon had Hitler isolated from everyone except those who favored his own ideas and programs – except for Eva, who had access to Hitler day and night. He also controlled the purse strings of the Nazi treasury as well as the private fortune of Hitler. When Eva needed money, Schaub told her to ask Bormann for it and not to bother Hitler. Schaub was working in conjunction with Bormann and they thought they could bring Eva to her knees. Bormann intended to make her grant him concessions and favors before he doled out any money to her. Eva, however, solved the problem so quickly that both Schaub and Bormann were taken by surprise. She shopped in Berlin and in Munich at the best clothing stores, buying hundreds of dollars' worth of dresses, lingerie, shoes and other apparel, and sent the bills to the Reich Chancellery in Bormann's name. The next time she was with Hitler at the Berghof and Bormann was within earshot, she said, '*Du*, I hear that Bormann is buying his mistress an entire new wardrobe. Where does he get the money?'

Hitler was irritated with Bormann at the time because he had read a letter from Bormann to his wife in which he had bragged about seducing his mistress, brazenly telling his wife the details of what happened while they were in bed together and how much he had enjoyed it. Hitler did not approve of this 'kiss-and-tell' technique, especially in a married man. But it was Gerda Bormann's reply that really amazed and disgusted the Führer. She wrote, 'I cannot be angry with you. You should see to it that one year she has a child and the next year I have one. In that manner you will always have a wife that is serviceable.'

Hitler thought all this was rather sordid, so when Eva told him that Bormann was buying his mistress a new wardrobe, he was furious. He demanded that Bormann bring him the Nazi financial records so that he could examine them closely to see if the party was paying for the purchases. Bormann knew when he was beaten. He had not yet paid Eva's bills because he had intended to negotiate a deal with her. He felt she was telling the Führer too much about the suffering of the people of Munich during the war and he wanted her to stop. But now he was trapped. If he told Hitler that the clothing bills were actually Eva's, Hitler would just nod and say 'Pay them!' He always did. If he tried to keep the bills from Hitler until he had forced Eva to knuckle under to him, Hitler would be suspicious and think they really were for clothing for Manja Behrens, his mistress, and he would be in trouble. He chose the first path and, as he had surmised, Hitler ordered, 'Pay them! Eva can buy anything she wants and when you get the bill, pay it promptly. Do you understand?' Bormann understood and Eva never worried about money after that incident.

Eva still had to watch her every move, however, because Bormann patiently stalked her, seeking revenge. He overheard her mention to Himmler that an aunt of hers, a nun, was distressed because the SS intended to confiscate her convent's buildings. Before Himmler could grant Eva a favor by canceling the order, Bormann had the nuns evicted and sent to a small village in the mountains south of Munich. There was nothing Himmler could do. He, too, feared the ruthless power of Bormann. As he told Eva, 'All I can do now is make certain your aunt has warm clothing. I cannot rescind Bormann's order.' During the nightly walk to the dinner table with Eva on his arm Bormann would often refer to the 'icy cold winds of the Alps which are bitter enough to freeze a nun's bottom.'

Quite often Speer and Eva together were able to countermand some of Bormann's orders issued in the name of Hitler but of which Hitler had never heard. Bormann had been placed in charge of the huge building project on the Obersalzberg. Every time Speer observed plans for a structure he didn't like or for the raping of the landscape, he would protest to Hitler. Eva would agree and Hitler, who had a very high opinion of Speer's artistic talents, would call Bormann to task and the changes Speer suggested would be made. This, of course, made Bormann furious but he rarely showed his anger in front of Hitler. After Speer became Minister of Armaments and Munitions he paid no attention to any directives issued to him by Bormann. He took orders only from Hitler. If Speer had trouble getting an appointment to see Hitler, Eva took care of the matter. They worked very well together and Bormann shied away from a direct confrontation with both of them in front of Hitler.

Bormann's great patience was rewarded early in 1944, however, when Speer became ill. He was rushed to a hospital in serious condition, the result of fatigue with the added symptoms of pulmonary embolism. Bormann wasted no time in getting into action. He arranged through Himmler to have Dr Karl Gebhardt, an SS Gruppenführer, put in charge of Speer's case. With Gebhardt doing the diagnosis – he said Speer had muscular rheumatism – and prescribing the treatment, Speer's condition got steadily worse. Within twenty days he was at the point of death. Meanwhile, Bormann, through lies, was able to convince Hitler that Speer was not as loyal as he should have been. Speer, who was unable to defend himself, was soon put out of the running as far as any influence with Hitler was concerned. Far more important to Eva and to Speer's family, however, was the fact that Speer seemed to be dying. Eva suspected Gebhardt and after a long discussion with Hitler she managed to get his permission to have another medical specialist check Speer. Dr Friedrich Koch, an internist from Berlin, was sent to Speer's bedside by Eva, and after correctly diagnosing embolism began a series of treatments and prescribed medication which eventually had Speer back on his feet. With the help of Eva, Speer was soon back in the good graces of Hitler although Bormann had managed to eliminate most of Speer's allies in Hitler's inner circle. The struggle continued as before, except that the Eva–Speer forces were somewhat weakened.

Eva had one advantage in the struggle with Bormann: she was always thinking of what would be best for Hitler, both for him personally and for his career. She was not selfish, she did not try to pile up wealth in her own name, she did not try to become a powerful leader in the Nazi hierarchy. She subjugated her own desires and pleasures to those of the man she loved, and Hitler understood this. Bormann, on the other hand, desperately sought to become the master of the Nazi Party, the one individual under Hitler who could give orders and expect them to be obeyed by every member of the Nazi hierarchy. He was ruthless, self-centered, crude. Though Hitler appreciated Bormann's loyalty and reliability, he sensed the man's ruthlessness and, in fact, used it to great advantage during the long years Bormann was at his side. Yet Hitler refused to designate Bormann as his successor because he believed so thoroughly treacherous an individual would not make a good leader. A follower, yes; a leader, no! By permitting Bormann so much power under him, however, Hitler jeopardized Eva much more than he ever realized. He only smiled when she hinted that she was afraid of Bormann and told her that there was no reason for her to be afraid. Didn't she know, he asked her several times, that Bormann wouldn't dare touch her or harm her in any way because of her special position? He hinted she was imagining things but Eva knew differently. She knew Bormann wouldn't dare move against her in an obvious manner that Hitler could detect but there were other ways that were not so obvious.

One of the ways Bormann tried to get at Eva was through another ally of his in the Hitler court, Dr Theodor Morell. Morell had an impressive educational background which included studying under the famous bacteriologist Ilya Mechnikov, a Nobel Prize winner. He was a devotee of the injection method of curing diseases, using drugs of all kinds on illnesses of all kinds, often to the detriment of the patient. Morell and his wife acted friendly toward Eva for the simple reason that they thought she could help them obtain favors from Hitler. When it became obvious that Eva had no intention of interceding with the Führer in order to help Morell become a rich man, the doctor turned against her and joined forces with Bormann, whom he recognized as the second most influential man in the Hitler court. One day after Morell had examined Hitler for one of the Chancellor's imaginary ills, Bormann told Hitler that Eva should also have a complete physical examination. Eva resisted this idea because she didn't trust Morell but Hitler was adamant, stating that he 'did not want to lose her'. A nurse who helped with the preliminary part of the physical examination of Eva, Ada Hocher, was ordered out of the examining room after she complained to Morell that he shouldn't give Eva an injection of a drug that would render her unconscious. Knowing that something was wrong but afraid to tell Hitler because of Bormann's custom of seeking revenge, Fräulein Hocher hurried to an SS officer she knew and explained the situation. On her way from the examining room she had seen Bormann entering through another door and she also told her officer friend this fact. Fortunately for Eva (but unfortunately for himself) the SS officer, a red-haired young Bavarian named Claus Kahr, was more interested in winning plaudits from Ada

Hocher than he was in avoiding a confrontation with Bormann and Morell. He hurried to the examining room, followed by the nurse, and walked in. According to Ada Hocher, Eva was lying nude on the examining table, unconscious. Morell was wearing rubber gloves and was preparing to inject some substance into her body. Bormann was standing beside the table observing the doctor. When the two men saw Kahr and the nurse they were startled. Ada Hocher quickly said, 'The Führer wants to see Fräulein Braun at once.'

Morell protested, saying that he was in the middle of his examination but the nurse covered Eva's body with a sheet and wheeled her from the room. Bormann never said a word. Ada Hocher stayed with Eva until she regained consciousness and explained what had happened. By this time the nurse was nearly paralyzed with fright, convinced that Bormann would have her killed, but Eva promised that nothing would happen to her as long as Eva herself lived. And nothing did, despite Bormann's efforts to have the nurse banned from the Berghof. Eva, knowing that Hitler would not believe Ada Hocher's story because he had too much faith in Bormann, was able to convince Hitler to keep the nurse on duty at the Berghof anyway. Eva watched over her carefully, warning both Bormann and Morell that the girl was her 'protégé'. The SS officer, however, was transferred from the Berghof the following afternoon by Himmler and neither Ada Hocher nor Eva ever saw him again. They suspected that Bormann had him executed.

What was Morell intending to do in the examining room? Through her own later investigation Eva was convinced that he meant to inject her with typhus bacillus. The reason she came to this conclusion was her knowledge of what had happened to Heinrich Hoffmann, one of Hitler's most trusted friends. When Bormann became unhappy about Hoffman's influence with Hitler he had insisted that the photographer have Morell examine him. Morell said after the examination that he could not find anything wrong but the final decision on Hoffmann's health status would have to await a bacteriological analysis which was being made in the Health Institute of the SS. A few days later Morell called him and said that the institute had found traces of typhus bacillus in his blood, that Hoffmann had Paratyphus B, the most dangerous form of the disease.

'Bormann has ordered that you stay away from Hitler until further notice. The Munich Public Health experts will come for you tomorrow morning. It will be necessary for you to be kept in isolation and under observation.'

Hitler had such a horror of germs that he even avoided shaking hands with people. When Bormann told him that Hoffmann was a possible typhus carrier, the Führer banned Hoffmann from the Berghof, the Reich Chancellery and his Munich apartment. For six months Hoffmann fought the accusations of Bormann and Morell, based on the false medical report, but it was only during the latter days of the war that he was permitted to see Hitler again.

In 1944 and 1945, when Hitler's fortunes ebbed and many 'friends' deserted him, Bormann and Eva remained at his side. Bormann spent most of his time eliminating or seeking revenge on his enemies, while Eva spent most of her time comforting Hitler and trying to help him face defeat. Bormann convinced Hitler that Göring had deserted him in the bunker in Berlin and had seized power illegally; accused Himmler of trying to arrange a separate peace with the Allies so that he could save his own life; and completely discredited Goebbels. Eva, however, was beyond reproach and Hitler appreciated her more than ever during this critical period. He listened to her advice, took comfort in her encouragement and trusted her more than anyone – even more than Bormann. In the last months of the war Eva influenced several of Hitler's decisions either directly or indirectly. It was through her adept maneuvering that the Allied prisoners-of-war Hitler was holding as hostages in the Bavarian Alps were placed under the control of General Berger who would not execute them. She helped Speer avoid a direct confrontation with Hitler over the 'scorched earth' policy the Führer directed was to be followed as the German troops retreated. Eva knew that the German people still had to live in some manner even if the Third Reich didn't, and she spent hours explaining this fact to Hitler in an effort to change his mind. While she never completely altered his opinion, she did manage to soften his outlook toward his countrymen and, more importantly, divert his attention elsewhere so that he didn't check and find out that Speer was successfully resisting the policy. It was also Eva who spoke up when Hitler, at Bormann's instigation, ordered the tunnels in the Berlin area flooded. Thousands of German soldiers and civilians were using these tunnels as a refuge from the Russian artillery and Allied bombs but Hitler was willing to sacrifice them all in order to delay the approach of the Russian ground troops by a few hours. Eva managed to get Hitler to talk with several generals who opposed the idea, much to the chagrin of Bormann, and the order was delayed.

As the fortunes of war turned against Hitler, he looked more and more to Eva for solace. Even Bormann was unable to halt the Führer's growing dependence on her. He opposed Eva until the end but this was the one and only struggle within the Nazi hierarchy that he lost.

Part 4

THE
FINAL
YEARS

18
Love Under Fire

*In the autumn of 1942 the military initiative passed out
of Hitler's hands for the first time, never to return. He
began to pay the price for his treachery and violence. In
October the British 8th Army in North Africa broke
through the German defense lines at El Alamein and
began a persistent, steady advance. Two weeks later, on
November 7–8, 1942, Allied troops landed along the
coast of Morocco and Algeria and soon occupied all of
French North Africa as far as the Tunisian border. Ten
days after this operation three Russian Army Groups
attacked German forces near Stalingrad and in less than
a week had twenty-two German divisions surrounded.
The tide had turned.*

Now that Hitler had been proved less than invincible many of his associates began thinking more about their own future welfare than that of the Führer and the Third Reich. Eva, however, became stronger in her support as the situation deteriorated. As others in Hitler's entourage became suspicious of one another, began to doubt the Führer's leadership, and even plotted against his life, Eva tried in every way to bolster his flagging spirits and ego, to keep his appearance and posture in the image the German public expected of their Chancellor, and to calm him after his numerous spells of rage. More than ever she devoted herself to the man she loved, disregarding his motives and the morality of what he was doing. When his nihilism and destructiveness bent back in on him, she was right there at his side.

Whenever Eva was away from Hitler he worried constantly about her. He also began to talk about her more and more to his secretaries and other associates. One night when Eva was at her villa an air raid on Munich was announced. Hitler 'ran around like a lion in his cage and tried desperately to get in contact with Eva by telephone'. Later, after he learned she was safe, he told Frau Junge, 'She doesn't go into the bunker although I constantly ask her to do so. Her villa will some day fall in like a house of cards. Neither will she run over to my dwelling where she would be absolutely safe. Now, I've at least brought her to the point where she had her own bunker built at her villa, but instead of using it, she takes the whole neighborhood and goes up on the roof to see if the incendiary bombs have fallen on it. She is really a very courageous, proud woman,' Hitler continued. 'I have known her for more than ten years and as an employee of Hoffmann's she had to save a lot at the beginning. Yet she wouldn't permit me to pay for even a taxi. For days she slept in Hoffmann's office on a bench so that I could reach her by telephone because she had no long-distance connection at home.'

Frau Junge, since she was as young as Eva, was often the target of Hitler's conversation about his mistress. After several long conversations she became more bold and asked him, '*Mein Führer*, why haven't you married?' She knew that he liked to arrange marriages between others, that he was interested in his associates' marriages, and she couldn't understand why he himself refused to marry.

'I wouldn't be a good head of a family,' Hitler said slowly, looking at Frau Junge with his intent stare. 'I would consider it irresponsible of me to start a family when I cannot devote myself to my wife sufficiently. Besides, I want no children of my

216

own. I find that the offspring of geniuses usually have it hard in the world. One expects of them the same importance as that of the famous predecessor and doesn't forgive them for being average. Besides, they are mostly cretins.'

His devotion to Eva seemed to increase with each military defeat the German troops suffered during 1943 and 1944. While his tenderness and concern for Eva grew, however, his cruelty toward others increased in direct proportion. When General Friedrich von Paulus reported in January, 1943, that 330,000 troops of his German 6th Army at Stalingrad were suffering unbearably from the cold, hunger and epidemics, and that to continue fighting in such conditions was beyond human strength, Hitler refused to allow him to surrender to the Russians. Hitler's prestige as a leader meant more to him than the lives of the 330,000 German soldiers. He told Paulus, 'Capitulation is impossible. The 6th Army will do its historic duty at Stalingrad until the last man, in order to make possible the reconstruction of the Eastern Front.'

That same day he promoted Paulus to the rank of Field Marshal in an attempt to bribe him into dying on the battlefield. But Paulus was too humane to allow his men to suffer any longer and surrendered. When Hitler heard that Paulus had allowed himself to be taken prisoner he was furious. He felt his prestige had suffered and he screamed that the German generals were turning against him. 'He should have shot himself just as the old commanders who threw themselves on their swords when they saw their cause was lost.'

With each defeat Hitler withdrew further from his associates. At his field headquarters he took lonely walks around his compound, usually accompanied only by his dog Blondi. He ate alone a great deal, and when he did occasionally invite someone to dine with him he talked only about trivial matters, never about the serious decisions he had to make. Often he would eat in complete silence, not speaking to his guest or to the cook, Frau Manzialy, whom he liked very much. Though he trusted her, he still had much of his food tasted by others before he would eat since he was afraid his enemies might attempt to poison him. Once, late in 1943, he told Speer, 'One of these days I'll have only two friends left, Fräulein Braun and my dog.'

It was true that he was losing his 'friends' very rapidly. On July 25, 1943, Hitler received word that Mussolini had been dismissed by the King of Italy and placed under arrest. This was a profound shock to the Führer. Only six days earlier he had met with the Italian dictator at Feltre in northern Italy and the two men had expressed their mutual trust and their determination to win the war. Hitler felt his prestige was involved here because he had constantly referred to Mussolini as the one man to be trusted and had repeatedly stated that the Nazi and Fascist revolutions were the hope of the world. Now his Italian counterpart had been rudely arrested, shoved into an ambulance and taken to a hiding place. Worse yet, no Italian had fired a shot in protest. Hitler decided he had to make some move to prove to the world that he did not desert his comrades in time of trouble. 'Call Skorzeny to headquarters!'

In July, 1943, Otto Skorzeny, a six-foot-four-inch Austrian with a vivid dueling scar across the left side of his face, was the commander of the German Special Forces. A hard drinker and a hard fighter, Skorzeny had never flinched from any assignment but had to use all his will power the day he met with Hitler at Wolf's Lair to keep from starting when the Führer gave him his orders.

'I cannot and will not leave Italy's greatest son in the lurch,' Hitler told Skorzeny. 'I will keep faith with my old ally and dear friend. He must be rescued promptly or he will be handed over to the Allies. I herewith order you to carry out the task, which is vital for the war!'

Hitler did not even tell Eva about the plan for fear it would fail. On the afternoon of September 12, 1943, Skorzeny and his Special Forces used gliders and light planes to rescue Mussolini from a hotel on Gran Sasso, the loftiest peak in the Apennines, one hundred miles from Rome. Skorzeny took the exhausted *Il Duce* to the Hotel Imperial in Vienna, and within an hour Hitler was on the telephone congratulating him. He awarded Skorzeny the Knight's Cross and promoted him to Stürmbannführer of the Waffen-SS.

'You have been away from your wife too long, Skorzeny, preparing for this rescue. It is not good for a man to be away from his wife's bed that length of time. Go home and enjoy yourself and make your wife happy,' Hitler told him.

Eva met Skorzeny later when he went to the Berghof and they became close friends. He spent many hours with her while waiting to see Hitler, both at the Berghof and later in the bunker in Berlin. Eva nodded and smiled when she learned what Hitler had said to Skorzeny about his leave. She said, 'He understands. He understands.'

Hitler saved face by having Mussolini rescued but not much

else. He found the Italian dictator a shrunken, aging, scared man who merely wanted to retire to some quiet place with his mistress Clara Petacci. Disgusted with the change in *Il Duce*'s character, Hitler settled him at Gargnano on Lake Garda and kept him a virtual prisoner. When Mussolini protested that he could not order the execution of his son-in-law, the handsome Count Galeazzo Ciano, who had tried to escape to Spain or Argentina after Italy's fall, Hitler took care of the matter himself. With the same calm with which he had sent Ciano's wife, Edda Mussolini, flowers on her birthday in September, 1943, he ordered the death of her husband in January, 1944. Eva liked the handsome Ciano and had even told Hitler once that he should try to copy the debonair manner of the Italian count, but at the showdown she agreed he deserved to die. 'He arranged his own fate,' she told Skorzeny. 'He betrayed *Il Duce*, his wife and his children.'

The execution of Count Ciano reminded all of those under Hitler that they were utterly in his power. During the long winter of 1943–44 this apprehension was evident wherever Hitler went – Munich, Berlin, Berghof or Wolf's Lair. No one seemed comfortable any longer. Everyone was suspicious of everyone else. It snowed hard during December and January, weeks without stopping, and walls of snow virtually imprisoned those in the Berghof. Huge amounts had to be shoveled away every day to clear even a narrow path to the teahouse and open the other entrances and exits. Eva wanted to go skiing to escape the depressing atmosphere but Hitler wouldn't give his permission. 'You could break a foot,' he told her. 'It is too dangerous.'

He became more and more possessive as his troubles mounted. Eva had to be satisfied with long walks along the cleared paths.

While he worried about Eva, she also worried about him. She noticed that his hair was turning much more gray, that he seldom stood straight as he always had during the early years of the Third Reich, that his energy seemed to be waning. One day when she and Traudl Junge were alone, Eva asked, 'What do you think about the Führer's health, Frau Junge? I don't want to ask Morell. I don't trust him and I hate him.'

Traudl Junge was diplomatic in her answer. 'Fräulein Braun, I know less than you. You know the Führer better than I do and can deduce things he doesn't tell me.'

As though speaking to herself, Eva murmured, 'He has become so serious. He worries so much.'

'The army reports are enough to fill those responsible with worry,' Frau Junge replied and turned away.

219

Later that day in the teahouse Eva reproached Hitler. '*Du*, you are so bent over. Can't you straighten up?'

'That comes from carrying such heavy keys in my pocket,' he replied, then smiling, added, 'Besides I fit better with you. You wear high heels so you are taller. I bend over a little, and so we fit together very well.'

Eva sensed Hitler was mocking her because of her petite size and she quickly protested. 'I am not short. I am 1.63 meters, like Napoleon!'

'How do you know that?' Hitler asked.

Eva wouldn't admit she really didn't know Napoleon's height. 'Every educated person knows it.'

That evening Hitler was observed checking through the books in the library hunting for statistics on Napoleon's height, but fortunately for Eva he couldn't find the information.

Shortly before Christmas, 1943, Fanny Braun visited the Berghof. The Allied bombing raids on Munich and the fact that she hadn't seen Eva for quite some time induced her to make the trip. She rather dreaded though the long evenings at the Berghof when Hitler talked until the small hours of the morning and she and the other guests had to stay up listening to him. She liked her sleep and, in fact, required a lot of rest. Hitler greeted her with warmth and, to her surprise, that evening he took her aside and said, 'I understand that you need a lot of rest.'

Embarrassed and confused, Frau Braun nodded. '*Mein Führer*, I sleep long hours in Munich, that is true.'

He took her hand and replied, 'I don't want you to mind me, Frau Braun. You go to bed early. I wish that I could sleep for as much as two hours at a stretch.'

It was during this visit that Frau Braun first noticed how ill Hitler seemed. Morell was treating him with injections and pills. At one time during this period he was administering twenty-eight different kinds of medicines to Hitler, many of which gave him more trouble than relief. Morell's penchant for injections was well known and talked about among Hitler's associates and especially Hitler's other doctors such as Brandt, Giesing and von Hasselbach. For over nine years Morell doped the Führer with drugs and medications every time he complained about something. If he was tired, Morell stuck a needle in his arm; if he was depressed the doctor gave him a stimulant; if he couldn't sleep, a sedative; if he had a speech to give, he got a shot before and after the talk. Hitler got a hypodermic needle for every ache and minor complaint involved in the average middle-aged man's existence.

Frau Braun noticed the effects of this therapy during her stay at the Berghof in December, 1943. She told Eva, 'The injection helps the Führer for a short time but when it wears off, he is worse than ever.'

Eva agreed but Hitler would not even listen to her warnings concerning Morell, telling her that she did not know anything about medicine and Morell was an expert. When Brandt, Giesing and Hasselbach analyzed one pill that Morell had prescribed for Hitler and discovered that it contained 4.0 milligrams of strychnine and 0.4 milligrams of atropine, they decided that they should tell Hitler the pills were doing him more harm than good. The amounts of both chemicals exceeded the safety level and could cause a progressive poisoning of the body if taken over a period of time. However, after they had given their facts to Hitler, instead of being grateful and getting rid of Morell, he accused them of professional jealousy and lying and had their names removed from his list of attending physicians! Hitler continued to depend on the numerous injections and pills prescribed by Morell.

Eva was also worried about the dangers Hitler faced while at his headquarters in the field. And she spent many long hours watching and worrying about the red reflection in the sky over Munich as the Allied bombers attacked the city. Unless it was foggy, the light from the fires could easily be seen from the Berghof. She could barely be restrained when the city was being bombed. Hitler had given strict orders that she was not to go to Munich while an air raid was in progress so she spent hours on the telephone trying to contact friends in the city. When she did complete a connection, she gave instructions about what she wanted done at her villa and asked for full eyewitness reports of the bombing. Once, however, when one of her best friends, the Munich actor Heini Handschuhmacher, was killed during an air raid, she ignored Hitler's orders and with her friend Herta Schneider and her sister Gretl went to the funeral services in Munich. When she returned to the Berghof she was badly shaken by what she had seen in the city – the devastation, the suffering, the dead and injured. Hitler listened to her report on the misery being endured by the population of Munich and vowed that he would pay back the Allies a hundredfold. He also forbade her to go to Munich again while the American and British bombers were in the area.

Another observer of the Allied attacks on Munich was Hermann Fegelein, a young Waffen-SS officer who was noted for his horsemanship, hard drinking and sexual prowess. He had learned his horsemanship from his father, who operated a riding school in Munich, and the other two talents he developed himself after he joined the Nazis. Tall, slender, a marvelous dancer and adept socially (unless he was drunk), Fegelein soon noticed the fun-loving Gretl Braun at the Berghof. His initial advances were strictly in keeping with his pattern of sexual conquest, but after the ambitious Fegelein gave the matter some thought, he could see many advantages to being married to the sister of Hitler's mistress. His references to Gretl as 'goose' quickly changed to 'my love' and by late spring of 1944 he had made up his mind – he proposed. Gretl was fascinated by the dashing SS officer who wore such gaudy uniforms and was sought after by all the un-married women at the Berghof (and some who were married). She asked her mother's advice about marrying him but her mother only shook her head, 'I don't know him.'

Gretl reminded Fanny Braun that she had introduced Fegelein to her at the Berghof but her mother couldn't recall him. The next day Fegelein showed up in person at the Braun household and asked for the consent of Fritz and Fanny Braun to marry Gretl. Hitler, he said, was delighted with the match, as was Eva. Taking him at his word, the parents gave their permission and eight days later on June 3, 1944, the couple were married.

The ceremony took place in the Salzburg town hall. Eva, as soon as she learned of her sister's wedding plans, had the entire staff of the Heyse fashion salon in Berlin come to the Berghof to make the wedding dresses. She also convinced Hitler to permit Gretl to have the wedding reception in the Eagle's Nest. It seemed that since she could not have a wedding of her own, she intended to lavish all her attention on her sister's. She persuaded Hitler to allow dancing at the reception, one of the few times he permitted dancing at an affair on the Obersalzberg during the war. She hired a band, made certain that there was more than enough drink and food and went out of her way to ensure that all the guests enjoyed themselves. For this night all the death and destruction outside the observation windows of the Eagle's Nest were forgotten. Even the hated Bormann forgot his ambitions for a few hours and drank so much champagne that he had to be carried back to his quarters. Hitler attended the reception but left early to return to the Berghof. The others, however, including Eva, stayed until dawn, dancing, drinking . . . and forgetting.

Three days later – on June 6, 1944 – the Allies invaded Europe. Hitler, who was still sleeping when the Normandy invasion was reported to the Berghof, was awakened and told the news. He got

so excited that he leaped out of bed and started out of the bedroom without getting dressed. It was Eva who stopped him.

'*Du*, on this important day of your life, it would not be right
for the greatest man in the world to be seen wearing his night-
clothes!'

Curiously, Hitler seemed more relieved than worried once the
Allied invasion had begun. He had been expecting it for so long,
wondering just where the Americans and British would land on
the coast of France. Now that the enemy troops were actually on
the soil of Europe, Hitler juggled his available divisions around
like chess figures. He didn't trust his generals and constantly
intervened and changed their battle plans. By the end of June both
the Russians in the east and the joint American-British forces in
the west were making sizeable advances against the German
ground troops – due, in large measure, to Hitler's inept handling
of the German military forces. On July 1, 1944, Hitler decided he
needed a rest from the forward headquarters where he had been
staying during June and he returned to the Berghof.

He was very depressed during the first two weeks of July. Eva
tried to cheer him up in her usual manner but was only partially
successful. During a late dinner with Christa Schröder, his secretary, Hitler told her, 'I feel that something is in the air.'

'Fräulein Schröder was puzzled. 'What do you mean, *mein
Führer*?'

'I am afraid something might happen to me and there is no one
else who can take over the leadership.'

The secretary, always outspoken and never timid of Hitler,
asked, 'Do you not have a successor in mind?'

'Hess is gone. He was insane. Göring wouldn't have the sympathy of the people. Himmler is a completely nonartistic person,'
Hitler said, dismissing the most obvious choices.

'But, *mein Führer*, being an artist is not necessary for a person
to be Chancellor,' the secretary said. 'One can always engage
capable people.'

Hitler frowned. 'It is not so simple to engage capable people,
Fräulein. If it was, I would already have hired them.'

'Who else do you have in mind as a successor then? Himmler is
most often named by the people.'

Hitler became very angry with his secretary when she mentioned Himmler's name a second time. 'Don't worry your head
any further about who should be my successor.'

It was obvious to Fräulein Schröder that he was insulted that
anyone would think he would be succeeded by Himmler – or any-

one. She changed the subject quickly.

At the moment Hitler and Fräulein Schröder were talking, a group of German army officers was putting the finishing touches on an assassination plan that they thought near-perfect. Count Klaus von Stauffenberg, a thirty-six-year-old colonel who had been wounded in action several times during World War II, decided that he would kill Hitler or die in the attempt. Aided by a small group of fellow officers, Stauffenberg put a bomb in his briefcase with a report he had to give to Hitler and headed for the Führer's field headquarters in East Prussia. His co-conspirators were strategically placed in Berlin and elsewhere in Germany awaiting word from him that Hitler was dead so that they could take control of their assigned areas.

As the conference was getting underway at the field head-quarters – 12.30 p.m. on July 20, 1944 – Eva and her friend Herta Schneider were swimming in the Königsee, near Berchtesgaden. It was a hot day and the sun was just right for getting a tan and for sleeping. Eva was on a raft several hundred feet from the shore resting before starting her swim back when she suddenly noticed a car approaching from the direction of the Berghof. She knew immediately that something was wrong. Diving into the waters of the Königsee, she swam as fast as she could toward shore.

A short time before Eva spotted the car, Stauffenberg had entered the conference room, spoke to Hitler and then placed the deadly briefcase with the bomb in it against a table leg near where the Führer was standing. The fuse mechanism had already been activated. Less than a minute later the would-be assassin left the room on the pretext of having to telephone Berlin . . . and kept on going toward his parked airplane. He had not yet reached the aircraft when the bomb exploded! Through the dust and smoke Hitler walked out of the shattered conference room. His pants were ripped, his hair partially burned away, his right arm hung useless at his side and he had a multitude of bruises.

The message given to Eva by the chauffeur of the car that arrived at the Königsee that afternoon was, 'There was an attempt on the Führer's life but he wants you to know that he is all right.'

Eva hurried back to the Berghof and desperately tried to reach Hitler by telephone but failed. By the time Hitler did contact her, she was nearly hysterical, certain that he was badly hurt or dead. Finally his voice on the telephone convinced her that the assassi-nation attempt had failed. When she saw his blood-stained uniform several days after the explosion, however, she nearly went into hysterics again.

'Only a miracle saved you,' she cried, holding his arm tightly. It was then that Hitler repeated one of his most quoted phrases:

I consider that it is by the grace of Providence that I have been chosen to lead my people in such a war. After my miraculous escape from death I am more than ever convinced that it is my fate to bring this war to a successful conclusion.

The Divine Providence that Hitler alluded to was certainly kind to him that day. Four of the twenty-four men in the room when the bomb exploded died, three others were injured seriously and the remainder were shaken and bruised.

Christa Schröder, who was at the field headquarters with Hitler, went to her room to compose herself after hearing of the attempt on his life that July afternoon. She wondered when she would see him again, what he would look like when she did see him. She was still worrying about his injuries when she was startled by the adjutant who knocked on her door.

'The Führer requests your presence at dinner,' Schaub said.

The secretary looked at the adjutant in amazement. 'The Führer is here? He can walk?'

Schaub nodded. 'The Führer will eat at 3 p.m.'

When she arrived at the dining room she was astonished to see how fresh and lively Hitler appeared. He greeted her in the same polite manner he always used with his secretaries and waited until she was seated before he sat down. He described to her how his servants had reacted to the assassination attempt. Linge had been furious and Arndt had cried. Then Hitler looked at Fräulein Schröder, remembering their earlier conversation about his successor, and said, 'Believe me, that is the turning point for Germany. Now it will go uphill again. I am happy that the *Schweinehunde* have unmasked themselves.'

The secretary was aware that Mussolini was scheduled to meet Hitler that afternoon but she assumed that the meeting had been canceled because of the attempt on the Führer's life.

'On the contrary,' Hitler said. 'I must receive him. What would the world press write if I didn't receive him?'

Hitler took Mussolini to the wrecked conference room and explained what had happened. Mussolini echoed the Führer's comments about his narrow escape from death. 'After what I have seen here, I am absolutely of your opinion. This was a sign from Heaven.'

Heavenly solicitation apparently did not extend to Hitler's health. Eva saw him only periodically during the four months after the assassination attempt, since he remained at the East Prussian field headquarters, but on each visit with her his physical deterioration was more marked. His hands shook, especially his left; his ears bothered him very badly and an examination showed that the tympanic membranes on both sides were broken; the on-and-off stomach cramps that had bothered him for years now became a constant nagging pain; and his head ached continually. Between the effects of the bomb and Morell's injections he was in very bad shape. In September Eva was notified that he was sick in bed and she was terrified.

'He has never been in that condition before,' she told Gretl. 'What shall I do?'

Hitler would not permit Eva to visit his field headquarters since he considered the area much too dangerous. There was nothing she could do but stay either in Munich or at the Obersalzberg and wait for word. He did telephone her every evening, but even the sound of his voice was not reassuring. He talked slower, his voice was husky. In October, Eva was told that the doctors had discovered a polyp in his vocal cords and they had operated. After that she couldn't even depend on his nightly telephone calls and it wasn't until November 20, 1944, when Hitler left the Wolf's Lair for the last time and went to Berlin that she was able to see him.

She was shocked at his appearance. He looked many years older than he had in early September. His face had the blue-gray appearance of death, he shuffled instead of walked and his hands shook much worse than before. He saw she was shocked. Smiling, he said to her, 'It is better that my hands shake than my head.'

Hitler discovered that Berlin had also been ravaged. A large part of the Reich Chancellery had been damaged by the Allied bombs and the surrounding area was a mass of rubble. By a quirk of fate his private quarters in the Reich Chancellery building were not destroyed and he and Eva spent their days and nights there until, on December 10, 1944, Hitler left for Alderhorst, his field headquarters in the west. Eva pleaded with him not to go, insisting that he could conduct military operations from Berlin just as well, but Hitler only shook his head. 'I must be in personal contact with my generals,' he said. 'They will no longer do what I order unless I am with them.'

When Eva scolded him, telling him that his health was more important to her than another victory on the battlefield, he stared at her for a long time before he answered. There was a deep, warm glow in his eyes and his voice became soft and quiet. 'You are the only one who would say that. You are the only one who cares.'

This was one of the most affectionate remarks he ever made to her in public. Germany was losing the war. Unless the army could reverse that situation soon, the Führer, the inner circle, the country, were doomed. Hitler's entourage pressed him for a winning strategy, a dazzling new plan that would bring Germany victory and save their lives and careers. Only Eva was concerned for him personally, and Hitler was touched.

The closest the German military forces came to reversing the tide was during their counteroffensive in the Ardennes Forest – the Battle of the Bulge – but it, too, ended in defeat. With the Russian forces pushing from the east in a new concerted drive to reach Berlin, and the Western armies headed full speed toward the Rhine from the west, Hitler decided to return to Berlin for his final stand. He moved into his private quarters in the Reich Chancellery, and during the Allied bombing raids he spent hours in the bunker underneath the building. Eva, when she received a telephone call from him informing her that he was there, quickly went to Berlin from her villa in Munich.

'This time you will stay with me,' she told Hitler when he greeted her in his second-floor quarters. 'I will take care of you. We will not part again.'

Late in January Eva's sister Ilse arrived in Berlin after she had been forced to flee from Breslau ahead of the advancing Allied ground troops. Eva arranged for her to stay at the still-standing Hotel Adlon and invited her to dinner at the Reich Chancellery. The two sisters were friendly but Eva knew that Ilse still disliked Hitler. When Ilse criticized the destruction of Germany, blaming it on him, they had a mild argument, but late that evening, when they parted, Eva kissed her sister warmly. 'Everything will be all right,' she said.

They never saw each other again.

On February 8, 1945, Hitler sent Eva to the Berghof on the pretext that she must get everything ready there in case he decided to move his staff to the Obersalzberg later. At first Eva was reluctant to leave Berlin and Hitler but suddenly changed her mind. She took her two dogs with her and many of her personal possessions such as jewelry and photo albums. Gretl, pregnant, accompanied her. Instead of going to the Berghof, however, Eva stopped at Munich. Gretl continued on to the Berghof to stay until the military situation was resolved and her husband, who was in Berlin with Hitler as Himmler's representative, could join her. She hoped it would be possible for him to be with her when the baby was born.

In Munich, Eva put her villa in order, arranged for friends to care for her dogs and visited with her parents. She also made a special trip through the rubble-strewn streets to spend an afternoon with her close friend Herta Schneider and her children, whom Eva loved very much. She was more affectionate than ever with the children that day and when she left the Schneider home to return to her villa, she kissed Herta. 'We have had such lovely times together.'

Herta nodded. 'I will meet you at the Berghof in a few days and we will go boating. The bombers will not bother us there.'

Eva smiled but said nothing. Later Fanny Braun said that if the American and British bombers continued to attack Munich, she would join Eva on the Obersalzberg, too. She noticed that Eva seemed more quiet than usual during her last visit to the Braun apartment in Munich and that her goodbye kiss was exceptionally long but she decided that it was because Eva was tired and depressed.

'A stay on the Obersalzberg will cheer you up,' she told her daughter. 'It will be nice and quiet after Berlin.'

Eva nodded but made no reply. She didn't want her mother or her father or Herta or Gretl or anyone else to know that she had no intention of continuing south to the Berghof as Hitler had ordered. She was going back to Berlin.

19
'For Better or for Worse'

*The cruelty of Adolf Hitler was never more in evidence
than during the last weeks of the Third Reich. He
ordered the death of Allied prisoners; directed that the
tunnels leading into Berlin be flooded despite the
German refugees huddled in them; outlined a 'scorched
earth' policy which would have left the country
uninhabitable for those who survived the war; refused
to enter into peace negotiations so that the massive
artillery and bomber attacks on Berlin would stop;
ordered teenage German boys to certain death in a last-
ditch stand against the advancing Russians; and
ordered the execution of his own brother-in-law. He
was vicious and vindictive to the end . . . except with
Eva Braun.*

Once Eva made up her mind to return to Berlin she quickly made the arrangements. Since Hitler did not know she was returning, and she did not want to alert him to the fact for fear he would try to stop her, Eva did not dare ask him to send his plane for her. Flying wasn't safe anyway because the sky was filled with Allied fighter planes and bombers. A lone Luftwaffe aircraft would be an easy prey. She finally talked a young Waffen-SS officer, Walther Galen, into driving her to Berlin in her black Mercedes-Benz.

It was a dangerous trip. The American 8th Air Force and 15th Air Force and the British Royal Air Force were out in full strength during March when Eva made her trip to the Reich Chancellery. On March 14, 1945, the day she left Munich, 1,246 heavy bombers of the 8th Air Force attacked high-priority targets all over Germany. Near Leipzig two Mustang fighters accompanying the bombers made a strafing attack on Eva's automobile but Galen saw them coming and managed to park under a viaduct. One tire was blown apart but there was a spare in the trunk and within an hour Eva was on her way north again. After another strafing attack outside Dessau when a P-38 pilot blew up a German army truck which Galen was following on the highway, the Waffen-SS officer decided to stop in a nearby wood and wait until dark before traveling any further. He and Eva were both weary and fell asleep. When they awoke it was nearly three o'clock in the morning, much later than Galen had wanted to continue toward Berlin.

At about the same time that Eva and her driver headed north again the heavy-bomber crews of the 8th Air Force were huddled in their briefing rooms in England looking at their maps. The chief target that day was the headquarters of the German high command at Zossen, twenty-eight miles from Berlin – almost in the direct path of Eva's Mercedes-Benz. Unaware of the armada of Allied bombers heading in her direction, Eva was relaxing in the rear seat of the automobile as Galen neared Berlin. Suddenly she sat up with a jerk as he brought the Mercedes-Benz to a stop.

'Get out and run for the shelter!'

Eva heard his warning and didn't hesitate. She opened the door of the automobile and raced toward a public shelter a few yards to her right. Just as she entered it, the first of the bombs exploded to the west. The 8th Air Force Liberators and Flying Fortresses dropped 1,400 tons of high explosive bombs in the vicinity of Berlin on that day, March 15, 1945, but Eva was about ten miles away from Zossen, the main objective of the bombers, and this distance saved her life.

After the Allied bombers had left the Zossen area on their way back to England, Eva and Galen drove the remainder of the distance into Berlin. She was stunned when she saw the city. The Reich Chancellery, which they reached by using the road through the gateway of the old Zossen Palace because the other streets were pitted with bomb craters, was in much worse condition than when she had left Berlin. There were huge holes blasted in all four sides of the building. The American Embassy was demolished, the city post office was badly damaged. Unter den Linden, the promenade that she loved and where she had spent so many hours walking while waiting for Hitler to complete his conferences, was practically obliterated. Tree trunks were scattered across it, bomb craters filled with water made it an obstacle course for any pedestrian brave enough to try and walk across it, and along one side there were sandbags piled high by German soldiers who hoped that they could hide behind them when the Russians arrived. The only trouble was that the soldiers, mostly teenage boys, didn't know from which direction the Soviet troops were advancing.

Eva went directly to Hitler's study in his private quarters of the Reich Chancellery which, despite the mounting damage to the structure, was still intact. Hitler was sitting on the blue-and-white patterned sofa when she entered the room and for a moment he just stared at her. Putting his trembling hands on the sofa, he pushed himself to his feet and walked toward her.

'I told you to go to the Berghof. It is . . . '

Despite his attempt to sound severe, it was obvious to everyone who witnessed the reunion – the secretaries, Schaub and Magda Goebbels – that Hitler was delighted to see Eva. When she took his hands in hers he smiled and motioned for her to sit down on the sofa. They sat there for most of the evening, talking about earlier days, looking at photograph albums, listening to records. When Eva left the room to wash up after her long and hazardous trip, Hitler bragged to his secretaries about her loyalty.

'Who else would come back to Berlin when they had the opportunity to go to the Berghof?' he asked several times.

The secretaries did not answer and Hitler did not press them. He knew very well that many of those in Berlin that night wished they were on the Obersalzberg, miles away from the attacking bombers and the advancing Russian soldiers. He himself still had

231

tentative plans to make his last stand in the mountains near the Berghof.

During the remainder of March, Hitler assured Eva that the city would not fall, that foreign troops had not marched into Berlin since 1806 and it would not happen again in 1945. She heard rumors that disturbed her, just as the appearance of the city had disturbed her upon her return. It was said that the Americans had crossed the Rhine over the bridge at Remagen and that the Soviet troops were closing in on Vienna and threatening to cross the Oder River. Despite the depressing news, Eva rarely took refuge in the thirty-room bunker fifty feet beneath the Reich Chancellery until the last weeks of March, when the attacks became more intense.

The bunker had two floors. Eva's and Hitler's quarters were on the lower floor, which was much more plush than the one above, which was used primarily for cooking, servants' rooms and guest accommodations. Eva lacked little in the way of comfort except, of course, the opportunity to see the sun and the stars. Her quarters were air-conditioned and carpeted and included a private bath and monogrammed furniture. She had a dressing room and a combination bedroom-sitting room, both of which were accessible from Hitler's study. Hitler's bedroom was on the opposite side of the study and beyond it was a map-conference room and a special room for Blondi, his dog. The study, where he and Eva spent many hours during the final days of the Third Reich, had a writing table, a couch, a small table and several upholstered chairs. Here Hitler kept Anton Graff's portrait of Frederick the Great, a picture he took with him whenever he moved his headquarters. There was a private vestibule off the main corridor that led to Eva's and Hitler's quarters. On the opposite side of the corridor were Goebbels' study, Morell's bedroom-sitting room, the elaborate telephone exchange which kept Hitler in contact with officers in the field until the end, various other offices and the stairway leading to the upper level.

The corridor itself was nearly ten feet wide and paintings, predominantly by Italian artists, were hung along its length on both sides. It was in this corridor on the lower level that many of Hitler's visitors waited for their turn to see him during the last days. At the end of the corridor was a circular stairway of thirteen steps which led to another corridor on the upper floor. This one was furnished with tables and chairs and was used as a general-purpose dining room. Four rooms on the upper level were used for kitchens, three for servants' quarters, one for storage and four for the guests who came to the bunker and stayed overnight. Both floors were connected by a labyrinth of tunnels with the main bunker under the Vossstrasse where Hitler's entourage was quartered. Eva rarely went to the main bunker because she did not feel safe there. The concrete was less than ten feet thick, not nearly enough to deaden the sound of the exploding bombs.

Most of the time Eva remained in her own quarters or in Hitler's. Not even the depressing atmosphere in the underground headquarters as the military situation worsened could deter Eva from maintaining her appearance. She applied makeup carefully, kept her fingernails well manicured and wore a different dress as often as possible. She even managed to smuggle in hairdressers among the multitude of officers, ministers and their wives, and other visitors who came to the bunker during late March and early April. She not only tried to look her best, she also acted her best. While others were morbid, quiet, pessimistic, Eva continually tried to establish a more lighthearted atmosphere around Hitler. She knew time was running out but she never gave up trying.

On April 1, 1945, she was in her combination bedroom-sitting room when Schaub announced that she had a guest. A moment later Heinrich Hoffmann entered the room.

'Heinrich!'

They embraced in silence for several seconds. Eva had not seen Hoffmann for six months, not since Morell and Bormann had convinced Hitler that the photographer had paratyphus.

'Have you seen the Führer?' Eva asked.

Hoffmann shook his head. 'Not yet. I have fifty documents with me proving that I never had paratyphus but when I tried to show them to the Führer, he backed away from me and would not talk to me.'

There were tears in the photographer's eyes as he stared at Eva. 'Me, the Führer's closest friend, can't even talk with him.'

Eva motioned for him to sit down. 'I will talk with the Führer.'

She disappeared into Hitler's study and was gone for several minutes. When she returned, she was smiling.

'We will have tea with the Führer at three o'clock. There is just one condition – do not mention your supposed illness.'

Hoffmann updated Eva on the news from Munich, including the information that her mother was well and that her father was on duty at a military hospital in the Munich area. He told her he had heard that Gretl was 'getting bigger' every day while she awaited the birth of her baby at the Berghof but he had no news about Ilse. By the time the adjutant arrived to tell them Hitler

233

was waiting for them in his study, Eva was in better humor than she had been for days.

Hoffmann and Hitler talked as though there had not been a six-month hiatus in their association. While Eva listened, the two men discussed art, the paintings Hitler still wanted for his personal collection, Hitler's favorite photographs – everything except Hoffmann's supposed illness and the military situation. Eva was delighted in the change that came over Hitler as he joked with Hoffmann about the photographer's added weight since the last time he had seen him, about his love of liquor and women and his large inventory of obscene stories. She later told Frau Junge that she had not seen 'the Führer in such good spirits since his days at the Berghof during the early part of the war.' Hitler, the teetotaler, even insisted that Hoffmann have several drinks after they had finished their tea. When it came time to part at five o'clock in the morning of April 2, Hitler solemnly shook hands with his long-time friend from Munich, gripping Hoffmann's hand for several long moments. Then, without a word, he abruptly turned and walked into his bedroom.

Hoffmann stayed a few minutes longer with Eva, long enough to ask her if she wanted to accompany him back to Munich. Eva shook her head.

'I will stay with the Führer.'

The rotund photographer shrugged. He was an ardent Nazi and considered himself one of Hitler's closest personal friends, but he had no intention of staying in Berlin until it was too late to get out.

'I'll see you later,' he told Eva as he kissed her on the cheek.

'Perhaps.'

One of the brightest moments in the bunker during April was when news was received that Franklin D. Roosevelt had died. But the excitement didn't last long; no one really thought the death of one Allied leader could change the course of the war. It did give Hitler a few cheerful hours contemplating the historical parallel with the death of the Czarina at a crucial moment, which saved the kingdom of Frederick the Great. Eva, ultimately more realistic, was more interested in Hitler's upcoming birthday. On April 20 he would be fifty-six years old and she wanted to celebrate the event. She was worried, however. The Führer was losing his temper more often as the days passed, going into a tantrum at the slightest provocation. He constantly screamed at General Hans Krebs, the new Army Chief of Staff, General Wilhelm Burgdorf, the army adjutant, General Karl Koller, the Chief of

234

Staff of the Luftwaffe, and Heinz Lorenz, from the Ministry of Propaganda. He even had a three-hour verbal battle with General Heinz Guderian during which he bellowed so much his voice became hoarse and his throat sore. Quite often he was insulting to the secretaries and Eva had to try and smooth matters over after he left the room. She sensed that his lack of control was hurting his image as a strong leader, that the loyal officers and others in the bunker were quickly losing respect for him. That is why she wanted to stage a birthday celebration in his honor, to establish him once again as the 'Great One'.

A birthday party in an underground bunker in the midst of the brutal bombardment of a city and country was no easy thing to manage. But Eva was so intent on giving Hitler some pleasure on his birthday that she never considered how grotesque this affair was bound to be. She invited all the Nazi leaders, and for the last time Speer, Goebbels, Bormann, Göring, Himmler, Ribbentrop and many lesser Nazi officers joined together. Their presents were not as lavish as in past years but Hitler did receive two gifts that he appreciated. One was a painting of his mother and the other was a portrait of Eva in a jeweled frame. He put them both in his study so that he could see them several times a day as he passed through the room. As the guests greeted him and wished him good fortune in the future, Hitler tried to conceal his physical infirmities. He braced himself against a couch in order to reduce the shaking of his body but he couldn't control his hands. They shook as though he had palsy. Eva stood beside him and tried to divert the guests' attention from the Führer as soon as they had greeted him but she was only partially successful in this maneuver. They were all shocked at the wreck Hitler had become and this shock was mirrored in their expressions.

Hitler left the party early and Eva accompanied him to his quarters. She was disappointed her effort had turned out so badly – Hitler was melancholy, brooding, so dejected he had not even noticed the new dress of silver-blue brocade that she had saved for the occasion. Nor did she dare mention the dress for fear he would go into a tantrum and accuse her of criticizing his manners. So far she had escaped being the target of his anger but she was not confident that she would escape much longer. In fact, she was not confident of anything now that Hitler no longer acted as though he believed in victory. In a sudden impulse Eva decided to have one last fling, to enjoy herself once more as she had in earlier days in Munich at the *Oktoberfest* when she danced, drank and sang all night.

After returning from Hitler's quarters Eva suggested to the guests that they leave the bunker and go up to the Führer's apartment – or what was left of it – in the Reich Chancellery and continue the party. The living room of the apartment was still intact, but bare since the furniture had been moved into the bunker. Only a large round table remained in the center of the room. At first everyone was reluctant to leave the safety of the bunker even though there was no Allied air raid in progress. Eva and several of the younger Waffen-SS officers went up the steps alone, carrying a phonograph with them and a supply of food and drink. Within a few minutes the others followed, lured by the opportunity to get out of their 'concrete prison' for a few hours and forget disaster with 'wine, women and song'. Morell, dejected and scared because that very morning Hitler had ordered him to leave the bunker after accusing him of injecting him with morphine so that he could be taken out of Berlin against his will, followed Eva. So did Bormann, afraid he might miss overhearing some remarks detrimental to Hitler which he could report back to the Führer. Traudl Junge went up to the party because she was young enough to want one last fling. Soon the majority of the guests were crowded into the old living room, dancing to the single record Eva had brought along for the phonograph, a record which repeated over and over that 'blood red roses tell you of happiness . . .'

Eva danced with everyone, not knowing or caring what man took her in his arms that night. Between dances she and the other guests drank champagne and as the night passed a giddiness came over all of them. Their shrill laughter echoed in the room, passed through the holes in the Reich Chancellery walls and drifted out to the black streets of Berlin. Once in a while, when an artillery shell burst in the city, the guests would be quiet for a moment, but only for a moment, and then the laughter and talking would resume. No one spoke about the war, or of victory or defeat. They just danced, drank champagne, laughed and listened to the record chant on and on about the red roses of happiness. Not until the sun came up on the morning of April 21, 1945, did Eva and her guests leave the battered Reich Chancellery building and retreat down the steps into the bunker again. The party was over.

Eva knew that there had been a conference between Hitler and his officers immediately after his birthday reception but it wasn't until the next day that she heard of Hitler's decision to stay and die in Berlin. She had thought that he was going to withdraw to the Obersalzberg and that the German Army would make its last

236

stand in this mountainous area. When she awakened early in the afternoon, she discovered a mass exit from the bunker was in progress. Göring, in fact, had begun the procession to the Berghof late the night before. Hitler had bid him an abrupt farewell, not mentioning their long years of association or the great victories they had once shared. The Führer was angry with him because his Luftwaffe had failed to protect Germany; he was glad to see the 'fat one' go. Albert Speer also left Berlin after trying to convince Hitler not to order a 'scorched earth' policy for what remained of Germany. Eva hated to see him go and was especially disappointed that she had not had the opportunity to bid him farewell. Himmler departed for his quarters at Ziethan Castle, not mentioning to Hitler his personal plans to end the war through negotiations with Count Folke Bernadotte of Sweden. Ribbentrop was preparing to leave the bunker when Eva awakened. Before he left, however, he stopped to see her.

'You are the only one who can take the Führer away from here,' he told Eva. 'Tell him that you want to leave Berlin with him. You can thereby do Germany a great service.'

Although she was shocked that Hitler intended to stay in the bunker until the end, she didn't reveal her emotions to Ribbentrop.

'I will not tell the Führer a word of your proposal,' she replied. 'He must decide alone. If he thinks it is right to remain in Berlin, then I will stay with him. If he goes, I'll go, too.'

Ribbentrop just shook his head, kissed Eva on the cheek and left.

Others also left the bunker that day, while the roads were still open and escape was possible. Fräulein Wolfe, Hitler's long-time secretary, and Christa Schröder both departed, as did Morell, the deposed physician. Many of the staff officers rushed to head south before the Russians arrived.

Later that afternoon Hitler met with his two remaining secretaries, Traudl Junge and Gerda Daranowski (who had married General Eckhardt Christian a few months earlier), Fräulein Manzialy, his favorite cook, and Eva. He announced that within an hour an airplane would arrive in Berlin to fly them out of the city to the Berghof.

'All is lost, hopelessly lost,' Hitler told the four women. 'It is best that you go to the Obersalzberg immediately.'

He turned to leave the room but Eva quickly walked to his side and took both of his hands in hers. As though speaking to a sad child, she said, 'But you know that I'll stay with you. I won't let myself be sent away.'

At that moment Hitler leaned over and kissed Eva on the lips, the first time any of those present had ever seen him do such a thing in all the years they had known him. Just before Eva and Hitler left the room together the two secretaries and the cook told him that they, too, intended to stay with him. His powerful attraction for women was still intact even in his hour of defeat.

At dinner that evening Hitler gave each of the women a small cylinder that resembled an ornate lipstick holder. Opening one, he deposited a small phial from it into his hand. Indicating the golden-colored liquid in the phial, Hitler said: 'This is potassium cyanide. There is enough in the phial to kill any man or woman. I suggest that you keep it with you from now on to use if and when you want to do so.'

This was his subtle way of warning them that they might prefer poison to the treatment they could expect from the Russian soldiers if captured alive.

Once she had made the decision to stay and die in Berlin with Hitler, Eva did not isolate herself in her quarters and brood. She was determined to 'act like a lady until the end'. She set two goals for herself: to keep Hitler as happy as possible under the circumstances; and to make all necessary personal preparations for the end. No longer could she hope to become the official 'First Lady' of Germany because she knew that Hitler was not going to have any country to rule within a matter of days. She knew now she would never be his wife. All her personal objectives, which in earlier years had seemed so important, were now forgotten. She thought only of her man – Hitler – and her relatives – her parents, Gretl and Ilse.

She admitted to Speer when he made a dramatic flight to visit Hitler one last time on April 23 that her most difficult task was to retain her self-control.

'One needs courage when death is near. I hope that my courage does not fail me at the end,' she said when Speer visited her in the bunker for the final time. Suddenly she brightened. 'How about some champagne for a farewell drink? And some food. You must be hungry after your flight.'

Speer had seen most of the others in the bunker that night – Goebbels and his wife, Hitler, the various generals, Bormann – but in his eyes only Eva was composed and calm. The others were either drunk or drugged or in a stupor because of their fear of approaching death. When it came time for him to leave, Eva made one last parting remark: 'Why does the killing continue? It's all for nothing.' She was the only one in the bunker who mentioned anything to Speer about the suffering of others.

Whenever it was possible during the final week of the battle for Berlin, Eva slipped out of the bunker to walk in the Reich Chancellery garden. She had always loved springtime, the mild air, the warm sun, but in April, 1945, there were deep holes in the new grass where the Russian artillery shells had landed and empty cans and bottles, broken branches and crushed flowers were everywhere. Several times she was forced to run for shelter when the Russian shells landed nearby, and finally, on April 25 she decided that it was not safe to go outside anymore.

In the midst of the general despair and destruction Eva remained optimistic. When Göring sent a message by radio that since Hitler had decided to stay in Berlin, he took it for granted that the Führer expected him to take over 'total leadership of the Third Reich', Hitler went into a rage and ordered his arrest. Eva managed to calm him during a conversation in his study later. While the others listened in silence she diverted his mind from the Göring affair.

'Say, do you remember that statue in the Foreign Office garden?' she asked Hitler. 'It would look wonderful standing beside the pool in the garden of my Munich villa. Please buy it for me after we leave Berlin.'

Surprisingly, Hitler gave the ridiculous request serious consideration. 'But I don't know to whom it belongs. It is probably state property. I couldn't just take it and say you can put it in your private garden if it is state property.'

Eva laid her hand on his arm and replied, 'Oh, if you succeed in beating back the Russians and free Berlin then you can make an exception.'

Hitler gave a short laugh and muttered, more to himself than to the others in the room, 'The logic of women!'

Later in the evening, when once again he began ranting about 'the traitorous Göring', Eva changed the subject to other matters. She walked over to him and pointed to several red and blue spots on Hitler's gray field uniform coat.

'Look, you are quite dirty! You mustn't do everything like old Fritz [Frederick the Great] and run around as unkempt as he.'

Hitler protested her rebuke mildly. 'But this is my work suit. I can't put on an apron when I go to a conference and have to handle colored pencils.'

During this last week Eva showed the same quiet composure

239

and muted gaiety that she had exhibited during most of her association with Hitler. Hanna Reitsch, the famed German aviatrix, saw Eva when she flew General von Greim to the bunker on April 26 after Hitler had appointed Greim to replace Göring. Eva was by far the calmest of the bunker occupants, much more composed than Frau Goebbels. Fräulein Reitsch noticed that when Eva was in Hitler's presence she was always charming and thoughtful of his every comfort, well dressed and as attractive looking as was possible under the circumstances. She seemed to take the prospects of dying with Hitler quite matter-of-factly, with an attitude that seemed to say, 'Has not our relationship been of many long years' duration and did I not try to commit suicide when he tried to get rid of me? This will be a much easier and more proper way to die.'

When Hanna Reitsch and Greim flew out of Berlin at Hitler's orders between midnight and 1 a.m. on April 29 Fräulein Reitsch carried a letter that Eva had written to her sister Gretl. The letter was never delivered but Fräulein Reitsch recalled that it stated:

I must write you these words so that you will not feel sad over our end here in the shelter. It is rather we who are filled with sorrow because it is your fate to live on into the chaos that will follow. For myself I am glad to die here; glad to die at the side of the Führer; but most of all glad that the horror now to come is spared me. What could life still give me? It has already been perfect. It has already given me its best and its fullest. Why should I go on living? This is the time to die; the right time. With the Führer I have had everything. To die now, beside him, completes my happiness. Live on as well and as happily as you can. Shed no tears nor be regretful over our deaths. It is the perfect and proper ending. None of us would change it now. It is the right end for a German woman.

20
'Until Death Do Us Part'

One day early in his career Hitler gave Ernst Hanfstängl and his wife a lift across Munich in his car. During their conversation Hitler told Hanfstängl: 'There are two ways of judging a man's character; by the woman he marries and by the way he dies.' In late April, 1945, it was time for Adolf Hitler to do both.

On April 25, while Eva stood nearby listening, Hitler gave precise instructions to his valet, Heinz Linge, about destroying all his personal effects after his death except for the Graff portrait of Frederick the Great – 'Hans will fly it out of Berlin after I am gone.' He was referring to Hans Baur, his personal pilot.

Everything else – papers, letters, photographs, official documents – was to be burned. When he went into detail about how he intended to shoot himself after taking poison and how he wanted his body burned, Eva, still dry-eyed but shaken, turned and walked out of the room. She intended to die with him but she did not want to talk about death. Later, however, she told Frau Junge, 'I want to be a pretty corpse. I'm going to take poison.' She took the brass tube with the phial of cyanide out of the pocket of her elegant dress and examined it carefully. 'I wonder whether it hurts. I am so afraid of having to suffer for a long time.'

The secretary tried to cheer Eva up by saying that Hitler had promised her there would be no pain, but then she excused herself and went to her own room. Both Frau Junge and Fräulein Manzialy had decided to try and escape from Berlin after Hitler's death rather than commit suicide. Later Gerda Christian joined in the plan. They intended to remain loyal to Hitler as long as he was alive but agreed that once he was dead their obligation to him ended. Whether they could get out of the inferno alive or not was problematical.

Eva never doubted that she would end her life when Hitler ended his but the suspense was hard on her nerves. Every time the news about the military situation was bad, Hitler murmured that the time had come, that under no circumstances could he wait too long and be captured alive. The next hour, when the news was good, he would postpone ending his life, grasping at the thought that by some miracle he might yet be successful in defeating the Russians, that the Allies might finally understand that their real enemy was Russia and help him drive the Soviets out of Germany. Each time he wavered one way or the other Eva stood by and waited for his final decision.

'If only it was finally over,' she murmured to Frau Junge after one such incident. 'I am so horribly worried about it.'

On April 26 a diversion took Eva's mind off her fate for a few hours. Two young Waffen-SS orderlies, Grossman and Busse, decided that since it appeared they were going to die defending Berlin they would like to get married to their long-time girl-friends. The two fiancées had joined the orderlies in the bunker. When the orderlies tried to see Hitler they were told that he was much too busy to talk with them. They then contacted Eva, told her their problem and asked if she could obtain permission for them to marry in the bunker.

Eva nodded. 'I will speak to the Führer. Wait here.' Within a few minutes she was back. 'The Führer is delighted to give his permission. If any of the parents wish to attend the ceremony, the Führer will send an armored car for them.'

Hitler and Eva both attended the double wedding that afternoon and afterwards extended their felicitations to the two young married couples. Erwin Jakubek, a waiter who also attended the ceremony, nudged Gerda Christian and pointed at the Führer and Eva. 'They are deeply moved by the wedding.'

The secretary, flippant until the very end, grinned. 'If Eva ever thought the Führer would marry her, she knows better now. Time has run out.'

She was wrong. Two days later, on April 28, Eva received a message from Grossman, one of the orderlies who had been married in the bunker. She hurried to Hitler's study where the Führer was sitting and staring at the portrait of Frederick the Great. After kissing him on the cheek, she read Grossman's note to him: 'If I am killed in battle now I will die happy because I was permitted to marry my sweetheart and the Führer congratulated me personally.'

Hitler nodded but said nothing. However, when Eva held the note to her breast and murmured, 'I am so happy for them,' Hitler rose shakily from his chair and walked to her side. He had a message in his hand, too, but he didn't show it to Eva. Actually the message was tantamount to his death sentence because it notified him that the army of General Walther Wenck, upon which he had depended to save Berlin, no longer existed. Instead he leaned over and whispered into her ear.

Frau Junge, who was at the other end of the room, saw Eva step back and stare at Hitler in amazement. He nodded as though to reassure her and then turned and went out the door calling for Goebbels. Eva, her eyes shining, walked over to Frau Junge and said, 'Tonight you will certainly cry.'

Frau Junge thought she meant that she and Hitler were going to commit suicide that evening, in that case she couldn't understand why Eva seemed so happy. Was she looking forward to dying? As she went into the corridor she heard Goebbels issuing orders to several Waffen-SS soldiers to go to a certain Volkssturm detachment on the Friedrichstrasse and bring back Walter Wagner. At the time the name meant nothing to Frau Junge but later she remembered that Wagner had married the Goebbels years earlier. During the remainder of the afternoon and early evening Eva stayed in her own quarters, which was unusual. Frau Junge and the others were accustomed to having her around, asking questions or trying to cheer everyone up when the news was bad. Eva's isolation further convinced the secretary that the end had come, that before the night was over both Eva and the Führer would be dead. Just before midnight Eva stepped from her room dressed in Hitler's favorite dress, the black silk one with the pink shoulder straps. She wore black suede shoes, a pearl necklace around her neck and a platinum watch with diamond numbers. In her hair was a gold clip. She looked so beautiful that Frau Junge leaned over to Gerda Christian to whisper, 'Why is she dressed so well to die?'

A few minutes later Walter Wagner arrived. He was a justice of the peace who had been drafted as a soldier to help defend Berlin. After Goebbels' messengers had located him and explained he was needed to perform a marriage ceremony, Wagner had gone to his home and obtained the necessary documents. It wasn't until he arrived in the bunker that he realized he had been summoned to marry the Führer and Eva Braun. He was so shocked to find himself in front of the Führer that he fumbled with the papers for several minutes. Finally Eva said, 'Herr Wagner, can we get on with the ceremony? It is getting late.'

Wagner nodded and placed the two-paged marriage document on the small table near where he was standing. Asking the necessary questions one by one, he filled out the document in a methodical manner that made Eva more nervous than ever.

'Please hurry,' she pleaded. Overhead she could hear the steady rumbling of the Russian artillery shells and the explosions of the Allied bombs. She had waited years for this wedding and it was obvious that she wanted it completed before it was too late.

Wagner was nervous, too. He didn't bother filling in the blanks asking for the names of Hitler's father and mother nor did he date the marriage document until after the ceremony. On the line asking for verification of Hitler's identity the harried justice of the peace scribbled, 'Personally known'. He did, however, take the time to ask Eva for her identity card, since he was not acquainted with her, and he filled in her birthplace and the names of her parents. Goebbels was a witness for Hitler and, ironically, Bormann stood beside Eva and was her witness during the ceremony. To Eva's surprise, her most hated enemy seemed to enjoy the affair and was the first to congratulate her after the marriage. The four were asked to sign the document in the proper sequence at the end of the second page: Hitler, Eva, Goebbels and Bormann. Eva nearly signed 'Braun' but caught herself and wrote 'Hitler' in a firm hand. Then, as though an unseen witness were showering them with the traditional rice, a particularly close explosion above-ground shook flakes of white cement from the ceiling of the bunker onto Hitler and Eva.

The wedding party retired to Hitler's study for the *Hochszeits-mahl* (wedding breakfast). It was now nearly 2 a.m. in the morning of April 29, 1945. The two secretaries, Colonel von Below, Goebbels and his wife, Bormann, and Fräulein Manzialy followed the elated Eva and the subdued Hitler into the room where champagne, wine and sweets were waiting. Hitler usually didn't drink any wine but to celebrate his marriage he took a glass of sweet wine and joined in the toasts to his wife. After the others had finished offering their congratulations the Führer stood up at the end of the table and made a short speech. He recalled that he had been best man at Goebbels' wedding and now Goebbels had repaid the debt by being his best man. He paused a moment and then added that his wish had always been to return to his hometown in Austria and settle down with Eva to the life of an average citizen. He had hunted for a place to build a home in that area several times during the war, a place where he could spend the last years of his life in peace, but he had not found a suitable spot. Now, he said, it appeared that he would not need such a place.

To the small audience in the room the thought of the Führer leading the peaceful life of an ordinary citizen was fantastic. They dismissed it as a fantasy induced by the sweet wine Hitler was drinking.

There was one minor irritation during the wedding party that bothered Eva. She couldn't understand why Hermann Fegelein, Gretl's husband wasn't present. She remembered that she hadn't seen him for two days, and as Hitler continued reminiscing about the war and what he would have done had he been victorious, Eva slipped around the table to the chair next to Frau Junge. 'Have you seen Fegelein?'

Frau Junge shook her head. She didn't know where he was, hadn't seen him for at least twenty-four hours.

Before Eva could question the secretary further Hitler turned to Frau Junge and said, 'Come, we must finish our work.'

While Hitler had been waiting for Wagner to arrive to marry him and Eva, he had begun dictating his last will and testament to Frau Junge. Now he wanted to complete the task before it was too late. Eva returned to her own room to await Hitler, but shortly after putting on her negligee she received an urgent written message which was delivered by a guard. It was from her brother-in-law, Hermann Fegelein. 'Eva, tell the Führer that I'm innocent. Beg him for a reprieve for me until I can prove my innocence. Please. I'm in Reich Chancellery garden under guard.'

The shocked Eva immediately checked with Bormann in an effort to determine what kind of trouble Fegelein had become involved in that could be so serious. Bormann was delighted to tell her, confident that at last he could hurt her. Two nights ago, he said, Fegelein had slipped out of the bunker and had gone to his private house on the Kurfürstendamm. He had changed from his uniform to civilian clothes and was getting ready to escape from Berlin and go to Berghof. From the Berghof, Bormann explained, Fegelein intended to go to Spain or Argentina. Hitler had noticed his absence, however, and sent out several members of his bodyguard under the command of Standartenführer Hoegl to the Kurfürstendamm where they discovered Fegelein and brought him back to the bunker.

'So?' Eva asked Bormann. 'That is reason enough to shoot him?'

Bormann grinned. 'A few hours ago Heinz Lorenz brought the Führer a Reuters report that stated Himmler was negotiating with Count Bernadotte to surrender Germany to the Allies! Your brother-in-law, as Himmler's liaison officer, undoubtedly was in on the plot. It is too bad.' Shaking with laughter, he turned away from Eva.

Eva interrupted Hitler while he was still dictating his last will and testament but it was useless. He ignored her plea that Gretl was expecting a child soon, despite the fact that he had always liked Gretl.

'We can't allow family affairs to interfere with disciplinary action,' Hitler bellowed at his new wife. 'Fegelein is a traitor just as Mussolini's son-in-law was a traitor and you know what happened to him.'

Eva recalled very vividly what had happened to Count Ciano. She also recalled that she had agreed with Hitler's decision to execute him. 'Then you will execute Hermann?' Hitler nodded.

Eva returned to her own room and wrote a final message to Gretl's husband, who was waiting in the Reich Chancellery garden with the firing squad: 'I can do nothing.'

Within a matter of minutes Hermann Fegelein was shot to

death near the same statue that Eva had asked Hitler to obtain for her private garden in Munich. Gretl was a pregnant widow at the age of thirty.

While Eva cried in her room, Hitler completed his dictation to Frau Junge, unconcerned over one more death sentence that he had pronounced. He was interested only in having his last will and testament in proper form before the hour came to pronounce his own death sentence. In his private will he wrote:

Although during my years of struggle I believed I could not undertake the responsibility of marriage, I have now decided at the end of my life's journey to marry the young woman who, after many years of true friendship, came of her own free will to this city, when it was already almost completely under siege, in order to share my fate. At her own desire she will go to her death with me as my wife. This will compensate us for what we both lost through my work in the service of my people.

What I possess belongs, in so far as it has any value at all, to the Party. Should this no longer exist, it belongs to the State, and should the State also be destroyed, any further decision from me is no longer necessary.

The paintings in the collections I bought over the years were never acquired for private purposes, but always exclusively for the establishment of an art gallery in my native town of Linz. It is my heartfelt desire that this legacy shall be fulfilled.

As executor of this document I appoint my most faithful party comrade Martin Bormann. He is authorized to make all decisions which shall be final and legally binding. He is permitted to give everything of value either as mementos or such as is necessary for the maintenance of a petty bourgeois household to my brothers and sisters, and also above all to my wife's mother and to my faithful co-workers male and female who are all well known to him, principally my old secretaries, Frau Winter, etc., who have assisted me with their work over many years.

My wife and I choose death to avoid the disgrace of defeat or capitulation. It is our wish to be cremated immediately in the place where I have done the greatest part of my work during the course of my twelve years' service for my people.

It was after four o'clock on the morning of April 29 when Hitler finished his last will and political testament and had them witnessed and signed by Bormann and the others. Eva, her eyes red from crying, was waiting when he reached their quarters. For the first time they went to bed together as man and wife. Their wedding night was punctuated by artillery and bomb explosions.

Eva appeared in the corridor of the bunker shortly after 11 a.m., well groomed and happy. No one knew how to address her, and when the orderlies and adjutants stammered a greeting she smiled and said, 'You can call me Frau Hitler if you want.'

She joined Hitler, who was already at the breakfast table, and poured herself a cup of tea. Just as she was lifting the cup to her lips, Linge, the valet, hurried across the room carrying a sheet of paper. Without a word he handed it to Hitler and walked away. Hitler read the message, so engrossed in it that he spilled his tea all over his pants. Eva grabbed a towel and started to wipe the liquid from his clothing but he just shook his head and handed her the sheet of paper. It was a Reuters dispatch which stated:

Benito Mussolini is dead. Captured by Italian partisans as he attempted to escape into Switzerland from northern Italy, he was taken before a tribunal and sentenced to death. In the village of Dongo the sentence was executed by partisans who machine-gunned him in the back. His mistress, Clara Petacci, who was with him at the time of the attempted escape, was also captured and also killed with the ex-Duce. Their bodies were taken to Milan and subjected to public degradation. After being dragged through the streets they were hung head downward in the public square where thousands spat at and reviled the corpses.

Hitler looked at Eva. 'They will not do that to us. Our bodies will be burned.'

Eva shuddered involuntarily at his words and Frau Junge heard her mutter, 'Don't say that. I don't want to think about it.'

Hitler shrugged but said nothing. After drinking another cup of tea he started to rise from the breakfast table just as Dr Ludwig Stumpfegger, the doctor who had replaced Brandt and Morell, walked into the room. Hitler called to him. 'Would my dog Blondi respond to the cyanide the same as a human?'

'Yes, *mein Führer*.'

Hitler reached down and scratched Blondi, his inseparable companion for so many years. Giving her one final pat, he told Stumpfegger, 'Take Blondi out and give her a phial of the poison.'

Eva watched until the dog disappeared down the corridor, then dropped her eyes to her plate. A few minutes later there was a loud barking, which soon faded to complete silence. Stumpfegger returned to the room and said, 'The dog is dead.'

Eva fingered her small phial and kept staring at the table.

248

Hitler, however, asked the doctor if a man would still have the strength to pull the trigger of a revolver after he drank the poison. When Stumpfegger said that he would, Hitler looked at Eva. 'We will take the poison and then use our pistols. That will make doubly certain that we will not be captured alive.'

Eva, twisting her handkerchief into a knot, said, 'Yes, yes, we will be certain.'

Hitler then called a German soldier to the breakfast table and gave him instructions to kill the five puppies that had been orphaned by Blondi's death. After making certain that matter was taken care of, Hitler reread part of the testament Goebbels had written while he and Eva were asleep:

The Führer has ordered me, should the defense of the Reich capital collapse, to leave Berlin, and to take part as a leading member of a government appointed by him. For the first time in my life I must categorically refuse to obey an order of the Führer. My wife and children join me in this refusal . . .'

At that moment six small coffins were carried into the bunker and Eva, knowing that they were for the Goebbels' children, left the table and hurried from the room. As she stepped into the corridor, however, the children called to her and ran to her side. She kissed each one and continued on to her bedroom, recalling the many times she had sung them to sleep. Now they were scheduled for a sleep from which they would not wake.

For the remainder of that day, a Sunday, Hitler took care of the few remaining military and political matters in his collapsing Third Reich. He made certain that Admiral Karl Dönitz was appointed his successor; ordered Himmler's arrest; mandated that Göring remain a prisoner; and emphasized that Otto Skorzeny, the German commando leader who had rescued Mussolini, should prepare a final defense against the Allies at the Alpine Redoubt south of Munich. While he was handling these matters Eva went to bed and it wasn't until after 3 a.m. that Hitler joined her for their last night together.

Eva arose early, so early that she heard Otto Guensche ordering that jerricans full of gasoline be placed near the bunker exit. She went directly to her own bedroom and called Frau Junge to join her. After the young secretary arrived, Eva opened her closet door, exhibiting the silver fox coat that she loved so much. 'Frau Junge, I would like to give you this coat as a farewell gift.'

Frau Junge thanked her but shook her head. 'I don't think I will have need of it.'

Eva approached the young secretary and embraced her. 'Please try to get out. Perhaps you can still get through. If you do, greet Bavaria for me.'

Frau Junge began to cry softly and left the room.

Hitler got up at noon and went directly to the conference room to check on the Russian advance. The news was all bad. Soviet guns were shelling the Reich Chancellery steadily and Soviet troops were fighting in the underground tunnels at Friedrichstrasse. That meant that the enemy was within a block of the bunker. He immediately left the conference room after studying the reports and summoned Hans Baur, his first pilot, to the study. 'Baur, I would like to take my leave of you.'

The pilot, though he had momentarily been expecting word that Hitler had committed suicide, tried to talk the Führer out of killing himself. He offered to fly him to Argentina or Japan or Arabia, stating that he still thought he could pilot a plane out of Berlin. Eva, who had joined the two men in the study, watched Hitler eagerly, but when the Führer waved aside Baur's suggestions, her smile faded.

'The war is over now that Berlin is finished,' Hitler said, 'and I stand or fall by the capital.' He took the portrait of Frederick the Great down from the wall and handed it to Baur. 'Take this with you. You deserve it.' Hitler turned, grasped Eva's hand and said to her, 'Now all I have is you.'

Baur saw her smile and nod.

At 2.30 p.m. on April 30, Eva and Hitler had lunch with Frau Junge, Frau Christian and Fräulein Manzialy. As usual, Hitler ate no meat. Instead he had a small dish of spaghetti. Eva had tea, nothing else. The smell of gasoline had swept down through the bunker from the Reich Chancellery garden entrance to the underground shelter and sapped her appetite. She was well aware of why the gasoline had been brought to the garden. After they had finished eating Eva went to her bedroom, Frau Christian to her quarters, Frau Junge to a small office across the corridor and Fräulein Manzialy to the kitchen to start preparations for the evening meal – even though it was obvious that neither Hitler nor Eva would be alive at the dinner hour.

At 3.30 p.m. Guensche announced throughout the bunker that the Führer wished to bid farewell to everyone and would be in the corridor within a few minutes. At approximately 3.45 Hitler, with Eva on his arm, appeared in the bunker corridor. Eva's hair was freshly washed and beautifully waved. She was wearing Hitler's favorite black dress and shoes she had bought in Italy. On her wrist was the platinum wristwatch studded with diamonds that Hitler had given her several years earlier. While Hitler's face was solemn, Eva was smiling. Only the moisture in her eyes revealed her true feelings at that moment – calm, composed, quiet . . . and afraid.

Those who were left in the bunker bid the couple farewell, some with obvious relief that now they were free to try and escape, others in near-panic. Frau Goebbels pleaded with Hitler not to kill himself, while her husband watched impassively. Goebbels had already decided that his wife, his children and himself would die shortly after Hitler was pronounced dead. Frau Christian took this final opportunity to announce to Hitler that she intended to try to escape from the bunker, that she was not going to take the poison. Hitler merely nodded. Frau Junge quietly said, 'Farewell.' Eva nodded and then kissed her.

'Tell everyone in Munich farewell,' she whispered. 'Tell my parents I love them.'

Then it was time to go. Hitler took Eva by the arm and together they entered the study. Just before the heavy iron door closed behind them, Eva turned, looked back at Frau Junge and smiled.

It was a short wait for those outside the door. Within a few minutes a single pistol shot was heard, and then complete silence. When the door was opened, there was a heavy bitter almond smell. Hitler was slumped on one end of the blue-and-white upholstered couch, blood running down his face from the single bullet he had fired from his Walther 7.65 pistol after he had swallowed the poison.

On the other end of the couch Eva was reclining as though asleep. Her little revolver was lying beside her, unfired, and beside it was her pink chiffon scarf. The empty phial that had contained the cyanide was on the floor near her left foot. She was dead, but she was still smiling.

Epilogue

After Eva and Hitler died and their bodies were burned in the Reich Chancellery garden, the other women in the bunker were left alone to decide their own fates. Frau Goebbels knew what she had to do, and with the help of Dr Stumpfegger she murdered her six children. She then joined her husband in the Reich Chancellery garden, and after Dr Goebbels shot himself with his service pistol, Frau Goebbels put the phial of potassium cyanide Hitler had given her between her teeth and bit hard. She fell dead at approximately the same spot where Eva's body had been burned the previous day.

Frau Christian left the bunker in a group led by Otto Guensche to try and pierce the Russian lines surrounding Berlin. A beauty with flawless complexion and near-perfect facial features, she would have been a prize catch for the women-starved Russian soldiers. After several narrow escapes on the way out, however, Frau Christian reached the American Zone safely.

Frau Junge donned men's clothing, slipped out of the bunker and mingled with the refugees fleeing Berlin. She reached Munich without being captured by the Soviet troops. Fräulein Manzialy, the cook of whom Hitler had been so proud, wasn't so lucky. She was last seen on the outskirts of Berlin being carried into a house by a Russian soldier while his eager comrades followed in line. Perhaps she used the poison at the last moment.

Fräulein Wolfe and Fräulein Schröder had departed Berlin before the death of Eva and Hitler and they survived the war. So did Hanna Reitsch, who piloted the last plane out of the capital. Eva's sister Gretl was at the Berghof when the fighting stopped and Ilse was in the Munich area, as were Eva's parents. Leni Riefenstahl survived to face a life of controversy in the film industry because of her association with Hitler.

They each had shared in the triumph of Hitler and, in the end, they shared in the tragedy of Hitler . . . as did Eva.

The Musmanno Archives

Michael A. Musmanno was a naval aide to General Mark W. Clark at the end of World War II. At his headquarters north of Florence he heard so many conflicting stories about the death or the escape of Adolf Hitler that he recommended to his Navy superiors that Hitler's end be fully investigated. Musmanno himself was given this assignment, including the authority to interrogate anyone he believed might have information about Hitler. Later, as an official U.S. Navy observer at the International Military Tribunal trials at Nuremberg, he had access to many individuals involved with the Third Reich. President Harry S. Truman appointed Musmanno as a judge at the Nuremberg war crime trials, which followed the I.M.T. trials, so that he even had additional time to interview and observe former German officers, Nazi officials and German civilians. From May, 1945, until the summer of 1948 Musmanno interviewed over two hundred persons who had known Adolf Hitler and Eva Braun, checking –and rechecking conflicting information, sorting the verified from the unverified facts. Consequently, the Musmanno Archives contain a wealth of information concerning the viewpoints and opinions of those persons who knew Hitler intimately and give a fresh, clear, verbal portrait of him and his associates.

In 1961 Musmanno was an important witness at the Eichmann trial and helped convict the former Nazi official. At the time of his death on October 14, 1968, Musmanno was a Pennsylvania State Supreme Court Justice. He was buried in the Arlington National Cemetery with full military honors.

Permission to use selected interviews from the Musmanno Archives was granted by William F. Cercone, Judge, The Superior Court of Pennslyvania, who has jurisdiction of the files.

It will be noted that even in the years 1945–1948, shortly after the death of Adolf Hitler and Eva Braun, eyewitnesses to the events of history differed in dates, times and other facts. Each was convinced that his facts were correct and the facts of the others wrong.

MUSMANNO ARCHIVES: VOLUMES IV AND XII

Excerpts from Interviews with Frau Winter

(Hitler's Housekeeper at his Munich Apartment)

In answer to my question about how Hitler behaved towards Eva, Frau Winter said that he was very affectionate towards her when they were in the Munich apartment. He used to lecture her on smoking, telling her the bad effects of nicotine. Yet Eva chain-smoked.

* * * *

'Hitler did not like Emmy Göring. She acted too much the "high lady, i.e., the First Lady of the Reich". Hitler did not like such women who called themselves by the titles of their husbands.'

* * * *

Q. When did Eva come to live in the Munich apartment?

A. It was only during the war that she got a room at her disposal. And when, during the war, she did not want to go home or couldn't go home because of an air raid, she just stayed there. She had a villa nearby in Wasserburgerstrasse. She was either escorted home or she remained with the Führer.

* * * *

She herself [Frau Winter] took the newspaper to Geli in Hitler's Munich apartment the day Geli died. She did this every morning. At that time the apartment had not been remodeled and the one apartment had two families living there, in two wings. In one wing, she, her husband and the Führer were living and in the other another family. Geli had a room with them. Geli's door was locked that fateful morning and since she did not answer Frau Winter's knock, Frau Winter called the police. When the door was forced open, they found Geli had shot herself.

* * * *

Q. Who are the two children pictured with Eva Braun so often?

A. These two children are Frau Schneider's. Frau Schneider was a good friend of Eva.

Q. When did Eva go to Berlin for the final time?

A. Eva stayed in Munich until September and then she went to Berlin and was there all the time except for a few days at Christmas. Hitler did not stay in his field headquarters after July 20, 1944. He went to the Reich Chancellery. He stayed in the old Reich Chancellery in Berlin. Eva Braun stayed there, too, and had two or three rooms.

Q. Did you go to Berlin during that time at all?

A. No.

Q. Where are the parents of Eva Braun living? Are they still alive?

A. They lived in Rupoldingen, near Traunstein. Ilse, the older sister of Eva, who was married in Breslau, is in Munich. Gretl's address is Garmisch.

Q. Have you seen the Braun parents since the end?

A. Not since the end but previous to the end.

Q. What kind of work did Herr Braun do?

A. He was a post office inspector. Now he is an unskilled laborer in Rupoldingen.

Q. Do you know whether the parents benefited very much because of the relationship with Hitler? Did they get a nice home? Was Herr Braun treated well?

A. Eva was able to make them nice presents which the parents would not have had if he had to get them on his inspector's salary. They couldn't have afforded them. She could support them quite well and did.

Q. Did all the party leaders and government ministers know about the relationship between Hitler and Eva Braun?

A. Well, those close associates knew. The others suspected, however. She never took part in the party receptions or other affairs.

Q. Yes, but she was at the Berghof.

A. Yes, but on the Berghof there was only the intimate circle and, even there, she did not appear at the public receptions.

Q. Would that mean people like Göring, Ribbentrop, Himmler and Hess knew about her?

A. Göring was at the Berghof often; also Himmler and Ribbentrop. They knew.

Q. Were you ever told or was it said among those whom you know that you must never mention Eva Braun's association with Hitler?

A. No, never. It was not prohibited.

Q. It was just generally understood?

A. One did not discuss it quite automatically. Yet, it was not prohibited to talk about it.

Q. The mere fact that Hitler did not take her anywhere in public of itself indicated that he did not want any talk about her. Is that correct?

A. Maybe, yes. I never worried my head about it. She was there and that was that.

Q. But so far as the German people were concerned, Hitler did not want them to know that he was interested in any particular woman?

A. That's possible. Nobody knew that he was, either, not even in Munich. He did not want Eva in public because of the rumors. That proves to me that he wanted her for himself and that he did not wish the public to learn about her.

Q. Did Hitler receive other women in his apartment in Munich?

A. Oh, yes. He received many women but none of them stayed overnight except Eva Braun.

* * * *

MUNICH, WIEDENMAYERSTRASSE 43, SEPTEMBER 3, 1948 (*This interview was conducted for Musmanno by a Miss Billig* – AUTHOR'S NOTE)

After I left you in the cab going one way and I the other, I went to that boardinghouse recommended by Hotel Gruenwald but it seemed so strange, so indefinitely queer that I decided not to stay there. I asked the cab driver to take me to my sister's place. Since she was vacationing on the Lake of Constance I had the room to myself. Dumped down my things and went to Frau Winter's place to pick her up for dinner. I knew that she would never talk with Herr Bronner around her in the same manner that she would with me alone with a good dinner and a few glasses of wine inside her. Went to the Hotel Rosengarten and ordered dinner – goose, *hors d'oeuvres*, and wine. First of all, she said that the time was not yet right to discuss anything. However, after she had eaten she apparently felt better and settled down to a long speech. She said to me: 'Now I will tell you everything.'

First, she told me that she had been to the Brauns' lawyer in order to testify against the published diary of Eva Braun that Luis Trenker said was authentic. There she met Ilse Fucke-Michels who told her very crossly, 'Why did you have to talk about my sister's suicide attempt? Nobody knew about it. Anyway, the way you tell it is not true at all. It was quite different.' Frau Winter insisted to me that it happened just as she told the story, that the Führer had come to her after it happened and said, 'What a foolish thing to do. What shall I do now? I cannot have a scandal.'

Frau Winter said that she was angry with Ilse at the lawyer's office after she bawled her out about mentioning Eva's suicide attempt so she told Ilse that Eva had not been a good influence on Hitler. She said, 'After all, every woman has some influence if she is close to a man as Eva was close to Hitler and she should have influenced him about the things she knew were wrong.' Ilse was very angry at the remark.

Frau Winter said that it is so ridiculous for the Braun family to go and be de-Nazified by the Spruchkammer since, after all, Eva was their daughter, they associated with her and they profited quite a lot from this association. 'I am so furious when I hear what so many people say before the Spruchkammer now,' Frau Winter said. 'Some of them now say that when Hitler ordered them to go see him, they slammed the door when they went in so

258

that he would see how annoyed they were. Pooh! If I would tell what I know lots of them would get five or ten years in jail for how they acted. I remember quite a few people who begged me to make it possible for them to have an interview with the Führer. Almost whiningly they begged me. Now they say differently.'

Frau Winter says that for three months after Geli Raubal's death, hardly anyone could speak with Hitler. He was so embittered, so cross, that he was very unjust to everyone. He thought only of his grief. Then Hoffmann tried to take his mind off his grief and invited him to the theater, placing Eva Braun next to him on purpose. According to Frau Winter, when Hitler returned home from the theater he said: 'Well, they meant well. They placed the "little Braun" next to me and she prattled on and on all night. At least she took my mind off certain things.' And thus they went on meeting, Frau Winter said, until she got a room in his apartment.

I asked whether she knew if there was any truth to the story that Hitler would not allow Geli to marry anyone. 'Yes,' she said, 'that may be true. You see, when Geli came to us she was only 22 years old, but she looked younger and she was quite heavily built. The Führer did not want her to marry so young and, after all, he was in love with her himself. He never went out with anybody but Geli at that time. I am positive about that. She was not his right niece; she was the daughter of his half-sister and I believe he could have married her. At that time, however, he did not want to marry anyone.'

Before Geli appeared, Frau Winter explained, Hitler had a girl friend called Ada Klein. She was a very charming lady, also rather young, but when Hitler could not make up his mind to marry her, she married someone else. She married a certain Walther. She was very happy with him and both of them admired Hitler very much. In 1944, however, Ada Klein gave Frau Winter a letter to give to the Führer personally, warning Frau Winter not to allow the letter to fall into the hands of Martin Bormann. Frau Winter gave it to Hitler at the Berghof and they read it together. The letter stated: 'My Führer, you know that my husband and I admired and still admire you very much but we are nearing our end. This war is lost. That bad spirit around you, Bormann, ought to be removed. Unless you do that none of us see any hope for any improvement ever. We suppose you know all the things he has committed but unless he goes you are doomed and so are all of us.'

Frau Winter emphasized to Hitler that Bormann must not be shown the letter. Hitler agreed but that night he flew to Berlin. Frau Winter was worried that Hitler might have left the letter behind and she knew that if Bormann saw it Ada was doomed. So she rang Fräulein Wolfe and asked her to check among the Führer's correspondence to see if the letter was there. Fräulein Wolfe found it and immediately hid it from Bormann, returning the letter to Hitler when he returned from Berlin. When Hitler saw Frau Winter the next time, he thanked her for reminding him of the letter because, as he admitted, it would never have done to have Bormann read it. Frau Winter explained that she then told Hitler, 'Mein Führer, you really should get rid of that man. Why do you keep him?'

Hitler answered, 'Bormann is the only man I can trust to carry out my orders.'

Frau Winter added that the Führer may have meant that Bormann was the only man that would carry out the criminal orders that Hitler passed on to him.

Ada Klein had some girl friends, among whom were the sisters Epp. They were dancers in a Munich cabaret show and the Führer liked to go to the cabaret. He fell in love with Lola Epp who later married a certain Herr Berum, a Norwegian. They lived in Oslo. Later Lola returned from Oslo, divorced from her husband, and tried to get Hitler to marry her. Hitler had no interest in a divorced woman. Besides at that time he already had Eva. There were no more women in his life outside Eva Braun after the war started. Eva was not very intelligent. She was just a pretty doll. When she was with Hitler she talked about her friends, about the parties she had attended, about the artists she had talked with, and the film actresses and actors she knew. She never did any serious talking as far as Frau Winter knows and she often wondered how the Führer, who had a serious mind, could put up with Eva's conversation. Once she asked him and he said, 'Eva keeps my mind off things which I don't want to think about. She gives me a rest.'

After Hess had gone, then Bormann came into the picture. When Hess flew away, the Führer kept walking up and down the room, shaking his head and saying: 'I cannot understand it. After all, if he thinks he ought to put things right, why did he not discuss it with me first? Now I have not only lost a party comrade, I have lost a brother.' Frau Winter is of the opinion that Hess had a good influence on Hitler. They talked for hours sometimes. Hess was the only one who really stood up to the Führer and wasn't insulted when Hitler became furious and called him names. Then, when Bormann got into the picture, the Führer became different according to Frau Winter. He was not as jolly any longer. He was gloomy and often wouldn't talk. By the way, Frau Winter does not believe that Bormann is dead. She said that she wouldn't be surprised that if the Russians take over Germany, Bormann will be Commissar of Munich. She thinks that many people will not talk today because they fear that Bormann will return and take revenge if they do. Few believe that he is dead. Erich Kempka talked with Frau Winter and told her that he had tried to break out of Berlin with Bormann but he had been wounded and knocked unconscious. When he woke up again,

Bormann had vanished and he had presumed that he was dead. Others, however, think that Bormann made good his escape.

'That Bormann was evil all though,' Frau Winter insisted. 'I often told the Führer in the beginning what I heard about Bormann, the letters I received from people telling me how he was terrorizing the country. The Führer would ask Bormann in my presence about these matters and Bormann would deny them. Hitler would then ask his adjutants to investigate further but they were afraid of Bormann and would say that Bormann was innocent. They were all telling lies.

'I said to Hitler once when the towns were being so heavily bombed that he should go out and see all the misery and then he would stop the war.'

The adjutants came to her and warned her never to say anything like that to the Führer again. They said it would be much better if he did not see the towns. Frau Winter said that she didn't say anything to Hitler again because he always gave the order to somebody else to investigate what she told him and they, of course, told him wrongly. 'Perhaps,' she said, 'he knew it all but just wanted me to believe it was not true. If people say now that they could not talk to the Führer, the generals and adjutants who are saying that in the trials, they lie. One *could* talk to the Führer. I often talked to him. He was mistrusting and had things investigated by the wrong people but I could talk to him. I stopped telling him things, however, because I was tired of being called a liar all the time.'

In the spring of 1944 she was up at the Berghof. Eva had adjusted herself to her position. She was very 'high-hatted' sometimes, particularly with those she thought weak characters, according to Frau Winter. 'Once Frau Bormann was at the Berghof shortly after having a new baby. She was not feeling well but she had to stay up as long as the other guests. Eva asked for coffee, then for milk. Eva didn't like the milk so Gerda Bormann had to get her another glass of milk. Eva always had wishes,' Frau Winter explained. 'I finally told Frau Bormann to go to bed, that I would oversee things, but she said she did not dare to go to bed because her husband would be angry.'

When Frau Winter moved to help Frau Bormann, her husband said, 'A housewife has to stay up as long as the high guests are still up.'

Frau Winter vows that Eva must have seen the condition of Frau Bormann but she paid no attention and chased her around as much as she could. Frau Winter says she couldn't stand it any longer and left.

Frau Winter: 'Although Eva did not see too much of the Führer sometimes, he made up for this by spoiling her terribly. She could have everything and she took advantage of it. She was very prattling and childlike in his presence, sometimes even a bit subdued. When she was alone in Munich, however, or at the Berghof when the Führer was away, she threw one party after another. All her young friends came and she flirted terribly. She did everything she was not allowed to do – danced, drank, smoked. She had no inhibitions because of her position with Hitler. She often did things that were not right for her lover's position. Of course, only those around her knew it and they were afraid of her and would not tell Hitler. I heard a lot from her maids at the Berghof.

'Leni Riefenstahl loved the Führer deeply. Before her marriage she came to Munich often. I knew her well and she often cried when talking to me. She asked me whether she should marry the Führer or not. She loved him very much and even would have stayed with him as his "friend" but he did not ask her. She knew nothing about Eva and I did not tell her. All of a sudden Leni married this Jacob fellow. I think she still loved the Führer. He liked her but never paid much attention to her.

'I am sure that if the war had not come he would have gotten rid of Eva somehow. She loved a luxurious life and if he had paid her off or made it possible for her to live a comfortable life, she would have left him. But the war strengthened her position since she was the only one Hitler really trusted and she must have known a lot of those things we hear about now.'

Frau Winter then made the observation that she was always surprised that Hitler's girl friends all come from the lower or middle classes. He could surely have had better connections but somehow his taste didn't run that way. Perhaps they did not admire him enough.

(Frau Winter obviously did not like Eva Braun. She was jealous of any woman whom Hitler liked since she considered herself his 'favorite' – AUTHOR'S NOTE)

MUSMANNO ARCHIVES: Volume VII

*Interrogation of Gottlob Berger,
General of the Waffen-S.S*

NUREMBERG, APRIL 20, 1948, 2.00 p.m. (*Describing his meeting with Hitler in the Berlin bunker on the night of April 22, 1945 –* AUTHOR'S NOTE)

Q. Were you alone with Hitler?

A. Yes, Hitler was alone. Nobody was with him. Then came the much maligned Eva Braun. Please write this, too. I must stand up for this woman in one thing. It would not have been possible for me to take care of this prisoner-of-war matter if it wasn't for Eva Braun who always made it possible for one to approach Hitler from the back, so to speak.

Q. You mean Eva Braun made it possible?

A. Yes, made it possible for me to get to him unofficially. Burgdorf and Fegelein were absolutely masterful in keeping Hitler away from people and they had all made up their minds to get me responsible for this prisoner-of-war matter. That is, force me to comply with the order. Eva Braun came in with the written documents. That was the regular document paper with the heading 'Führer' and 'Reich Chancellor' and he signed them. His signature was strangely small. It consisted of mere periods which didn't hang together very well. And it was noticeable that the signature dropped down at an angle of forty-five degrees. I had these orders up to the ninth of May.

Q. And did those orders call for the execution of the prisoners-of-war?

A. Yes, those three orders. I showed these orders to General Patton.

Q. Well, how did Eva Braun help you in this case? You say that she was of assistance to you but she brought in the orders which were to further embarrass you?

A. I meant to say these orders were not dangerous. I could carry them out or not because between me and Adolf Hitler there were 650 kilometers.

Q. Now you used the phrase 'the much maligned Eva Braun'. What have you to say good about Eva Braun?

A. I didn't know her before I became chief of the SS main office. When I needed help, I asked her and she could be convinced if the reason was good. For instance, I always told her the following: 'My dear young lady, you are certainly concerned with seeing that Hitler enters into history as a decent man. Now a lot of blood has been shed. That is the human reason but I have a very realistic reason, too. I have drafted about 10,000 people into the Waffen-SS. Of course, the Western Powers now undertake to take reprisal measures and they are directed against the men of the Waffen-SS who were once drafted by me in order to use a last reservoir of elite troops against Bolshevism. People must despair of me. I can't do it.' And she always realized what I meant and she always managed to get me an interview with Hitler. Often I had to wait a long time in the bunker but I always got to see the Führer.

Q. Did she participate in Hitler's official life?

A. I didn't hear anything about it.

Q. Well, the fact that she would get you in to see Hitler on official matters would show that she had some interest in his official business.

A. You want to know whether she had an influence on him? Yes, at that time she definitely had an influence on him.

Q. Do you think she had a personal interest in Hitler's official life or was she concerned only about his personal and intimate companionship with him?

A. In my opinion this was a purely personal relationship because if she had been in on the official life, one would have heard of her sooner.

MUSMANNO ARCHIVES: VOLUME VII
Interview with Erich Kempka
(Hitler's Personal Chauffeur)

MUNICH, AUGUST 19, 1948

After I listened to Maja Kempka's remarks and complaints for several minutes, Erich Kempka finally came into the room. He heard his wife mention Henriette Hoffmann, the photographer's daughter, and Kempka immediately began talking about her, too. He told about the time Hoffmann's daughter, wife of Baldur von Schirach, asked Hitler at the Berghof: '*Mein Führer*, don't you think it is detrimental to my husband that he has only the title of Gauleiter in Vienna whereas here in the Third Reich he is the Reich's Youth Leader? Can't you do something about that?' Kempka said Hitler turned and walked away. He then called von Schirach to him and told him that unless his wife removed her 'warpaint' – silver eyelids and painted eyelashes – they would have to leave. And he told von Schirach that if he had any wishes concerning his position, he should not send his wife to plead his case for him.

I now asked Kempka what he knew about the various women around Hitler. He said that he had been driving for the Führer since 1932 and he had to say that there was never anything with women except Eva Braun and that only started officially in 1936 when Hitler's sister left the Berghof. At that time, Eva Braun became the official hostess at the Berghof with her apartment next to the Führer's apartment. However, when dignitaries arrived she was never seen. At those times she often slept in the Bechstein Haus or Bormann Haus on the Obersalzberg.

Kempka said that in 1932 they were driving up north during an election campaign and they met the Baroness Laffert who was a beautiful blonde girl of seventeen years. Hitler was fascinated by her and he exclaimed over and over in the car: 'She is beautiful, isn't she? Oh, she really is a beauty.' He invited her to Munich several times for tea but he never met with her alone. There was always an adjutant present. She was heard to remark by one adjutant that she was sick of the long tea hours and that all Hitler did was pat her hand. They finally parted.

Also in 1932 he first met Leni Riefenstahl. Hitler was very im-

264

pressed by her beauty and talent but they did not see each other very often.

Kempka said that as long as he drove Hitler – since 1932 – there was never a woman in Hitler's car except Eva Braun. Hitler took her home when they had been with Hoffmann which was not far from his Munich apartment. They acted very official. She got out of the car and the Führer wished her a good night's rest. She would say: 'Good night, my Führer. Sleep well.' And that was all. Kempka never saw Hitler kiss her or be affectionate to her. Kempka said that Hitler was very careful about his actions in public. At that moment Kempka's wife interrupted the interview and said, 'Oh, Erich, don't tell such lies. You were not the "public". Why don't you tell that after you put the car away, Hitler would walk back to the door where she was waiting for him?' Her husband just smiled.

Kempka said that Christa Schröder liked to drink cognac. One night late in April, 1945, after she had downed a considerable amount of cognac, she came down the steps in the bunker with a large pile of letters and said she had cleared the Führer's desk. One letter Frau Kempka remembered was a letter from an artist friend who wanted to marry Geli Raubal and he wrote that she should leave her uncle, that he was a despot and a tyrant and that he had no right to keep her. She should marry him and they would leave Germany. He would take her to Argentina. Another letter of Hitler's to Geli revealed that he couldn't marry her because he had to sacrifice for his people but he wanted to keep her. Frau Kempka stated that she thinks Geli knew something was 'going on' between Hitler and Eva Braun and that made her desperate after being told that he must live only for his people. So she shot herself.

According to Kempka, Eva's mother told him that she had only learned about this going on between her daughter and Hitler one year later when her daughter came to her and told her if they did not like it, she would leave. Eva told her mother that she could never leave Hitler. Fanny Braun told Kempka that she was not at the Berghof very often. The last time she was there was when her daughter Gretl married Fegelein. She then realized and noticed how ill Hitler appeared. Frau Braun also told Kempka that shortly before Christmas, 1943, she had been staying at the Berghof and since she loved sleeping and needed a lot of rest, it was difficult for her to stay up late and listen to Hitler talk. The Führer heard about it and told her not to mind him but to go to bed early. He then said to her, 'Oh, I wish I could sleep only for once two hours at a stretch.'

(*Erich Kempka has given many versions of his association with Hitler but because this interview was made shortly after the end*

MUSMANNO ARCHIVES: VOLUME IV
Interview with Gerda Christian
(Hitler's Secretary)

BERCHTESGADEN, JANUARY 26, 1948

Q. How did Eva Braun conduct herself towards the end? Was she brave?

A. Yes, she was brave and made no trouble.

Q. Were Hitler and Eva Braun married?

A. Yes. On April 28th there was the wedding late in the evening about midnight.

Q. The wedding? Was there any ceremony?

A. No ceremony. We had an invitation to go to Hitler's private room. Goebbels, two secretaries, Bormann, some generals. That was all.

Q. Who performed the ceremony?

A. The marriage registrar. But I was not there — only the registrar, Bormann and Goebbels. I saw them later, half-an-hour or so, for a few minutes.

Q. Did you congratulate them?

A. No. I said nothing because his wedding meant his death day. It was not the same as is usual with weddings. I could not say, 'I wish you all the best from my heart.' It was a death wedding.

Q. So that wedding was not very hilarious, was it? Not very gay? No drinking champagne?

A. Oh yes, I drank some champagne.

Q. Did they have champagne?

A. We had enough.

Q. I do not see that even with the fact that it meant death that there could be no happiness about it.

A. We were happy. If I drink three glasses of champagne then it is not like a funeral, let me tell you. Hitler never drank alcohol. I saw him drink some sweet wine. Not often, though. He did not smoke either and he never ate meat.

Q. Well, you say that the wedding was on the night of the 28th at about midnight.

A. Yes, and we had a gathering and we had a meal together.

Q. What was his attitude?

A. He talked about former times. He had been a witness to Goebbels' wedding and they discussed things which happened during Goebbels' time when he got married and he told about the war time when he was a soldier. He also said that it was his greatest wish to live near Linz, his home town. He had looked for a place where he would build his home and his great wish was to live there during the last years.

Q. Then about 4.00 p.m. on April 30th Hitler called you to the bunker corridor?

A. Yes, near his map room, in the conference passage.

Q. Did he say anything?

A. He just said 'goodbye'. He did not say *Auf Wiedersehn*.

Q. The word 'goodbye' is sad.

A. Yes. We told him we were not going to take the poison, that we wanted to get out. I told him that before. He ordered SS Obergruppenführer Mohne to take care of us and help us get out of the bunker.

Q. He did not expect you to commit suicide? Was it not his attitude that because he did so, the others should do the same?

A. No.

Q. Was Eva Braun with him? Did she speak?

A. She only said 'farewell'.

Q. What was his expression? Just solemn, not sad?

A. He was very solemn.

Q. And how was Eva Braun?

A. She was very pale but she was composed.

Q. How was she dressed?

A. She wore a black dress.

Q. Did you know Fegelein? Do you think he was treated badly?

A. Yes. He was killed because of Bormann. I do not know what Bormann had against him but it was typical of Bormann.

Q. What I do not understand is: If Hitler loved Eva Braun and Eva Braun was the sister of Fegelein's wife, why did she not help?

A. Hitler had the opinion that Fegelein was a traitor.

Q. Was Fegelein a traitor? Did he try to run away?

A. Perhaps. He belonged to Himmler, not Hitler.

MUSMANNO ARCHIVES: Volume XI

Interrogation of Heinrich Hoffmann

(Hitler's Photographer)

Nuremberg, July 19, 1948

Q. What is your full name?

A. Hoffmann, Heinrich.

Q. What is your permanent address?

A. Munich, Klugstrasse 47.

Q. Your daughter is married to Baldur von Schirach?

A. Yes.

Q. When did you first meet Hitler?

A. 1923.

Q. Where was this?

267

A. This was in Munich.

Q. And what were the circumstances under which you met him?

A. I was a press photographer trying to get his picture.

Q. When did Eva Braun come to work for you?

A. It must have been in 1929 or 1930.

Q. How did she happen to come to you for employment?

A. She came to me as every other girl offering her services as an assistant. She didn't know very much. She had been educated in a convent. After leaving the convent she had been trained for typing and bookkeeping. Then she came to me, quite a simple girl, to sell cameras. I had such a shop at the time.

Q. This was in Munich in 1929?

A. Yes.

Q. And was she very capable in the store?

A. Not especially, not outstanding.

Q. Was she a very attractive girl?

A. She was a very pretty girl, a 'chocolate beauty'.

Q. I don't understand the expression. What is a 'chocolate beauty?'

A. Sweet. Pretty in a sweet way.

Q. Blonde?

A. Blonde.

Q. When did Hitler first meet her?

A. It is difficult to say. Maybe around 1930, shortly after she came to me.

Q. Tell us the circumstances of this meeting.

A. Hitler saw her in my office and he talked to her for a few minutes. When he saw her the next time, he gave her some tickets to the theatre. Finally he invited her to go and see him.

Q. Where? Berghof?

A. In Munich, in his apartment. He was rather strict in that way. Someone else had to be present.

Q. Somebody in addition to Eva Braun?

A. Yes.

Q. A man or woman?

A. A chaperone. He was very cautious in those things at that time.

Q. In 1933 he was already Chancellor.

A. Yes, but that didn't matter in Munich because there he was always a private man. He never allowed anybody to take away his private life. Later, he went to the Obersalzberg and invited her there when he went down for a week-end.

Q. When did he first begin to receive her as a particular friend?

A. A particular friend? That all developed so slowly it is difficult to say.

Q. When did she stop working for you?

A. 1945.

Q. Come now, let's deal in facts.

A. April, 1945.

Q. Don't you know, Herr Hoffmann, that she was living with Hitler in Berlin in April, 1945?

A. She didn't get notice . . . I want to add something which seems important to me in order to clear this up so that we can understand it. I have got to tell it as you want to know it correctly. For practical purposes, she never left employment with me but when Hitler was on the Obersalzberg, she got leave for that time in order to be present at the Berghof. Only during the last years Hitler asked her to come to Berlin to see him. She was assigned to my shop always.

Q. I don't understand why you say she was 'assigned?'

A. When the compulsory labor assignment for women started, she was 'assigned' to my business.

Q. Did you see Eva Braun on your last visit to the bunker?

A. Yes, she was with us.

Q. Was she at the 3.00 a.m. tea party?

A. Yes, of course, and maybe one secretary and an adjutant. I think about four people. No generals or anybody like that. Only his intimate circle.

Q. Now, when Hitler first met Eva Braun did he show any interest in other women?

A. He liked women really. He was very attentive to them all.

Q. Did he go out with other women?

A. Not publicly, only privately.

Q. Do you know Eva Braun's parents?

A. Yes.

Q. Do you know the family?

A. Yes.

Q. Where is the family now?

A. Rupoldingen.

Q. Where is Gretl Braun?

A. I am not sure.

Q. You know that a diary has been published supposedly written by Eva Braun?

A. That Trenker diary is a lie from beginning to end. Everything.

(This is only a part of several interviews with Hoffmann. His testimony varied greatly from time to time — AUTHOR'S NOTE)

MUSMANNO ARCHIVES: VOLUMES III AND XI
Excerpts of Interviews with Traudl Junge

MUNICH, FEBRUARY 7 AND JULY 25, 1948

Q. Was Eva Braun overcome with emotion in any way during her last farewell meeting?

A. She was touched, moved, but not overwhelmed. She told me before, 'I am terribly frightened.' She told me this when we were alone. She kept up appearances for the others as if she was very much composed.

Q. Did you have the impression that she was really terrified? She was willing to do this but, on the other hand, had she all the fear that goes with a child crying in the dark?

A. Eva Braun was a woman who enjoyed life, loved to live, loved to laugh, loved beautiful things, beautiful clothes. I can really say that she loved life. Eva Braun was not the standardized National Socialist woman who had fought for any of the party ideas. She was only Hitler's follower because of his personality and only interested in him as a man.

Q. She was not concerned about the ideology of National Socialism?

A. No, not in the real sense of the word. She did live with the same ideas that Hitler did. She was, for instance, completely unpolitical. She never allowed any racial or political ideas to influence her in her relationship with Hitler.

Q. Was Hitler affectionate with Eva Braun?

A. At times. One evening Fegelein came down to the Berchtesgaden Hof and said that he was absolutely sick. We asked him what was the matter and he said, 'Oh, I had dinner with Gretl [his wife] and Eva and the Führer. The way Eva and the Führer are carrying on is sickening. They act as if they were a young cock and a hen.' When they were in a small circle he was usually very affectionate. He patted her hand, calling her 'my *patscherl*' which means 'my pet' in Viennese [sic]. He always urged her to eat this or that, saying, 'Now, my *patscherl*, eat this little morsel that is good for you' or 'have a little more of this or that.' She did not know anything about the military situation. Sometimes she would come to us secretaries and ask, 'Do tell me what is going on. He never tells me anything.' But in his private life she influenced him insofar as she told him what people to invite and what people she did not like to come.

Q. Did he like other women?

A. He had a foible for Frau Christian. He used to call her 'Dara'. But he never approached her closer than patting or kissing her hand. Frau Christian tried hard to get nearer to him but she did not succeed.

Q. Was Hitler emotional? Did you ever see him cry, for instance?

A. He cried twice to my knowledge. The occasion when Eva Braun said she intended to stay with him in the bunker until the end and the second time was after the wedding.

Q. Was there rivalry between Eva Braun and Frau Goebbels?

A. In what connection? Because of Hitler?

Q. Well, after all, Eva Braun must have regarded herself as the most important woman in Hitler's life and perhaps Frau Goebbels was jealous?

A. Eva Braun and Frau Goebbels only met when they ate with Hitler and that was on the Obersalzberg where Eva Braun was the mistress. There was no talk about rivalry and could not be since Frau Goebbels was only a guest.

Q. There is a story that Hitler refused to invite Frau Goebbels to parties because of her antipathy to Eva Braun.

A. At the time I was there I never heard anything of that. True, Eva Braun was not happy with Frau Goebbels. Maybe she had an inferiority complex because of Frau Goebbels. I don't know.

Q. How was Eva Braun dressed the night of the wedding?

A. She wore the dress which was Hitler's favorite. A black afternoon dress without sleeves, pink shoulder straps, two roses at the neck, a square neck and, over the dress, a little coat with long sleeves. The dress had a waist section and a wide skirt. It was made of dull silk. She wore black suede shoes with modern wedge heels, a kind of evening shoe, sandal form. In her hair she wore a clip, I believe of gold, and she wore a necklace but I can't remember what it looked like.

Q. Was she dressed the same on the day of her death?

A. I do not recall that. Maybe it was the same. In fact, she probably was since she had sent most of her dresses away. She had sent her things to Munich and the Obersalzberg.

Q. She could not have done that during the last two or three days because there was no way out. It must have been some time before.

A. I do not remember when she sent her dresses away. She sent her jewelry out on April 22 or 23 when she made up her mind to stay in Berlin so that her parents would have something to live on after the war.

MUSMANNO ARCHIVES: VOLUME IV
Excerpt of Interview with Julius Schaub

GARMISCH, MARCH 22, 1948

Q. Did Eva have any influence on Hitler?

A. Eventually Eva represented a certain power in the private circle of Hitler. If someone aroused her anger, woe to them. Eva didn't keep her criticism hidden even before Hitler. Her judgement on certain matters was respected in that circle of house guests in which she was authoritative. Yet, this influence was completely internal and had neither an effect on Hitler's decisions nor on his development. She could have, if she desired, used her influence with Hitler for many an order of good sense and humanity or against many a nonsensical order but Eva used her possibilities only seldom. It is too bad because she had a good influence on Hitler.

Eva's influence was limited to superficial things, however. When, during the war, women and girls began wearing long pants on the street, there was a great outcry from some German 'intellectuals'. The district Nazi leader of Garmisch banned the pants and Eva called the order to Hitler's attention. The Führer was furious, called it a ridiculous order. He said, 'How many women are there today who as air raid wardens meet catastrophe and danger like a man? Should I approach these women and tell them they can't wear pants?'

At once Bormann had to take care of the matter. That same night the responsible official of Garmisch, who lived in the neighborhood of Munich, was awakened from his sleep and had to make the situation right at once.

Similarly cutting into the personal rights of women was the ban by the Party office of the use of electric hairdryers by hairdressers. This was done to save electricity. Nor were the hairdressers permitted to color hair. Eva brought this silly saving measure to the attention of Hitler and he had the order rescinded at once.

'On the contrary,' said Hitler. 'Every woman should please her husband coming home on leave with a cared-for appearance. Unfortunately she will have enough to do to hide her prematurely gray hair as a result of the terrible events of the war. The gentlemen in the War Ministry are poor psychologists if they make the women, on whom everything depends, bitter through such nonsensical regulations.'

MUSMANNO ARCHIVES: VOLUME IV
Interview with Herr Braun and Frau Braun
(Eva Braun's parents)

RUPOLDINGEN, GERMANY (NEAR TRAUNSTEIN, SCHWABENBAUER) SEPTEMBER 4, 1948

Arrived at Rupoldingen at 9.00 a.m. and went to the Braun family residence. Herr Braun there, too, having arrived the previous night from Munich, where he had been to see the lawyer because of his daughter's alleged diary. I gave him the rest of the whiskey and he was very happy about it. He drank and drank and talked and talked so that I did not have much chance to talk to Frau Braun. When she mentioned that she did not have the money to go to Garmisch, I invited her to come along with me. I told her that I would pay all the expenses.

Herr Braun told me: 'I was a teacher at a technical school and only in 1936 did I become an assistant master of that school. The affair with Eva and the Führer had already been going on for some years. When this affair started, I had gone to the administrators for school affairs and I had told them that I was the father of the Führer's mistress and that I thought it was not right that I stayed in civil service. I was ashamed of my daughter's position. We come from a decent family, and when my daughter said to me when I asked her if it was true that she was the Führer's mistress: "Yes, and what about it? If you don't like it, I shall go." I was shocked. She was still at home at that time.'

Herr Braun said that he begged her to leave Hitler, to bring home any man, the poorest and the most simple one, and he would accept him, but not Hitler. Eva would not listen. He said that he did not want any further hostility between himself and his daughter when she refused to give up her romance with Hitler, so he kept quiet but continued to check on her. Before he became assistant master of the school, they said to him: 'Braun, you are a foreign body in our school. You must join the Nazi party.'

Herr Braun: 'You see, as ridiculous as it may seem, I was not a party member then. I disliked politics and my wife did, too, and we did not like Hitler because my wife's father was so much against him. Eva always wanted us to turn on the radio and listen to Hitler's speeches, because he was so wonderful, but we ignored her. We thought it was just a flapper's admiration, the same as all women liked him and fell for him. At that time we never listened to him, but later I did listen to some of his speeches and I saw how the unemployment was eliminated. I thought this was good, so when I was asked to join the Nazi party I made an application. At first they would not accept me because politically I was unreliable. Later I was accepted and then I was promoted to assistant master of the school.'

I asked him when he first learned about Eva's friendship with the Führer.

Herr Braun: 'Well, Frau Braun had better tell it.'

Frau Braun: 'We had taken our cars to Berchtesgaden, some friends, my husband and I. Formerly, Eva and Gretl always joined us, but they had changed. They no longer travelled with us. Eva was always talking about the Führer and admiring him, but I didn't think anything bad of it. That was in 1933, shortly after the seizure of power. We were in Berchtesgaden and suddenly I suggested that we go and see the Haus Wachenfeld on the Obersalzberg. People were talking so much about this place and I was curious. We drove up. And I must say I was very disappointed, for it was just a small house, nothing like later. Hitler had bought it when he was younger. Many people were standing

273

in front of the house, shouting that they wanted to see "our Führer". Well, I didn't want to see him, so I suggested we leave. When we came to Lambach, the roads were blocked off by the SS and we had a hard time getting through. The SS men said that the Führer was coming. We stopped at the Lambacher Hof for coffee, and just as we got out of our car, a large car drove up to the door of the Lambacher Hof. Eva stepped from the car with another girl. I rubbed my eyes. I thought I had not seen right. I went up to her and said: "Eva, you? What are you doing in this car." And my husband came up, too, and said to her very harshly, "Where have you come from and what does this mean?" She looked at us and said very flippantly, "I come from the Obersalzberg." She then walked past us and went into the Lambacher Hof. My husband wiped his forehead. Suddenly, another car drove up and the Führer got out of it. I stepped back into the crowd.'

Herr Braun: 'I went up to Hitler and said: "I am Eva's father." I waited for him to give me some explanation, but he only said: "Where is your Frau Gemahlin?" I looked for her but I couldn't find her. When I finally did locate her she said she felt so ashamed. She wanted to leave immediately.'

Frau Braun: 'I suddenly knew why Eva had talked so much about the Führer and why she always urged us to believe in him. As her mother, I now sensed that she was his friend, close to him.'

Suddenly, an adjutant came out when they were on the point of leaving and called loudly: 'The Braun parents, please!'

Frau Braun: 'I stamped my foot and said that I did not want to go in. But my husband convinced me that it would be better to do so.'

The Führer had vacated a chair next to his and Frau Braun sat down. He shook hands with her, standing up while she came in, and was seated. He talked of little things, nothing of importance . . . about the countryside, the cakes, the tea. He never looked at her directly. She noticed that he felt embarrassed and acted rather awkward. He said *Du* to Eva and that, of course, made it even clearer to Frau Braun that Hitler and her daughter were close. He was very attentive to Frau Braun, but while she waited for some serious words, some explanation, she never received them. When they broke up, Hitler dismissed everybody but kept Frau Braun with him. He walked her to the door after everyone else had left, not speaking, but before they passed through the door he took her hand, squeezed it three times very very hard, and looked at her.

Frau Braun: 'He looked straight through me as if he could look into my very soul. He never spoke a word. There was embarrassment and yet admiration in his eyes. We then left and Eva didn't say goodbye to us even. She just rode off with the Führer's column.'

At that time Eva was still living at home, and when she got home that night her father was very angry. When he asked her again if it was true that she was the Führer's mistress, Eva said that she was and 'if you don't like it I will leave'. According to Frau Braun's story, Eva moved out a short time later to a *Haeuserl* (little room) in Wasserburgstrasse. Herr Braun would not go there for some time, but when his wife told him that it was better to go there occasionally and be on good terms so that if she needed help they would know it, he agreed to go. Later they had tea with Eva almost every Saturday or Sunday. The mother was there more often than Herr Braun. Frau Braun was also at the Berghof quite often.

Herr Braun: 'When the Americans came at the end of the war, I was a major in the German Army, on the administrative staff of the hospitals. The Americans photographed me and they asked me why I was not a general. That surprised me. A few days later some other Americans came and they were very mean. They ordered all the good food and drink available. When I told them that if I gave all the food and drink to them the patients would not have much left, the officer in charge was very angry. He told me to shut up and get the stuff. I then told the officer that before I did anything I wanted him to know that I was Hitler's father-in-law. The American officer gasped and went out to talk with some others. They went away and I was not bothered anymore.'

Later, Frau Braun was arrested and locked up for three weeks. The Braun apartment in Traunstein was requisitioned.

Herr Braun: 'All the worries our children have given us. Ilse got divorced and then married the Reichgau leader of Breslau. That is, he married her thinking he would have a better chance for promotion if he married Eva's sister. Gretl went off and married that Fegelein whom we did not know and whom we disliked intensely when we saw him. And then Eva, of all girls!'

Herr Braun was very worried about his pension. He had forty years civil service and now they don't want to give him his pension.

Herr Braun: 'After all, I couldn't help it if Eva had a relationship with the Führer. I would much rather she had married some decent poor man.'

We then had to leave for Garmisch. At Traunstein we had lunch and I gave Frau Braun some wine, which made her rather hilarious. She began reminiscing about the good times she had with her daughter. I really don't know where to start with all the stories and episodes she told me. According to her own story, she never discussed these things with anybody before and she didn't want these stories to be misused. I assured her that nothing of the sort would happen. She said the Führer was always full of respect for her, but somehow she felt that he was embarrassed in her presence, that he realized that he was not doing right, not according to his own preachings.

When at the Berghof, she always sat at his right and Eva at his left. All the people thought that he was enjoying himself when he was at the Berghof, but she said that this was not so, that he worked most of the time. She and Eva saw him for the first time during meal hours – at lunch first. Then again in the afternoon for tea and in the evening at 9.00 p.m. or 10.00 p.m., usually for dinner.

Frau Braun: 'He was very thoughtful and considerate with Eva, and after lunch he always said to her: "And what is my *Patscherl* going to do now?" He was always stroking her hand. When he was reluctant to go for a walk, Eva would say: "It would please me so much and it would be good for you." Hitler would try to get out of it by looking down the table and saying to Dr Morell or Dr Brandt: "Doctor, what do you think I should do?" And Morell or Brandt would say: "Do you have any appointments?" Then Eva would interrupt and say: "No, don't try to get out of it." Usually Morell or Brandt would then agree that Hitler should go for a walk, and he did.'

Hitler would go up to the teahouse and back and then he would start work again. Eva took a two-hour walk every day, climbing and walking along until the two hours were up. That was a strict rule with her, and when Frau Braun was at the Berghof she insisted that she go along.

Frau Braun: 'Once the snow was so high, up to my knees, that I told Eva I could not continue the walk any longer. I was exhausted. Eva looked at her watch and said that we only had fifteen minutes longer, so I had to struggle through the snow with her until the two hours were up. But she enjoyed these walks.

'The Führer allowed Eva every pleasure. He wanted her to enjoy herself. She could buy what she wanted and she loved clothes. Whenever she had a new dress, she showed it to me, watching my face as I examined it to get a hint of whether I liked the dress or not.'

According to Frau Braun, Eva seldom went to a beauty shop. She did everything herself, including her hair, except when it needed bleaching. Then the hairdresser came. She used camomile baths to steam her face and other home helps to help stay beautiful for Hitler. Often, before she would leave her villa in Munich for the drive to the Berghof, Eva would wash her hair, put it in curlers, tie a scarf around it, and allow the hair to dry in the car during the trip.

Frau Braun admitted that in later years her daughter became more 'bossy' and sometimes arrogant.

Frau Braun: 'She loved to order her maid about. Sometimes, when we were going to the Berghof from Munich, she would order Paula, her maid, to pack sandwiches, tea, and chicken although she knew we would not eat it. The trip was too short. She just wanted to order the maid around. Frau Mittelstrasser was the female majordomo at the Berghof, and when there were large receptions there Eva did not bother about anything. She ordered Frau Mittelstrasser to take care of everything. She also had all the dresses made for the servants. She designed the dresses herself and she was there when the dressmaker tried them on the servants. She was strict with the servants and the dressmaker.'

In 1938 or 1939, Frau Braun said, Eva, Gretl, and she made a voyage to the North Cape on the ship *Milwaukee*. At that time, Eva had bought a lovely musk coat which was made in Munich. It was an evening coat with a little train, very soft and fluffy, and wide sleeves with a little tight edge on it. She wore it during the trip. The first three days Frau Braun got very seasick.

Frau Braun: 'When I was seasick, Eva said to me that if she got seasick she would not stay on the ship one day. She said she would telephone the Führer and he would send his seaplane for her. He would have, too. They had beautiful things on that ship. For breakfast alone there was a menu with eighty different things on it. We ate a lot but Eva never got heavier than one hundred pounds. If she weighed more than one hundred pounds she immediately went on a diet. She teased everyone on the ship. They had lovely parties. The Führer called every day. He always did regardless of where Eva went. If she was in Italy or up north, he rang every day. That's why she enjoyed her trips so much, because she knew where he was and what he was doing. He told her and she told him these things.'

Frau Braun said that when there were big receptions Hitler always invited four or five beautiful women. Once Eva asked whether, just this one time, she could attend and mix among the crowd. Hitler said: 'No, you cannot. You are too good for these people.' Frau Braun thought this was because Hitler wanted to keep her daughter as his little treasure, locked up from everybody so that nobody might soil her with his glances. When there was a large reception or party at the Berghof of an official nature, Hitler would send Eva to Bormann's or Speer's or Göring's home to stay until it was over.

Frau Braun sometimes heard rumors, and when she asked Eva why she had not told her mother, Eva would say: 'Oh, *Mutti*, I did not think it would interest you and, anyhow, there are some things which I will not tell to anybody.' Frau Braun is of the opinion that Eva knew some things were perhaps not as they should be, but she wanted to keep up appearances and did not want people to know that not all was as well as they believed. When Herr Braun was asked about his daughter's attempt to commit suicide, he got all flustered.

Herr Braun: 'There is nothing to the story.'

Frau Braun: 'Where did you learn about that? Nobody, but nobody, knows about that.'

Herr Braun: 'Oh well, I heard that Frau Winter told about it at Nuremberg. I heard about it from Ilse, but there is nothing to it. After Hitler's niece had committed suicide, Eva got hold of my Browning and then it went off. I asked her what she had done because she had fetched it from my night table. She said she had wanted to see what a thing like that which Geli had shot herself with looked like and it went off. There was no safety catch on it. That's all there is to it. It was not serious. She was up and about in no time. The Führer sent her beautiful roses and she soon got well.'

Often, Eva, Frau Braun, and Gretl went to Italy. They loved Italy. Once they went further south and they took a lot of clothes. They had innumerable trunks and among them they had thirty-seven pairs of shoes. When they had to change trains, everybody laughed at their large amount of luggage. They did not take a maid along, but went alone. Gretl would hand the suitcases out of the train window, Eva received them, and Frau Braun piled them on the platform until the porter came along with his handwagon. They used to go by sleeper, and one night somebody knocked at the door. It was the customs people. They were crossing the border. Eva and her mother shared a sleeper, Eva sleeping in the upper bed and her mother in the lower. Eva hated sleeping with somebody in a room since she could not bear to hear others breathe. She claimed she never heard her mother, however. They got up, put on their dressing gowns, and when the officials came in the hood on Eva's gown fell over her eyes as she fumbled for her luggage keys. She brushed it back, but every time she bent over to insert the key in the lock, the hood fell over her eyes again.

Frau Braun: 'I laughed and laughed. It took Eva so long that the custom officials finally gave up and left us alone. We went back to sleep.'

Eva and her mother used to sunbathe, swim, and dance a lot, but their main pleasure was shopping. Once they had some extra lira which they did not want to take back to Germany from Italy, so they decided to buy Italian stockings. They always sent Gretl into the store first because she spoke Italian. This time Gretl asked to see Italian silk stockings, but the saleswoman leaned over and said: 'Don't buy the Italian silk stockings. They are no good. It is better you buy the German "Elbee" stockings.'

These were the best silk stockings in Germany, which were exported to Italy. So they bought the German stockings.

Frau Braun: 'We thought it was a good joke on us. We went to Italy to buy German silk stockings.'

On their return trips to Germany from Italy, they always feared the customs because they had bought so many things which had to be declared. So Eva usually put her purchases into her mother's suitcase.

Frau Braun: 'She said that since I was an older lady they would treat me politely, that they wouldn't expect to find such finery in my luggage.'

Most of the time, however, Eva would telephone Hitler and he would send an SS man to the border to meet them.

Frau Braun: 'The SS man would talk to the customs people and, after a while, we would be allowed to pass through without paying any duty on the things.'

When the *Anschluss* united Austria and Germany, Eva rang her mother and asked her if she would accompany her to the border. She wanted to see what was going on. The mother agreed and Eva sent her car and off they drove to Salzburg. They did not intend to drive any further, so they did not take anything, not even a handbag. No toothbrush or money. When they came to Salzburg, they heard that the Führer had gone on to Linz to visit his parents' graves. They wanted to catch up with him because Eva wanted to see him. When they came into Linz, they learned he had just left the city and had gone to Vienna. Eva said: 'How about it, *Mutti*? Shall we go to Vienna?'

Frau Braun: 'I said I would go, but what about the driver? Eva said that the driver Junge could go on if he had a big meal. So she sent him into a restaurant and he had a big meal and we went on to Vienna that same night. We arrived in Vienna at 4.30 a.m. and the Viennese were simply potty with happiness. When our big Mercedes drove into town, the population opened the car door, pulled Eva out, and kissed and hugged her. They didn't know who she was, but we were Germans and they were showing us how they felt about the *Anschluss*.'

They learned that the Führer had gone to the Hotel Imperial, so they drove to another hotel. The hotel manager received them and gave them a suite, asking for their luggage.

Frau Braun: 'Eva quickly said that the luggage was in a following car. Actually we had nothing. We telephoned the porter and asked him to buy us soap and toothbrushes. He only got us one toothbrush.'

The following morning Eva rang the Hotel Imperial and asked for the Führer. The adjutant said to her: 'Oh, there will be a row because of your escapade.' Then the Führer came to the phone. He scolded her terribly, for Eva was very red in the face, and then she stamped her feet and said: 'Don't go on scolding me so much. It was not dangerous at all and, anyhow, *Mutti* is with me. She is standing right here beside me.' Apparently, the Führer told Eva how dangerous it was, for he had no idea how the Austrians would receive him at the border. It might not have been so joyful. It might have been the other way around, and after Eva told him that her mother was with her, the Führer said:

'She ought to have more sense than her daughter,' and he got more angry.

Frau Braun: 'Anyway, he sent for Eva and she went to his hotel. I went over later and just before lunch the adjutant came and brought Eva a check. When we had just started to eat, the adjutant came back and told Eva that Hitler was flying back to Berlin, that if she wanted to go she would have to leave at once. She put down her fork and left immediately. I called after her, telling her that I had no money and asking her what I should do. She had put the check the adjutant gave her in her coat pocket. She didn't even answer me, but apparently she gave the adjutant instructions because he later returned and handed me a check. I was able to pay for everything and stay a few more days in Vienna. And I had a lovely time.'

She said that when they were in Munich or in Berchtesgaden the Führer would often send his special train to take Eva up for a day or two. That was done very quietly. Hardly anyone noticed it, but Frau Braun knew. Hitler did not like Eva to make the trip by car or plane for fear she might get hurt.

Frau Braun said that when the Führer telephoned her Eva would always tell him her plans. He did not mind that she had big parties. He liked her to enjoy herself. Often there would be many young men flirting with her and she would go to her mother and tell Frau Braun to order them away.

Frau Braun: 'Eva was sometimes rather abrupt with me or to the maids. Later, she felt sorry. When she was abrupt to me on the telephone, within fifteen minutes she would sent me some beautiful roses or other flowers. Sometimes, when she scolded a maid, she would then spoil her unreasonably in an effort to make up for her temper.'

When I asked Frau Braun whether Eva ever showed any affection or sentimentality over the Führer, she said: 'No, Eva was not that kind of a girl. She was not sentimental and she would never show her feelings in the presence of other people. Hitler was very affectionate to her in his close circle, but not when there were many people. She never talked about her intimate relationship with him. She only told me, when the subject was broached, "There are certain things I just cannot tell." '

During the years just before the war and during the war, Eva never spent Christmas at home. Every year, eight days before Christmas, she arranged a party in her house in Munich. Her big bedroom was deprived of its furniture for this purpose and the room was festively decorated. She sang the song *Stille Nacht, Heilige Nacht* ('Silent Night') which Bormann had forbidden to be sung in all churches and schools. Eva said it would be sung in her house, and it was. All the servants and friends of Eva came in and got their presents, which she had wrapped personally. She also sent Christmas parcels to all the shop people who served her.

On Christmas Eve she went to the Berghof and decorated the hall, did the Christmas tree, and on Holy Eve she had all the families, all the servants, and all the children from the Obersalzberg come in for their Christmas. There again she gave presents to all of them. Every year she wore the same white dress.

Frau Braun: 'I asked her why she was never with Hitler on Christmas and she answered: "Leave be, *Mutti*. He had such a horrible Christmas when he was a young boy that he never wants to celebrate Christmas again. He must be alone at Christmas time." '

When, one day, Frau Braun was having tea in the teahouse on the Obersalzberg, Hitler, as usual, offered her the cake and cookies. He took them away from the waiter and handed them to her, piling her plate up high with all the things she particularly liked, saying: 'Now, madam, this is very good, you must try this, and how about that?' Her plate was so full she could hardly eat it all. Then, on that particular occasion, he said to her: 'Try my tea, it is tea made of apple peels and is really very good.' And he ordered another cup for her so she could try his tea. And Frau Braun said to Frau Mittelstrasser afterwards that the tea really was not so bad after all. Frau Mittelstrasser grinned and said: 'Don't you ever tell, because he doesn't know it, but the tea is not made of apple peels. It is real tea with some apple wine in it. It is Eva's idea.'

Frau Braun: 'I was always surprised that the Führer ate such a lot. He used to take a second helping of everything. If, for instance, he had a vegetable pudding – all kinds of vegetables steamed together and plenty of sauce – it was always served in such a way that he could take one helping on his plate, one helping prepared in such a way as to make a mould for his plate. He took first one, then the second one.

'One day we were having pork. I was pleased because I had not eaten pork in a long time. When I told the Führer, he said: "I wish I could eat it, too." I told him that I didn't think one dumpling, which was served with the pork, would do him any harm. The Führer looked down the table to Dr Morell and asked: "Morell, do you think I could eat one dumpling?" Morell looked at the dumpling and shook his head. "No, *mein Führer*, you better not. Afterwards you will have pain again." The Führer turned to me and asked me if I had heard what Dr Morell said. I nodded, but actually I don't see how anything could have been wrong with his stomach because he always had such a big appetite and I never heard Eva say that he suffered badly from pains in his stomach. You should have seen the enormous quantities of sweets he ate at tea time. Of course, I suppose he used up a lot of energy.'

According to Frau Braun, everyone hated Dr Morell. Eva tried to get rid of him. She would not allow him to touch her.

281

She often used to tell Hitler that the 'injection quack' would poison him with all the injections he gave the Führer. Hitler, however, would say: 'But, *Patscherl*, he does ease my pain and I feel so wonderful after his injections.'

Frau Braun: 'After the injections wore off, however, he would flop more and more. One could see that the injections harmed him. During the last year one could tell that he was not normal anymore in his thinking and reasoning. I thought for sure that Morell was a British agent who doped Hitler so much that he committed acts he was not responsible for any longer.'

(I assured her that he committed worse acts before he ever had any injections. She was silent but agreed afterwards that things happened which she did not know about.)

Frau Braun: 'Maybe that's why Eva often said there are things she would not talk about. Maybe she knew something. She always said that when the Führer was no more, she would not be anymore either. That's why I was not surprised when I learned over the radio that she was dead. She did not write to us anymore.'

Frau Braun said her daughter hated Bormann and she wanted to get rid of him. Once she complained to Hitler about Bormann and Hitler told Bormann, in her presence, about her complaint. Bormann assured the Führer that it was not true. After that she never said much about Bormann. She feared him.

Eva was very kind and good to children. She loved the Schneider babies. She often told Frau Braun wistfully: 'I wish I could have a baby, but he won't have any.'

Frau Braun: 'I will tell you something I never told anybody before. I am glad that Fegelein is dead. He was a bad person. We hardly knew him. Gretl came one day and asked whether she should marry Fegelein and I said that we didn't know him. Gretl laughed and said: "*Mutti*, I did introduce him to you at the Berghof." I met so many people there that I did not remember them all. Then Fegelein came and asked Herr Braun for the consent to this marriage and eight days later they were married on the Obersalzberg. I saw him then and one time later, when he took us to Zell am See. That is all. Altogether, we did not talk to him more than half an hour, but I did not like him. His mother is still alive and I don't like her either. There were rumors in the papers that the remains of Hitler and Eva had been buried in the same crater into which Fegelein had been put. I wish they would open the grave and prove whether Fegelein's body is in there or not. Nobody knows for certain that he is dead. If Gretl wants to marry again she must have proof.'

Frau Braun says that as a child Eva was very headstrong. She refused to do her homework. In the morning, before she went to school, she used to kneel down on the floor and write on a chair. In no time she had finished her homework. Sometimes she got extra homework for punishment, and shortly before leaving for school at 8.00 a.m. she would go to her mother, hand her a slip from the teacher, and say: 'Sign it quickly, please. I am late.' Frau Braun stated that she often had no time to examine the paper or the homework her daughter had written. Eva never asked her father because she was afraid of him.

In 1944 Fanny Braun was at the Berghof. After lunch, Eva asked the Führer to take a walk with her and her mother, but Hitler refused, saying: 'I can't today, *Patscherl*. Leni Riefenstahl is coming with her husband. She wants me to give him a decoration.' Eva and her mother went for the walk and when they returned Leni Riefenstahl had departed.

Frau Braun: 'Once Eva and I were sitting in a restaurant in Munich. At another table two girls were sitting and Eva pointed to them. "Look," she said, "there are the two English girls the Führer is doing such a lot for." These were the Mitfords, Diana and Unity. Unity was very much in love with Hitler, and in 1939 she attempted suicide in the English Gardens in Munich. Dr Brandt took her to Switzerland, where her father met her. When the Führer heard about the shooting, he said: "Poor thing. She takes it so much to heart that England and Germany apparently do not hit it off." '

Fanny Braun said Eva never cried, adding that her daughter really had no reason to cry. Hitler rang her every day, saw her often but not every day, sent his special train for her. She had everything and more than she wanted.

Frau Braun: 'Eva was sure the Führer was faithful to her.'

Eva's mother admitted that she had heard many stories about the first meeting between Eva and Hitler, but she knew the true facts.

Frau Braun: 'All the stories about Eva's meeting with Hitler are quite wrong, I tell you. I know of a witness who worked with Hoffmann and who volunteered to testify in behalf of Eva if he was ever needed. The story is as I tell it. One day Hitler came into Hoffmann's office, which he used for his work since he did not keep his own office then. Eva was standing on a high ladder getting something down from a high shelf. The Führer looked up at her and then went on with his work. Eva did not even notice him. Hoffmann called her down from the ladder and asked her to go across the street for beer and *Leberkaes* (Bavarian sausage). She came back with a big beer mug and the sausage, put it down on his desk, and wished him "good appetite". He looked up at her, staring so intently that Eva blushed. After that, Hoffmann invited both of them to his house quite often and that is how they first met.'

When she was asked whether Eva knew Geli Raubal, Frau Braun said: 'Yes, I think so, because she often talked about her. But I never saw Eva and Geli together and I do not know whether they met often.'

(Both Herr Braun and Frau Braun survived the war. At the time of the interview, in 1948, Herr Braun was doing common labor to make a living for the family. Gretl and Ilse also survived the war and were living in Germany at this time – AUTHOR'S NOTE)

MUSMANNO ARCHIVES: VOLUME X

Interview with Dr Karl Brandt
(Hitler's Personal Physician)

NUREMBERG, JANUARY, 1946

Whenever Hitler stayed at his mountain retreat, the Berghof became his love. It meant for him a break in his normal routine. It enabled him to lead the life of a private individual. Apart from the normal retinue of adjutants and officials, other guests were accommodated, either in single or double bedrooms, at the Berghof. As much as possible was done to separate the guests proper from Hitler's own officials, and it was only on rare occasions that they ever met. In this way, Hitler was able to enjoy to the full the company and confidence of his guests in complete privacy. Not only did the prominent personages such as Heinrich Hoffmann, Esser, and other high party officials play an important part in Hitler's life, but so also did other lesser men and women who were around him. For example, his host of women secretaries shared, in part, the intoxicating atmosphere of the Berghof. The Berghof was managed by an SS man and his wife, who, apart from their duties, were comparatively unimportant. The couple were accommodated in the side wing of the building. Eva Braun was lavishly installed in the main building. She had never before played the role of the housewife. It was only in later years that Eva aspired to become – and became – the leading lady of the Berghof. She charmed all guests and her convincing personality won her esteem and respect. It was not an easy task for Eva to please Hitler. To my knowledge, Hitler first met Eva when he was introduced to her by Heinrich Hoffmann, in whose employ she was at that time. It would appear that at this time Hitler was still very much under the influence of his niece, Geli Raubal, the daughter of Hitler's sister Angela. Moreover, Hitler was deeply indebted to his niece for her loyalty and comfort during the early years of his struggle. I've heard it said that Geli was an important woman of high and noble character and that her influence over all she met was hypnotic. Geli died in 1931 and it was said that it was suicide. Hereafter, Hitler never mentioned her name nor was the episode ever discussed. But I remember that the emotions with which Hitler spoke of her in early years amounted to the worship of a madonna. Her room in Hitler's Munich flat has been preserved and left untouched ever since. Moreover, Hitler requested that an exact replica of this room be built in his new home in Munich. It is odd that Hitler, feeling the deep devotion that he did for Geli, should have been influenced by the entirely different personality of Eva Braun. Perhaps it is the tragic perception hiding in Hitler's subconscious that made him exclaim, in 1934, that 'the greater the man, the more insignificant the woman'. By saying this, it seems Hitler was giving expression to the emotion that all great men with all their responsibilities had no right to bind themselves to an intelligent woman, not even in matrimony. A marriage for an intelligent woman must remain in the background or the affair must inevitably fail. The happier union would therefore be with a woman of modest, homely gifts who is satisfied with the normal, everyday fundamentals of home life, yet is ever prepared to welcome her partner.

In the case of Eva Braun, it appears that her assured charm and intelligence embodied just those qualities which formed a contented alliance between herself and Hitler. It is all the more astonishing that, in spite of the unfavorable influence of her relatives and friends, Eva underwent a complete change for the better while with Hitler. A change which, however, did not make a great woman but certainly transformed her into a lady. Eva was the daughter of a university teacher and, in consequence, she acquired a thoroughly sound education. Until her teens she visited a convent. My first impression of Eva was that she was a woman who had suddenly been transplanted into the whirl and scurry of society. With it went the fine clothes, luxury, and jewels, and her changing moods under which certain guests had to suffer. As the years went by, particularly during the early war years. Eva's character seemed to undergo a complete change. She grew more serious, busied herself more with the domestic affairs at the Berghof, and [with] the Führer's flat in Munich. At this period, she tried to understand the thoughts of the Führer, and to attain this objective Eva began studiously to read and improve her knowledge and general educational outlook. A stranger meeting Eva at this period would undoubtedly have gained the impression of a slightly spoiled young lady who, although not a great personality, was certainly gifted in her exceeding charm, manner, and vitality. At first glance, it would seem astonishing that this gentle person should possess such a strong character; rather, one would have expected to find a more obliging person. There can be no doubt that Eva was deeply in love with Hitler, whom, until recent years, she addressed as *Mein Führer*. True, Hitler was not the complete lover pictured in Eva's romantic heart, but he was a man to comfort her and care for her. Hitler always tried to make life for her with him as pleasant and happy as possible. He showered upon her every charm and kindness he could muster and allowed her to enjoy all of the small, daily luxuries which life at the Berghof could offer. Indubitably, it must have been difficult for Eva to fit in with Hitler's daily routine. Hitler's day was mostly taken up in conferences, one after the other, lasting until late evening. It was only after dinner that the small exclusive group of the inner circle had time for private conversation in the sitting area, where they often remained until the early hours of the morning.

Hitler and Eva were certainly bound together by a deep emotional understanding, and this is surely proven by the fact that he married her during the last hours of his life. It is quite natural that Hitler enjoyed the company of other women, but he always returned to Eva. Leni Riefenstahl was one of these women, and others were mentioned in the press, but only Eva remained at his side throughout the years. According to newspaper reports at the time, Hitler was the father of two children by Eva, but she never had any children. The two children said to be Eva's were those of Frau Schneider, a friend of Eva's who resided at the Berghof for many years. Eva Braun had two sisters, one of whom is Gretl, who married Hermann Fegelein last year, and Ilse. The latter played no prominent part in Eva's life and saw her only on rare occasions. Gretl, however, saw much of her sister, both at the Berghof and at the small villa they shared in Munich. Eva made great use of her younger sister, who served her almost as her personal maid. Even in the close circle of her own family, Eva played the role of the great lady. Her parents were modest people who led secluded lives and were never much in the foreground of Eva's affairs. At the beginning of the war, Eva's father volunteered to join the service, though he was already an old man in retirement. Finally, he was given the post of paymaster in the German army. Gretl Braun was generous and good-natured, but she was far too easily influenced by others. Her marriage was very possibly contracted in a mood of fancy rather than governed by the principle of love. Hitler was fond of Gretl and liked her company. He would often converse with her alone and enjoyed her good humor. Other women at the Berghof were not much of an influence on Hitler's life. They were there solely to be near their husbands, for it was Hitler's wish that, where possible, a man and his wife should live together. For that reason, extra rooms were added when the Berghof was rebuilt. My wife, Annie Brandt, belonged to this group. She had known Hitler since 1925, when she had been a swimming champion for several years in succession. Hitler always treated my wife in a friendly way, but she was never in the limelight because she did not want to be. Frau Speer was in a somewhat similar position. She never played any political part but was noticeable for her intentional reserve. Both my wife and Frau Speer became much more friendly toward Eva Braun in later years than was the case when they first met. Professor Morell and his wife joined Hitler's circle of friends in 1935. The professor, and particularly his wife, tried to be in the good grace of Eva Braun and, unlike other guests, they showered presents upon her – handbags, jewel cases, etc. This was not the custom at the Berghof until then. Frau Morell, whose past was not all that could be desired, found little in common with the other guests at the Berghof, and perhaps it was for this reason that she clung to Eva Braun. It is probable that through this connection Frau Morell tried to help her husband and his endeavor to become a director of a pharmaceutical firm. As a woman and a human being, Frau Morell did not impress me very much. The wife of the Reich leader Bormann came to the Berghof only occasionally. She was a modest woman and always stayed in the background. Moreover, her husband would have forbidden her to show any spirit of independence. She lived in a house with her children, only a few minutes away from the Berghof.

No prominent part was played by any of the feminine visitors. Hitler's lady secretaries played their own special roles. This was due to the fact that they were not only alternately away with Hitler on his journeys and were present during important events, but they also belonged to the private circle and so were allowed to share the social life at the Berghof. The oldest of Hitler's personal secretaries was Fräulein Johanna Wolfe, the former secretary of Dietrich Eckart. She has peculiar human qualities. Despite her high position, Fräulein Wolfe lived a very modest life, and whenever time allowed she would stay with her eighty-year-old mother. Fräulein Wolfe proved helpful at all times and showed the greatest tact in settling occasional disputes. Though somewhat of a melancholy character, she could show a great sense of humor. For Hitler, she proved the most loyal assistant, giving him her best regardless of her own health. Owing to heart trouble and a chronic gall bladder complaint, she was sometimes pushed into the background by younger secretaries – not always in a very nice way. Hitler, however, took a keen interest in the well-being of Fräulein Wolfe and arranged for her medical supervision and treatment. It seemed that Fräulein Wolfe's quiet and gentle manner brought her somewhat sentimental ties between Hitler and herself. Also her extraordinarily true and open character contributed to the happy relation between Hitler and his secretary. At the beginning of the war, Hitler employed two secretaries, one of which was Fräulein Wolfe and the other Fräulein Christa Schroeder. Only on rare occasions were they replaced by Fräulein Gerda Daranowski. Fräulein Schroeder was not only highly intelligent, but showed the high gift of handling people skillfully. She also was a most critical person and she was of enormous perseverance, and, to show one example I remember, she took dictation for several days and nights with very little rest. Up to the very last day of her secretarial work, she would not hesitate to express her views, even though they may have been against the beliefs of Hitler. At times this would lead to controversy and Fräulein Schroeder would voluntarily choose to stay away from the Berghof, or be made to stay away. Though she suffered greatly under this state of affairs, she would not give up her right to criticize Hitler, to the extent that it brought her into danger. As a human being, or indeed as a woman, she did not achieve any close communion with Hitler. In later years, Fräulein Schroeder was frequently under medical treatment. She had trouble with hormones, which necessitated long and continuous treatment at different health resorts. Fräulein Schroeder was popular with her colleagues and with Hitler's close associates. She was not a favorite of Hitler, however.

Fräulein Gerda Daranowski, who later married General Christian, one of Hitler's air force adjutants, played a special role in the circle of secretaries. She was an up-to-date woman with an enormous amount of vitality. The desire to ingratiate was evident. She was professionally efficient and her patience matched that of Fräulein Schroeder. But her character was directly the opposite. In her conversations with Hitler she was invariably in agreement with his views and avoided the slightest conflict of opinion. She certainly exercised a feminine influence over him. She did everything to heighten those sentiments. This was certainly not prompted by an altruistic motive. She desired to play a definite role around Hitler and obtain certain privileges. Here may be mentioned her marriage to the General-to-be, Christian, who was appointed chief of the operation department of the air force on Hitler's own orders and against the wishes and interests of Göring. One cannot but assume that Fräulein Daranowski, who remained Hitler's secretary even after her marriage, played a decisive role in his appointment. The relations between Fräulein Daranowski and Eva Braun, and vice versa, were naturally tense and Hitler knew it. This fact, however, exerted no influence during all those years, and during the time when Hitler was at his various headquarters, Fräulein Daranowski was always the center of attraction at the nightly talks. It must certainly also be attributed to her influence that Hitler, as the result of strong hints from Fräulein Daranowski regarding the poor state of health of Fräulein Wolf and Fräulein Schroeder, kept these two ladies absent from his headquarters quite often and made him insist on lengthy visits to health resorts for them both. Frau Christian appeared to have no particular affectionate relationship with her husband. Obviously, one can be mistaken on this point. She never bothered actively about the three children from his first marriage. After a few days these children were sent to their grandparents, where they remained.

A former servant of Hitler's, Junge, very soon married a secretary from the Führer's secretariat. Frau Junge, a native of Munich, was very young to find herself in this privileged position, but soon blossomed forth in her new surroundings. With her ability and charm, she soon found the right thing to say to everyone. Very shortly, she became one of those in Hitler's circle who would have been most missed. She combined naïveté with a freshness of youth that was irresistible. Hitler was fond of her, although he treated her somewhat in a fatherly manner. He often pointed out the similarities of personality between Frau Junge and Eva Braun.

Fräulein Manzialy was a native of Innsbruck. Her father was Greek and her mother Tyrolean. She had been a cook for a school in Berchtesgaden and then was employed by Professor Zabel at his clinic there. The professor, in the previous year, had prescribed a vegetarian diet for Hitler which Fräulein Manzialy used to prepare and send to the Berghof. Fräulein Manzialy sometimes visited the kitchen at the Berghof to prepare the meals. At this time Hitler was suffering increasingly from intestinal troubles and, as a dietary assistant, a half-Jewess who had come from Marshal Antonescu, was leaving, the choice fell on Fräulein Manzialy. Her appearance was quite plain and she would have passed unnoticed wherever she went. She was unbelievably humble and unobtrusive, but now and then she was present at the evening teas. She really only spoke when an answer was required. She took the trouble to make Hitler's meals nourishing and varied, which the scant possibilities open to her made very difficult. For instance, she prepared sweets with immense care. Hitler appreciated this and gratefully accepted this care for his person. Probably not a day passed without his referring to the coming meal and the surprises Fräulein Manzialy had in store for him. In this case the well-known phrase 'Love enters through the stomach' was true. Hitler often invited Fräulein Manzialy to eat with him, especially when he was away from the Berghof, using the pretext that she must taste her own dishes.

The ladies previously mentioned all played different roles during the war than those they played in peacetime. The fact that they had joined in the war as women meant that they had to become accustomed to a rougher way of living. From another point of view, the masculine, they also played a special role. Even for Hitler himself they provided pleasant entertainment, especially in the evening after the talks on the military situation were concluded for the day. Then began the so-called tea. All the ladies came to the tea together or attended it alternately. Some of them had already slept, since the teas often did not begin until after midnight, and they were fresh and lively. Certain of Hitler's personal staff and his adjutants also attended, but no army officers. Around the table there were about eight armchairs in which the guests sat. Fräulein Daranowski always sat on Hitler's left while on his right sat one of the other ladies. This was at his field headquarters, of course, not at the Berghof. The subjects discussed naturally varied. Occasionally some critical happening was discussed, but more often trivialities were the order of the day. It may be mentioned that Hitler's wolf dog played a perfectly unbearable role at these teas.

In Munich, Hitler's Prinzregentenstrasse flat was cared for by a married couple named Winter. The husband attended to all details, repairs, and concerns of the house. The main work, however, was done by Frau Winter herself, whose position was that of housekeeper. She had known Hitler for many years. She kept the flat in order and looked after Hitler in a general way when he was in Munich. She also cooked his meals for him, which usually consisted of eggs, vegetables, and salads. Over and above this, she played a certain role, owing to the fact that she recounted all the Munich gossip to Hitler and laid before him many appeals which were addressed to him. All this undoubtedly gave her a key position, if only one, from which she was able to influence Hitler regarding certain persons or their activities. One gained the impression that Hitler attached importance to her views and he himself often asked her for her opinion. When it became more widely known that Frau Winter was not just a lowly housekeeper, she was treated with a remarkable politeness and consideration by influential people. Gauleiter Wagner, for instance, kept her supplied with theater tickets. Frau Winter tried to pose as a lady moving in the highest circles, but she was good-natured and enabled many humble people to get certain favors and to obtain interviews – even with Hitler. Her relations with Eva Braun, whom she also looked after, were good. She answered the telephone; this alone made her position a very confidential one. Frau Winter was fairly well-known in Munich, and where this was not the case, she soon remedied it herself.

There were a number of women who were often mentioned by Hitler in conversation and who attracted his attention, owing to their peculiarities or their personalities. If, first of all, one mentions Frau Hess, it is because of Hitler's aversion to this woman. If any opportunity arose to express an adverse judgement when she was the object of it, he did. He characterized her as the type of man-woman whose ambition made her strive to dominate the man and therefore almost lose her own femininity. Her preoccupation with handicrafts, which Hitler did not share, is interesting but not important. Frau Hess, after many years of married life, had a child to whom she was devotedly attached. Hitler described her feelings as theatrical. She was the first to call Hitler 'Chief', the name by which he was known for many years among his immediate entourage. Whether there were other personal reasons for the unhappy relations between Hitler and Frau Hess I don't know. It is probable that this clever woman, with her sober outlook, could never have had any affinity with a man like Hitler.

Frau Troost, on whom Hitler had conferred the title of 'professor', was the wife of the architect Troost, who had designed the Nazi party buildings and the Art Institute in Munich. Frau Troost, while lacking any outward charm, had an intelligence far above the average. Ambitious and clever, she understood how, through her mutual and intellectual interests with Hitler, she could play a leading role, if not *the* leading role, in the art circles of Munich. She cruelly criticized people who stood in her way, and since Hitler valued her judgement, there is no doubt that she influenced to a considerable extent the artistic development in Munich. It was, of course, natural that she should be feared in these circles and harshly criticized in turn. She has a remarkably developed sense of color, and in the development of her late husband's work she has influenced the whole color scheme of the new public buildings in Munich as well as their interior architecture. She understood how to demonstrate to Hitler the effects of color gradations and she cared both for the heavy colors of the Markut period and for the finer shades of color. It was easy for her to secure Hitler's complete agreement. When he went to Munich, if it was possible, he always visited Professor Troost within the first few hours of his arrival; there he spent hours talking and discussing with Frau Troost and her colleague, Professor Gall, general matters, but especially subjects connected with art. It is natural that Frau Troost was almost always one of the guests invited to be present at the simple midday meals at the Osteria Bavaria in the Briennerstrasse. As she was usually the only woman present, she sat on Hitler's right hand; from there she and Hitler led the conversation.

Two elderly ladies were also members of the Munich circle. One was Frau Bruckmann, widow of the art publisher. Hitler sometimes visited her, and the hours spent with this witty woman, who was well into her seventies, always meant something special to Hitler, although the subject of their talks was doubtlessly mainly recollections. Yet the way of looking at things as shown by this woman was praised so highly by Hitler that he talked about it for weeks. The same applied to a Frau Hoffmann, who, in spite of her eighty years, had remained robust and cherished a special loving regard for Hitler. He thought nothing of traveling from Berlin to Munich to present his birthday wishes to her in person. She was one of the first party members in Munich and in Hitler's eyes this gave her great prestige. Neither of these two ladies played any political role.

The eight-day visit to Bayreuth for the Wagner festival provided the special interruption of the year's activities for Hitler. He stayed in an annex of the Haus Wahnfried, usually alone with his adjutant Schaub or Brueckner, and a servant. There was, on the ground floor of this annex, a fairly large dining room for fifteen to thirty persons, a correspondingly large lounge, and an open veranda which overlooked the garden. A covered way led to the

Haus Wahnfried, where the Wagner family lived. This was a happy time for Hitler. Apart from the musical impressions made on him by the opera, it was the proof of his friendship with the Wagner family. He had been on terms of friendship ever since the children were small. As the children grew up, he was drawn more intimately into the family circle. He was always ready to help Frau [Siegfried] Wagner with word and deed. A long, close friendship existed between Hitler and this wise and highly intelligent woman. It is difficult to describe how these two highly developed characters were complementary to each other except that both had the same deep reverence for Richard Wagner and his music. This had perhaps been the decisive factor in [Winifred's] marriage to Siegfried Wagner. She was, at that time, very young and doubtless very much under the influence of the great Richard Wagner. One may also assume with some certainty that the presence of Frau Cosima Wagner, so lively up to a very advanced age, was of significance in this circle. On social evenings in Haus Wahnfried, the most gifted theater folk were guests, constituting to quite an unusual degree all that was brilliant in the artistic life of Germany. It is important to emphasize this artistic atmosphere in order to understand how it was bound to attract Hitler. It was, of course, natural that Frau [Winifred] Wagner dominated the circle, for she had to fight in very difficult conditions in order to succeed in restoring the Bayreuth festival to its original conception. Whether relations between Frau Wagner and Hitler were consciously fostered by her in order to attain the fulfillment of her objective is hard to say. If that were the case, it would be indicative of Frau Wagner's cleverness rather than the nobility of her character. She did try to influence the political views of the Führer, but as she seldom saw Hitler in later years her influence was slight. Many of her friends signed petitions which were forwarded through my hands to Hitler. I know that the majority of them were concerned with political oppression against persons of half-Jewish blood. In such cases, Hitler always tried to settle the matter in the way she desired.

Frau Wagner's children were, with the exception of the eldest daughter, devoted to Hitler. Although she was just as intelligent as her brothers and sisters, she had been rather put in the shade. This discrimination, real or imagined, reached such a point that the eldest daughter went to Switzerland, once there, she quite often openly criticized Hitler. Publications in the press show how far she went. She claimed that since her mother was an Englishwoman, she regarded herself as English the same way that her brothers and sisters regarded themselves as German. This matter was never discussed in Haus Wahnfried in the presence of outsiders. Hitler undoubtedly saw a kind of high treason in this attitude of the eldest daughter and condemned it accordingly. He never discussed this matter in wider circles, but he occasionally criticized her during talks with his inner circle.

With his own relatives Hitler hardly had any contact. During the years 1932 or 1933 and 1936 his sister Angela kept house for him in Haus Wachenfeld, later the Berghof. In this house she was looked on as the housekeeper; she did everything possible to make life agreeable for her brother, whom she adored. She looked after him with a motherly care and he must have appreciated it very much at first. Owing to some tension, the origins of which are not known but which disappeared in later years, she left the Berghof. Angela married a Professor Hamitsch of the technical high school in Dresden and remained estranged from Hitler for a long time. He, however, often spoke of her and her gift for running the household. He often mentioned his mother, to whom he was devoted. He described her as a simple and good woman who always brought up her children with great trouble and patience and always tried to help them. He often said that 'she would have been unhappy to see her son in such a position of great responsibility'. He intended to express his adoration for his mother by having the architect Glesser design and have erected on the banks of the Danube a tall tower hung with bells. The base was to form a mausoleum for the bodies of his mother and father.

(*Dr Brandt fell out of favor with Hitler in 1944 and later was condemned to death by the Führer. The end of the war prevented the carrying out of this death sentence* – AUTHOR'S NOTE)

Notes

References are given in abbreviated form. Interview dates are only listed for first references. 'M.A.' refers to the Musmanno Archives section of the present work.

14. *'take a bath, put on her best underclothes'* : From a copy of a letter by Eva Braun found by the OSS in Switzerland after the end of World War II.

14. *Though he liked his beer* : Interview with Ernst Solf, Munich, February, 1973. Solf is a former Bavarian restaurant owner, now retired.

14. *At twenty-five minutes past two* : Birth records of Eva Paula Braun are on file in Munich.

17. *They moved to a new apartment* : Gun, 25.

19. *'I will never stay here two years'* : Nina Garnier interview, Paris, February, 1973. Nina Garnier is presently a dress designer.

20. *'Your daughter is intelligent and ambitious'*: Records at the Catholic Young Women's Institute at Simbach.

21. *'If a few pfennigs of cosmetics will get me what I want'* : Hilda May interview, Ulm, Germany, February, 1973.

21. *Now she began to learn about a more sophisticated life* : Klara Oster interview, Bari, Italy, March, 1970. Klara Oster, the widow of an Italian industrialist, lives in Italy at present.

23. *'pretty'* : Hoffman, 160.

26. *His mother was Klara Pölzl* : Genealogists, both German and foreign, have attempted to give the Führer of the Third Reich an accurate lineage, but the records are imprecise and confusing. The facts included here are those provided by the latest research of government records and documents available in 1973.

27. *'Test drawing unsatisfactory'* : From the classification list of the Academy of Fine Arts, Vienna, Austria, 1907.

28. *'He hadn't much to say about it'* : Heinz, 102.

29. *After swearing the doctor to secrecy* : Krueger, 31. From 1919 until 1934 Dr Kurt Krueger treated Hitler at his office in Munich for a variety of actual and imaginary illnesses. In 1934 Krueger escaped from Germany and went to live in New York City, where he was interviewed by U.S. military and political officials interested in understanding

Hitler's personality. Most of the information in this book attributed to Krueger comes from his own book, *Inside Hitler*, which was published in 1941. Upton Sinclair, Otto Strasses and K. Arvid Enlind, M.D., a lieutenant colonel in the U.S. Army Reserve, also contributed to this book in various ways. However, the medical information about Hitler comes from Krueger and is based on his personal contact with Hitler during the years mentioned above. When the OSS made an analysis of Hitler during World War II in hopes of predicting his future actions, Krueger's material was studied closely.

29. *'If I don't have syphilis why am I totally impotent?'* : Krueger, 37.

30. *One of the first women* : Hanfstängl, 44. Ernst 'Putzi' Hanfstängl was a member of Hitler's intimate circle from 1922 until he was forced to flee for his life in 1937, after the Führer threatened to have him murdered. Hanfstängl, who was born in Germany, graduated from Harvard University in 1909 and for several years operated the New York branch of his family's art publishing firm. He returned to Germany in 1920 and met Hitler for the first time. He was instrumental in introducing Hitler to many wealthy and influential Germans, including the Bechsteins, and later handled foreign correspondents for Hitler because of his knowledge of the United States. After the war Hanfstängl wrote of his experiences in *Unheard Witness*.

30. *he met Elsa Bruckmann* : Hanfstängl, 44.

31. *Hitler injured his shoulder in the melee* : There is considerable confusion and controversy over just what happened after Hitler escaped from the putsch scene. Konrad Heiden, in his *Der Führer*, suggests that Hitler stayed with Erna for forty-eight hours. Ernst Hanfstängl states that while Hitler hurried to his sister's home at Uffing, it was his wife who took Hitler in and that his sister was in Munich at the time. It is known for certain, however, that Hitler greatly admired Erna Hanfstängl and had spent many hours in her company.

32. *twenty-five million gold marks* : Payne, 223.

33. *Captain Ernst Röhm . . . had been publicly chastised* : Ludecke, 353. Kurt Ludecke was an early financial supporter of Hitler and the Nazi Party. Later he was imprisoned by Hitler and escaped to the United States. In 1937, while living at Sea Spray Inn on the Dunes in East Hampton, Long Island, he wrote his memoirs.

33. *'Such elements are unusable in time of peace'* : Trevor-Roper, 153–56.

34. *'Do you know the audience at a circus is just like a woman?'* :

Oss interview with Ernst Hanfstängl in the United States during World War II.

38. *He periodically published illustrated books :* Hoffmann, 63.
39. *Eva was standing near the top of a ladder :* Frau Franziska Braun told about the initial meeting between Eva and Hitler in an interview at Rupoldingen, Germany, near Traunstein, Schwabenbaurer, on September 4, 1938 (M.A., 274ff).
41. *Dr Joseph Goebbels had been appointed Minister of Propaganda :* Lochner, 13.
42. *Yet she couldn't forget the look in his eyes :* From a secret psychological report written in 1943 for the OSS which attempted to apply psychoanalytic insight to warfare. This secret report on Hitler was compiled under the direction of Walter C. Langer at the behest of William J. ('Wild Bill') Donovan, who headed the OSS at the time. A quarter of a century later parts of the report were declassified and published. In March, 1973, Albert Speer stated to me: 'The so-called analysis by Walter C. Langer seems to me rather superficial, which is understandable because it couldn't draw on immediate sources. Eva Braun once made the observation to me that Hitler, when he was approximately fifty years old, left her the choice to leave him because he couldn't give her what she, as a young woman, could expect from him.' Dr Werner Maser, professor at the Munich Institute for Politics, told me in May, 1973: 'The report is nonsense. It has nothing to do with the facts. Langer invents tales to be able to "prove" his thesis about Hitler's youth and sexuality. Hitler's sexuality was absolutely normal.'
42. *'Hitler? I would not walk on the same side of the street with him' :* Braun interview.
43. *an American banker named Owen D. Young :* Bullock, 145–46.
44. *'I would like to have you come to the house tonight, Eva' :* Hoffmann, 161.
45. *'At one time I was a pupil of Professor Heinrich Knirr's Academy' :* Ibid., 48.
45. *'My bride is Germany' :* Ibid., 141.
46. *'Often when he intends to stop at our house' :* Ibid., 161.
47. *'the barren hero' :* Hanfstängl, 130.
50. *The apartment in Munich was divided into two wings :* Frau Annie Winter interview, Munich, March 30, 1948 (M.A., 254).
51. *Geli was interested in a musical career :* Ludecke, 420.
51. *He arranged for her to start singing lessons :* Hanfstängl, 129.
52. *Gunther . . . was completely misled by Hitler's public actions :* Gunther, 7.

52. *Hanfstängl . . . considered Hitler unorthodox sexually* : Hanfstängl, 129.
53. *The proof he sought* : Ibid., 170.
54. *He did admit, however, that for a time Hitler was in love with his niece* : Hoffmann, 150.
55. *Frau Winter, Hitler's housekeeper* : Frau Winter interview, March 30, 1948.
55. *Ada Dort, who became acquainted with Geli* : Ada Dort is now a retired voice teacher living in Paris. Interviewed at the Prince de Gaulles Hotel, Paris, February, 1973.
55. *A former SA officer who guarded Hitler's apartment* : Wilhelm Stocker now lives in Spain. He is one of several former Nazi officers still interested in German politics. Interviewed at the Palace Hotel, Madrid, 1973.
56. *When he took her home* : Erich Kempka interview, Munich, August 19, 1948 (M.A., 263ff.).
56. *Another party member who felt the wrath of Hitler* : Otto Strasser interview.
57. *She often talked about Geli with her mother* : Braun interview.
57. *'We were walking in the English Gardens'* : Ada Dort interview.
58. *. . . Heinrich Hoffman took Eva to* Fasching: Julius Schaub interview, Garmisch, March 22, 1948. Julius Schaub was Hitler's personal adjutant for many years (M.A., 273ff.).
59. *They joined the driver of the black Mercedes-Benz* : Ludecke, 522.
59. *That evening Geli went to the Munich Playhouse* : Julius Schaub interview.
59. *She then notified her husband* : Frau Winter interview, March 30, 1948.
60. *The* Münchener Neueste Nachrichten *reported the tragedy* : September 19, 1931.
61. *she was the one woman he trusted* : OSS report, 1943.
61. *. . . Maja Kempka, the attractive wife of Hitler's chauffeur* : Erich Kempka interview.
64. *A closer analysis reveals a much different Hitler* : Bullock, 187.
64. *He was so uncompromising on this subject* : Gun, 67.
65. *When Geli was living at the apartment on Prinzregenten-strasse* : Ibid.
66. *One such individual was Wilhelm Brückner* : Ibid., 69.
66. *During the early months of 1932* : Krueger, 267.
67. *'I had almost decided to let matters lapse between us'* : Ibid., 284.
67. *'From what you have told me'* : Ibid., 284.
67. *. . . Albert Speer, a close associate* : In February, 1973, I visited Albert Speer at his home in Heidelberg. We talked for several hours about Eva Braun. Speer and his wife knew her well. He was one of the last persons to see

her alive. He told me that his opinion of her had changed during the long years since the end of the war; he now considered her much more intelligent and adroit in her relations with Hitler than he had previously assumed. Speer said that her ability to devote herself entirely to Hitler's career without developing ambitions of her own after she became his mistress was the mark of a great and unusual woman. He liked her very much.

68. *Hitler had made a cult of the music* : Stevenson, 36.

69. *Winifred used the intimate form* du: OSS Report, 1943.

69. *Winifred Wagner had visited Dr Krueger in Munich* : Krueger, 314.

70. *Frau Winter, the housekeeper at Hitler's apartment in Munich* : Frau Winter interview, September 3, 1948.

70. *The photographs in her personal albums* : The National Archives in Washington, D.C., are the repository for the photograph albums of Eva and Gretl Braun. Gretl's albums are covered with a cloth bearing a floral pattern. The pages were originally separated by transparent protective paper; most of these protective covers are now missing. Eva's albums have two different types of covers. The albums that contain pictures of her parents, relatives and childhood friends are covered with blue leatherette. The albums that she kept after meeting Hitler have expensive ivory-colored leather covers with her initials in gold on the front. One of these albums has a flower pressed into it. Eva seems to have liked children; there are numerous pictures of children, including those of Bormann, Goebbels and the children of the village of Berchtesgaden. Surprisingly, there are also many pictures of Hitler with children in the albums. I had the impression from the numerous photographs in the Braun albums that Eva's parents were taken care of very well by Hitler despite their protests, after the war, that they seldom associated with him.

71. *While this political intrigue was in progress* : Bullock, 208.

74. *Lying there, still conscious but bleeding badly* : Hoffmann, 115.

75. *As Fritz Braun told inquiring neighbors* : Braun interview.

75. *He told Hoffman* : 'She did it for the love of me' : Hoffmann, 162.

81. *'I am an old man'* : Trials of War Criminals . . . Nuremberg Proceedings, Part XVI, 272.

81. *Paul Harns, a former waiter at the Carlton Hotel café in Munich* : Paul Harns interview, Munich, February, 1973. Paul Harns was one of Hitler's favorite waiters, not only because he served well and quickly, but also because he was an ardent Nazi. He, too, gave the dejected Hitler encouragement in December, 1932, though he later

wished he had done just the opposite – in 1940 he was drafted into the German army and lost his leg while fighting in Poland. He knew Eva Braun well during the years 1933–40. He liked her very much. He said that even after she became the 'First Lady' of the Third Reich, albeit secretly, she was still friendly and unassuming when they occasionally met in Munich. Harns is retired and still lives in Munich.

81. *Another witness to Eva's exhortation about Hitler's great political future* : Maria Paith interview, Madrid, February, 1973. Maria Paith was a hostess/waitress at the Osteria Bavaria in 1932 and knew Eva well. Only after the war did she realize that Eva was the mistress of Adolf Hitler. She left the Osteria Bavaria in 1934, worked for a time at Der Peterhof in Munich and then went to Berlin, where she was employed at the Kaiserhof Hotel for a short time. In 1940 she moved to Spain, where she now lives.

83. *Shortly after noon on January 30, 1933, Adolf Hitler was named Chancellor of Germany* : Bullock, 250.

84. *As he told Heinrich Hoffman* : Hoffmann, 162.

84. *As Frau Winter said bitterly* : Frau Winter Interview, August 21, 1948.

86. *When Eva celebrated her twenty-first birthday* : Gun, 100.

87. *Coincidentally, that Sunday* : Braun interview.

92. *Kurt G. W. Ludecke, one of the early Nazis* : Ludecke, 747.

92. *Dr Kurt Krueger, the medical expert* : Krueger, 427.

92. *Later, Ernst Hanfstängl*, 279.

92. *Some months later he was summoned to Berlin* : Ibid., 293.

93. *She once confided her fears to Harns* : Paul Harns interview.

94. *She told Harns early in June, 1943, that she was 'nothing but a prisoner'* : Ibid.

95. *My dear Chief of Staff* : Published in the *Völkischer Beobachter*, the Nazi newspaper, January 2, 1943.

96. *Göring had met her while he was in Sweden* : Frischauer, 29.

97. *Later, Goebbels publicly confessed* : Ludecke, 770.

98. *Then, about the time Eva was eating her breakfast* : Payne, 271.

98. *Hitler so ordered* : Ludecke, 772.

99. *He was given a tea party in the Chancellery garden in Berlin* : Bullock, 304.

100. *'The man is mad'* : Braun interview.

102. *'The Jew is the incarnation of egoism'* : Bormann, 115.

102. *Heinrich Himmler, the Reichsführer of the SS* : Gun, 156.

103. *If Eva needed any evidence of Hitler's strong feelings* : Kohler, 151.

104. *Once when they were alone* : Krueger, 325.

105. *He was referring to an episode* : OSS report of an interview

with A. Zeissler, Hollywood, California, June 24, 1943.

105. *'I believe in a divine commandment' : Bormann.* 116.

106. *In turn, Eva seldom brought the subject up to Ilse* : Paul Harns interview.

106. *She had once been good friends with Pearl Sklar* : Pearl Sklar interview, Bari, Italy, March, 1970. Frau Sklar, at the time of the interview, was eighty-eight years old and living on a small income from an apartment building she owned. She remembered Eva Braun very well and said that she liked her. 'She was a very kind young girl and spent many hours with me because she knew I was lonely. This was before she met Hitler. I think she was fooled by that man just as most Germans were at that time.' She is convinced that her life was saved by Eva Braun because most of her Jewish friends in Munich from that period died in concentration camps before the end of World War II.

106. *'What about Frau Sklar?' Eva asked* : Frau Sklar related during the interview that Hoffmann told her about his conversation with Eva Braun. He told her about the incident after the war, when she returned to Munich for a visit.

107. *Dr Eduard Bloch had also treated Hitler's mother* : Colliers, March 22, 1941.

108. *Former Gestapo officer Otto Beck* : Otto Beck was interviewed by the author at a villa on the outskirts of Madrid, Spain, in February, 1973. Beck, a tall, slender German who deals in real estate (and possibly still has ties with ex-Nazi officers scattered around the globe, since he is very knowledgeable about their present whereabouts), talked freely about his activities with the Gestapo. He did not know to whom Himmler was referring as a 'stupid cow' until after the war ended; he then discovered that Eva Braun was often called this by those who were jealous of her.

109. *She did hint to him several times* : Heinrich Hoffman interview, July 19, 1948, Nuremberg, Germany (M.A., 268ff.).

111. *Hitler believed that every woman was unreasonable* : Bormann, 201.

112. *Gradually she became more and more depressed about Hitler's indifference and expressed her growing disillusionment in her diary* : National Archives, Washington, D.C., Record Group 242. When, in 1935, Eva Braun laid her diary beside her on the bed after taking an overdose of Phanodorm, it was open to the entry of May 28. After her sister Ilse found her unconscious, and before Dr Marx arrived, Ilse quickly took the twenty-two pages from the

diary and put them in her pocket. She did not want the real reason for Eva's illness to become known. So no one discovered the reasons for the suicide attempt at the time. Later Ilse gave the diary pages back to her sister and Eva kept them at Obersalzberg. Several days before she died (in 1945), Eva wrote a letter to her other sister, Gretl, asking her to destroy the diary. Instead, Gretl and Ilse smuggled the diary into Austria, where it was found by the Americans in 1945 in the possession of the mother of an officer of Hitler's guard. The Americans sent the diary to the United States as 'plunder of war' and it lay in the National Archives for nearly a quarter of a century, unbeknown to historians and researchers. Even Ilse and Gretl Braun were unaware of its location. The diary was finally 'found' and authenticated and is published here in its entirety. The translation here reproduced is by Dr Werner Maser of the Munich Institute for Politics, Munich, Germany.

117. *'I detest women who dabble in politics'* : Bormann, 206.
118. *On March 4, 1935, the British government announced that it was going to increase its armaments* : Bullock, 332.
119. *Hitler's apartment was being remodeled* : Speer, 77.
123. *'It's a fact,' Hitler stated, 'that women love real men'* : Bormann, 141.
124. *Lilian Mina, a young dancer* : Lilian Mina interview, Munich, February, 1973. Fräulein Mina remembers the Braun sisters well. She recalls that at the time Gretl seemed more lively and fun-loving than Eva. When she noticed that a man was slipping into the Braun sisters' apartment by a side door late at night, Fräulein Mina teased Gretl about it. Instead of taking the teasing lightly, the usually good-humored Gretl became angry and walked away. Eventually Fräulein Mina and Gretl became friends again, but Gretl never explained about the stranger's nightly visits nor identified him as Hitler. Shortly after the argument the two Braun sisters moved to their new villa and Fräulein Mina seldom saw either of them again. Today Fräulein Mina operates a small resort hotel in Switzerland.
125. *The house had been designed by a Munich architect* : Julius Schaub interview.
126. *He could convince her that she was young and beautiful* : Interview with Dr Werner Maser at his home in Speyer, West Germany, on February 14, 1973. Dr Maser teaches at the Munich Institute for Politics. His subjects include: Hitler, National Socialism and the Führer legend. Maser obtained his material in an unusual way. He masqueraded as an American soldier and marched

302

into the Berlin store house, which the U.S. Army had captured, where a large number of the National Socialist documents were kept. He found more than a thousand written items, among them the official diary of the Nazi Party for the years 1920–21.

127. *'It is better we go there occasionally and are on good terms with her'* : Braun interview.

127. *One of these artists*: Hans Kelter interview, Paris, 1973. Herr Kelter, who now lives in Paris, does not like to publicly recall his friendship with Eva Braun. He did admit, however, that before he learned that she was Hitler's mistress he was very interested in her. According to Herr Kelter, Eva's personality was warm and friendly and she was very easy to talk to on a variety of subjects. Herr Kelter observed: 'Why she would fall in love with a man such as Adolf Hitler will always be a mystery to me.'

128. *Another man who professed to be interested in Eva Braun*: Julius Schaub interview.

129. *Your Excellency the Chancellor* : The Denazification Tribunal Files, Munich, 1948.

130. *Instead, she also wrote a letter to Hitler* : Braun interview.

130. *Before Dr Kurt Krueger fled from Germany* : Krueger, 307.

131. *Krueger agreed with Kaiser Wilhelm II* : Krueger, 435.

134. *Many Germans considered her Hitler's mistress* : Luis Trenker interview.

134. *'It is to her advantage not to deny the rumor'* : Frau Christa Schröder interview, Berchtesgaden, May 22, 1945. A copy of this interview is on file at the University of Pennsylvania Library. Frau Schröder was one of Hitler's personal secretaries from 1933 until his death. Since she spent long hours with him, both in Berlin and in his field headquarters during the war, and participated in conversations every night after his official duties ended, she knew a great deal about Hitler. She was also very well acquainted with Eva Braun.

134. *Eva, however, saw a dangerous rival in the beautiful Leni Riefenstahl*: Julius Schaub interview.

135. *As the first step in his plan* : Hanfstängl, 202.

136. *'If Riefenstahl can't manage this, no one can'* : Ibid., 203.

136. *Often in private so that not even his immediate staff knew what transpired between them* : OSS Report, 1943.

138. *Eva arrived in Nuremberg with Frau Schaub* : Julius Schaub interview.

139. *The film premiered on March 28, 1935* : WCBS-TV's 'Camera Three' program. Leni Riefenstahl's career has been seriously affected by her work during the war with Hitler and the Nazis. Amos Vogel, author and film critic, stated (in the May 13, 1973 issue of the New York *Times*)

that the 'Camera Three' program televised in the United States in 1973 was a 'whitewash of a great and dangerous film artist responsible for one of the most notorious masterpieces of world cinema.' Since 1945 Leni Riefenstahl has glossed over the part she played in glorifying Hitler and the Third Reich, saying that she was a naïve young girl who did not know any better. Most historians do not agree with this theory, but they all agree that as a film-maker she had few peers. Today she lives in Munich and is interested in filming the tribes of Africa. She married her late husband, Major Peter Jacob, in 1944.

139. *Frau Schaub often stated :* Julius Schaub interview.
139. *'I have commissioned so many men to make a film' :* Ibid.
140. *Yet she was the one person :* Mandell, 290.
140. *'I had the whole thing in my head' :* Gordon Hitchens, *Film Comment,* III, No. 1, Winter issue, 1963, 4–11.
141. *She had discovered that Leni Riefenstahl was amorously linked with many men :* Mandell, 290.
141. *She used it so cleverly :* Paul Harns interview.
142. *Udet was the type of freewheeling individual :* Interview with former Luftwaffe Captain Otto Wagner, Berlin, March, 1970. Captain Wagner was a test pilot who worked closely with Ernst Udet in developing new aircraft and new aircraft components. He spent a great deal of his off-duty time with Udet and came to know him very well. Since both men were bachelors, they often entertained their women friends at the same places in Berlin, drinking and dancing until the early morning hours. Wagner had many interesting stories to tell about Udet's personal life.
142. *According to rumor, Leni Riefenstahl had been with him during his last days :* Frischauer, 190.
147. *When Hitler went to his home on the Obersalzberg :* Bormann, 136.
148. *When Hitler was released from Landsberg Prison :* Bullock, 134.
148. *The Platterhof was an old farmstead :* Ludecke, 489.
149. *Martin Bormann, who, like Eva, was seldom noticed by the average German citizen :* Albert Speer interview. Speer considered Bormann ruthless and cruel, a schemer who built a wall around Hitler that very few people could penetrate. Bormann took care that Hitler would hear only what he wanted him to know. The fact that he was a manipulator of great magnitude was not understood by the German public or even by some of Hitler's closest associates. Bormann remained almost as well hidden as Eva Braun, according to Herr Speer, as far as the ordinary citizen was concerned. It was only after the end of World

War II that Bormann's real 'power behind the throne' was recognized.

151. *The Berghof had fourteen guest bedrooms :* Interview with Dr Karl Brandt, Hitler's personal physician. Dr Brandt was also Hitler's Commissioner for Public Health. However, after the assassination attempt in 1944, he told Hitler that the pills given him by another doctor, Dr Theodor Morell, were poisoning his system. Hitler became furious and eliminated Brandt from his inner circle. Herr Speer gives Dr Brandt credit for saving Speer's life when he was ill in January, 1944; at the time, Speer was being treated by another German doctor who was gradually causing Speer's condition to get worse. Later, after Brandt submitted a report to Hitler on the serious medical situation in Germany, Hitler ordered his arrest and charged him with high treason. Only the defeat of Germany prevented his execution in the spring of 1945 (M.A., 288ff.).

151. *Guests at the Berghof were given a list of rules to follow :* Kohler, 93.

151. *Once, at dinner, when he noticed the print of her lipstick on a napkin :* Traudl Junge interview (M.A., 270ff.).

152. *These men, and the other men and women hired to serve at the Berghof :* Interview with Fritz Utel, Berlin, March, 1970. Herr Utel was an SS member who was assigned to the Berghof during the years 1936–41. A small, slender man with impeccable manners, Utel was considered an asset to the staff at the mountain retreat and was retained there by Hitler much longer than was customary (the usual assignment was for a single year). He was a waiter, personal bodyguard, gate guard, door guard and general handyman at the Berghof during this period. He saw a great deal of Eva Braun, although his personal contact with her was limited to a few formal conversations. He believes she influenced Hitler more than most people assumed, especially in the area of domestic matters. Utel says that she often interceded on behalf of her friends and acquaintances and voiced their grievances. He states that there is no doubt in his mind that Hitler loved Eva as deeply as it was possible for him to love anyone. In 1970 Herr Utel was a security guard for a wealthy industrialist in West Germany.

152. *Hitler's secretaries accompanied him to the mountain retreat :* Dr Karl Brandt interview.

153. *'You had better marry her before you go away' :* Ibid.

154. *On her first trip to the Berghof, Frau Junge was excited :* Traudl Junge interview.

155. *Fräulein Manzialy, who prepared Hitler's meals, was quite plain :* Dr Karl Brandt interview.

156. *She was very proud of her slim, dainty figure* : Traudl Junge interview.

156. *She often asked Paul Harns whether he thought Hitler was only using her* : Paul Harns interview.

157. *It came at the 1935 Nuremberg rally* : Julius Schaub interview.

159. *. . . Sauckel delighted in having all the foreign females medically examined* : Bormann, 528.

160. *During one of their intimate conversations* : Julius Schaub interview.

160. *Ludwig Kreiger, an official stenographer from the Reichstag* : Ludwig Kreiger interview, Palace of Justice, Nuremberg, January 28, 1948.

160. *On a trip to Munich, Eva stopped at the Sahn Studio to have her photograph taken* : Interview with photographer Sahn. Munich, July 28, 1948.

161. *Even Albert Speer's mountain guide suspected Eva's relationship with Hitler* : Albert Speer interview.

161. *She grew more serious and assumed more authority over domestic affairs* : Dr Karl Brandt interview.

162. *Eva finally learned her lesson by observing Hitler's reaction to Marion Schoenemann* : Ibid.

163. *The only house she could enter socially was Heinrich Hoffmann's home* : Julius Schaub interview.

163. *'Hitler now took care that Eva was recognized and respected within his inner circle.'* Saturday Evening Post, December 16, 1939.

163. *The observant Frau Junge once noted* : Traudl Junge interview.

164. *'I don't understand why you women must always change'* : Ibid.

164. *For years Eva had her clothes made to order in Munich* : Julius Schaub interview.

164. *On another occasion she and Gretl went to the famous leather store Lederer in Berlin* : Gun, 174.

165. *Once when she had combed it into an upswept style, Hitler was disconsolate* : Traudl Junge interview.

165. *His day was mostly taken up with one conference after another* : Dr Karl Brandt interview.

167. *The affair gradually developed into a contented alliance* : Ibid.

167. *In a letter to his wife Gerda* : Trevor-Roper, 19.

169. *'Women have a talent'* : Bormann, 285.

170. *Unity Mitford was the exact opposite of the type of woman who usually attracted Hitler* : Julius Schaub interview.

171. *The first time Eva saw Unity Mitford in person* : Hoffmann, 164.

171. *He and his guests usually stayed in an annex of Hans Wahn-fried :* Dr Karl Brandt interview.

172. *Whether he thought Eva was at the concert nearby :* Monita Garnier interview, London, March, 1970. Miss Garnier was formerly a maid for the Wagner family at Bayreuth and was acquainted with most of the famous guests who attended the Wagner Festival every year. A native of Paris, Miss Garnier was brought to Germany in 1930 to add sophistication to the Wagner household staff. She liked Eva Braun very much and thought she was kind and considerate to the servants, whereas Unity Mitford was much more reserved and snobbish. Miss Garnier was one of the few persons who ever heard Eva give Hitler a 'bawling out' (her words). At the 1936 Wagner Festival Hitler was very abrupt with a singer whom he did not like personally ; Miss Garnier later heard Eva tell him in a very blunt way that 'he had acted like a spoiled baby and if he didn't acquire some manners he would go down in history as the most ignorant and impolite chancellor that ever held office in Germany.' According to Miss Garnier, Hitler didn't argue with Eva. He just nodded. In 1970 Miss Garnier was living in a small hotel just off Trafalgar Square, London.

173. *Hitler had a rule that no one could discuss politics during mealtime :* Speer, 74.

173. *During the Czechoslovakian melee Unity lost her camera :* Frau Winter interview, September 3, 1948.

173. *She and her mother were sitting in a restaurant in Munich :* Ibid.

174. *Unity was a direct pipeline to the British leaders :* Hoffmann, 165.

174. *So accurate that in 1942 :* Bormann, 513.

174. *'I dream of an impregnable and invincible alliance' :* Hoffmann, 165.

176. *As she told Hitler later, 'All guests at the Berghof must be treated properly' :* Traudl Junge interview.

176. *Throughout the summer of 1939 . . . he stayed at the Berghof planning his military moves :* Bullock, 505.

176. *While she understood his reasons for seducing Unity Mitford :* Traudl Junge interview.

177. *He gave her what he considered kindly and well meant advice :* Hoffmann, 166.

177. *When some of her Nazi friends visited her :* Julius Schaub interview.

178. *Once she was home, she was arrested under Security Regulation 18B :* Ibid.

178. *While Eva had always known that Hitler was using Unity Mitford :* Paul Harns interview.

178. *he revised his will in 1938, placing Eva first in the list of beneficiaries :* The 1938 will was discovered after the war by an East German worker among the rubble of the Reich Chancellery. He kept it until his death, when his wife turned it over to West German officials. A copy of the will is at the Hoover Institution on War, Revolution and Peace, Stanford, California.

179. *In one breath he would swear that the 'Ten Commandments are a code of living to which there is no refutation' :* Bormann, 70.

179. *With the next breath he would state, 'I've much more respect for the woman who has an illegitimate child than for an old maid' :* Ibid., 286.

180. *'I'll give you good advice,' he told Kempka. 'Get a divorce' :* Erich Kempka interview.

180. *With Goebbels, Hitler reacted in just the opposite manner :* Albert Speer interview.

181. *Wilhelm Brückner, an early Nazi Party Member and one of Hitler's adjutants :* Otto Skorzeny interview, Madrid, Spain, February, 1973. I met with Otto Skorzeny in his office in Madrid to get his personal opinion of Eva Braun and as many details as possible about her affair with Hitler. Skorzeny was not the least reluctant to talk about the era of the Third Reich. Among many of the subjects we discussed was the Brückner affair. Skorzeny was very fond of Eva Braun and told me that he had many long conversations with her, usually while waiting to see Hitler. He thought that she was very beautiful and that 'Hitler loved her as much as he could love any woman.' Skorzeny said that Eva Braun influenced Hitler a great deal, not directly in planning political or military actions, but indirectly by subtly leading his thoughts into certain directions that pleased her. However, he does not believe that she tried to influence Hitler in major matters, but rather matters in which she had a personal interest. Naturally, with an adventurous soldier such as Skorzeny, the matter of women and sex was discussed. He scoffed at the suggestion that Hitler was not interested in sex. Skorzeny told me that after he had rescued Mussolini from Gran Sasso, Hitler summoned him to Berlin to personally congratulate him for his successful operation. The Führer said: 'You go to your wife for a few days now. You have been away from her too long and it is not good for a man such as you not to be with your wife for too long a time. A man needs a woman periodically.' Skorzeny, a hard-boiled soldier who commanded the German Special Forces (commandos), is one of the few persons still living who was a personal acquaintance of

both Hitler and Eva Braun. Like Albert Speer, he was
with the pair until very shortly before their death.

182. *One of Hitler's rulings on love probably changed the course of
     history :* Otto Skorzeny interview.
183. *It was Eva who gave him the idea of how this could be ac-
     complished :* Paul Harns interview.
184. *Alfred Jodl, a military officer :* Alfred Jodl's diary [unpub-
     lished version].
184. *As Hitler told Eva after he had read the police file on Erna
     Grühn :* Paul Harns interview.
185. *Once again Himmler was ordered to check the files at the
     Berlin police headquarters :* Otto Skorzeny interview.
190. *less than eight hours later Hitler personally crossed the
     frontier :* Bullock, 433.
191. *Eva decided she wanted to share Hitler's triumph :* Braun
     interview.
192. *After he had berated her for a few minutes :* Ibid.
193. *The Germans were unaccustomed to formal state visits :*
     Dollman, 115.
194. *Later he told Eugen Dollman :* Ibid., 117.
194. *'I will be back at a decent hour' :* Julius Schaub interview.
195. *'In inviting me on the evening of October 17' :* François-
     Poncet's official report (1938), Ministère des Transports,
     Paris, France.
197. *In fact, the family spent so much time at the Berghof :* Julius
     Schaub interview.
197. *'Don't tell the Führer' :* Braun interview.
198. *Eva asked to use a telephone :* Paul Harns interview.
198. *Hitler telephoned her every day she was away from him :* Frau
     Winter interview, September 3, 1948.
198. *Once when she complained that Goebbels was demanding
     that all women forgo cosmetics :* Albert Speer interview.
201. *Yet, the man who became the most important Nazi leader
     after Hitler was barely known to any :* Ibid.
202. *When, late in the war, Hitler decided to use thirty-five
     thousand prisoners-of-war as hostages :* Gottlob Berger
     interview (M.A., 262ff.).
202. *The other person in Hitler's inner circle :* Otto Skorzeny in-
     terview.
203. *He had done so since his days as a member of the Freikorps :*
     Hugh Trevor-Roper, *New York Times Magazine*,
     January 14, 1973.
203. *Albert Speer, however, thought that Bormann . . . finally
     drove Hess to the foolhardy flight :* Albert Speer interview.
204. *Hitler also ordered that Frau Hess be evicted from her Berlin
     quarters on the Wilhelmstrasse :* Stevenson, 55.
204. *Once when she complained that Bormann was harassing the
     churches in Munich :* Braun interview.

205. *Speer had always been friendly with Eva*: Albert Speer interview.

206. *By 1943 Bormann had reached the status of personal secretary to the Führer*: Trevor-Roper, *New York Times Magazine*, January 14, 1973.

206. *Hitler was irritated with Bormann at the time*: Ibid.

207. *Hitler thought all this was rather sordid*: Stevenson, 43.

207. *He chose the first path*: Gerhardt Frisch interview, Paris, March, 1973. Prior to World War II, Frisch was an accountant with his own office in Augsburg. When the war started he became an SS officer. His primary assignment was to help Himmler maintain financial control of the organization and, while doing so, to spy on the other Nazi leaders for Himmler. Himmler sent him to the Berghof several times a year to check on the money spent to feed, house and otherwise maintain the SS contingent that was on duty there. At the same time, according to Frisch, his orders were to learn all the facts he could about Bormann's manipulations of Nazi Party money and Hitler's private funds. It was during one of his stays on the Obersalzberg that Frisch discovered Bormann's plan to withhold money from Eva Braun until she agreed to cooperate with him. Frisch now works in a Paris bank.

208. *Bormann's great patience was rewarded early in 1944, however, when Speer became ill*: Albert Speer interview.

208. *Eva had one advantage in the struggle with Bormann*: Otto Skorzeny interview.

209. *One day after Morell had examined Hitler for one of the Chancellor's imaginary ills*: Ada Hocher interview, Munich, February, 1973. Fräulein Hocher was a nurse who resided in Berchtesgaden and was often summoned by the doctors at the Berghof to help out when an extra nurse was needed. She was about the same age as Eva Braun and the two became friendly. Fräulein Hocher was in love with a young SS officer, Claus Kahr, and they planned to marry. After the incident at the Berghof – she managed to stop Dr Morell and Bormann from injecting Eva Braun – she not only lost her lover, she also lost her freedom. She was a virtual prisoner at the Berghof, where she felt protected under the watchful eye of Eva Braun. She was afraid to live at home in Berchtesgaden for fear Bormann or Himmler would take their revenge and murder her. After the war she changed her name and continued in the nursing profession. For several years she lived in Geneva, but she returned to Germany in 1969. She still believes Bormann is alive and fears for her life.

210. *The reason she came to this conclusion* : Hoffmann, 218.
216. *Hitler 'ran around like a lion in his cage'* : Traudl Junge interview.
216. *'I wouldn't be a good head of a family'* : Ibid.
217. *'Capitulation is impossible'* : Evidence given by General Friedrich von Paulus at the Nuremberg Trials. *Trials of War Criminals* . . . Nuremberg Proceedings, Part VI, 262.
217. *'He should have shot himself'* : *Gilbert*, 17–22.
217. *'One of these days I'll have only two friends left, Fräulein Braun and my dog'* : Albert Speer interview.
218. *In July, 1943, Otto Skorzeny . . . was the commander of the German Special Forces* : Otto Skorzeny interview.
219. *With the same calm with which he had sent Ciano's wife, Edda Mussolini, flowers* : Ibid.
219. *'You could break a foot'* : Traudl Junge interview.
219. *'What do you think about the Führer's health, Frau Junge?'* : Ibid.
220. *Later that day in the teahouse Eve reproached Hitler* : Ibid.
220. *Shortly before Christmas, 1943, Fanny Braun visited the Berghof* : Erich Kempka interview.
220. *Morell was treating him with injections and pills* : Musmanno, 52.
221. *When Brandt, Giesing and Hasselbach analyzed one pill that Morell had prescribed for Hitler* : Ibid., 53.
221. *Eva was also worried about the dangers Hitler faced while at his headquarters in the field* : Traudl Junge interview.
221. *He had learned his horsemanship from his father* : Musmanno, 124.
222. *She asked her mother's advice about marrying him* : Braun interview.
222. *Eva, as soon as she learned of her sister's wedding plans* : Julius Schaub interview.
223. *'Du, on this important day of your life'* : Otto Skorzeny interview.
223. *During a late dinner with Christa Schröder* : Christa Schröder interview.
225. *Christa Schröder, who was at the field headquarters with Hitler* : Christa Schröder interview.
225. *'After what I have seen here, I am absolutely of your opinion'* : Bullock, 744.
226. *When Eva scolded him* : Traudl Junge interview.
227. *'This time you will stay with me'* : Julius Schaub interview.
230. *She finally talked a young Waffen-SS officer, Walther Galen, into driving her to Berlin* : Walther Galen interview, Berlin. March, 1970. When and how Eva Braun arrived in Berlin for her final stay has been a matter of controversy. Both Trevor-Roper and Bullock, in their respective books, say that she arrived at the bunker after Roosevelt's death on

April 12, 1945. Gun, in his book, states that she arrived in March but that Junge drove her to Berlin in her Daimler-Benz. In 1970, through the help of an acquaintance in the American Embassy, I interviewed Walther Galen, who told me that he had taken Eva Braun from Munich to Berlin in March, 1945, in a black Mercedes-Benz which belonged to her – or one that she had the use of (he said it is possible that the car belonged to Herta Schneider). After interviewing him I checked with other sources, including Albert Speer and Otto Skorzeny, and while they could not verify all of Galen's facts, they stated that, for the most part, his story sounded authentic.

231. *Hitler was sitting on the blue-and-white patterned sofa*: Julius Schaub interview.

232. *The bunker had two floors*: Musmanno, 11.

233. *On April 1, 1945, she was in her combination bedroom-sitting room*: Julius Schaub interview.

234. *Hoffmann and Hitler talked*: Traudl Junge interview.

234. *The rotund photographer shrugged*: Heinrich Hoffmann interview.

235. *Hitler left the party early and Eva accompanied him to his quarters*: Traudl June interview.

237. *Eva hated to see him go*: Ibid.

237. *'You are the only one who can take the Führer away from here'*: Ibid.

237. *'All is lost, hopelessly lost'*: Ibid.

238. *At dinner that evening Hitler gave each of the women a small cylinder*: Musmanno, 41.

238. *She was determined to 'act like a lady until the end'*: Otto Skorzeny interview.

238. *'One needs courage when death is near'*: Albert Speer interview.

240. *Hanna Reitsch, the famed German aviatrix*: National Archives, Washington, D.C., Captured German Records Division, Interrogation Summary No. 1, October 8, 1945.

240. *I must write you these words*: British Intelligence Subcommittee Report, Interrogation Report No. 167, October 5, 1946. Hanna Reitsch and General von Greim read the letter, but instead of delivering it, they tore it up. They believed that the letter was too dramatic, that if it fell into Allied hands Eva Braun would appear a martyr.

241. *One day early in his career*: Hanfstängl, 147.

242. *Later, however, she told Frau Junge, 'I want to be a pretty corpse'*: Traudl Junge interview.

243. *Erwin Jakubek, a waiter*: Erwin Jakubek interview, Munich, August 1, 1948.

243. *Two days later, on April 28, Eva received a message from Grossmann* : Musmanno, 159.

243. *Frau Junge, who was at the other end of the room, saw Eva step back and stare at Hitler* : Traudl Junge interview.

244. *Wagner nodded and placed the two-page marriage document on the small table* : Musmanno, 162.

246. *Eva returned to her own room and wrote a final message to Gretl's husband* : Ibid., 149. The entire Fegelein incident is rather confusing and has been reported in various ways down through the years. This version came from the Musmanno Archives and had been verified in its important aspects by Otto Skorzeny.

247. *Although during my years of struggle* : The William R. Philp Collection, Hoover Institution on War, Revolution and Peace, Stanford, California.

248. *Benito Mussolini is dead* : Reuters, April 28, 1945.

248. *'Would my dog Blondi respond to the cyanide the same as a human?'* : Musmanno, 180.

249. *After the young secretary arrived* : Traudl Junge interview.

Bibliography

BULLOCK, ALAN. *Hitler: A Study in Tyranny*. New York: Harper & Bros., 1962.

CHILDS, DAVID. *Germany Since 1918*. New York: Harper & Row, 1971.

COLLIER, RICHARD. *Duce*. New York: The Viking Press, Inc., 1971.

DILL, MARSHALL, JR. *Germany: A Modern History*. Ann Arbor: University of Michigan Press, 1961.

DOLLMAN, DR EUGEN. *The Interpreter*. London: Hutchinson & Co., 1967.

FRISCHAUER, WILLI. *The Rise and Fall of Hermann Goering*. New York: Houghton Mifflin Company, 1951.

GILBERT, FELIX. *Hitler Directs His War*. London: Tandem Books, 1950.

GUN, NERIN E. *Eva Braun: Hitler's Mistress*. New York: Meredith Press, 1968.

GUNTHER, JOHN. *Inside Europe*. New York: Harper & Bros., 1933.

HANFSTÄNGL, ERNST. *Unheard Witness*. New York: J. B. Lippincott, 1957.

HEIDEN, KONRAD. *Der Führer*. Boston: Houghton Mifflin, 1944.

HEINZ, HEINZ A. *Germany's Hitler*. London: Hurst & Blackett, 1934.

HITLER, ADOLF. *Hitler's Secret Conversations*. New York: Octagon Books, 1973.

HOFFMANN, HEINRICH. *Hitler Was My Friend*. London: Burke Publishing Company, Ltd., 1955.

HOLBORN, HAJO. *A History of Modern Germany 1840–1945*. New York: Alfred A. Knopf, 1969.

KOHLER, PAULINE. *The Woman Who Lived in Hitler's House*. New York: Sheridan House, 1940.

KRUEGER, KURT, M.D. *Inside Hitler*. New York: Avalon Press, 1941.

LANGER, WALTER C. *The Mind of Adolf Hitler*. New York: Basic Books, Inc., 1972.

LOCHNER, LOUIS P. (editor and translator). *The Goebbels Diaries*. New York: Doubleday & Company, Inc., 1948.

LUDECKE, KURT G. W. *I Knew Hitler*. New York: Charles Scribner's Sons, 1938.

MANDELL, RICHARD D. *The Nazi Olympics*. New York: The Macmillan Company, 1971.

MANN, GOLO. *The History of Germany Since 1789.* New York: Frederich A. Praeger, Inc., 1968.

MUSMANNO, MICHAEL A. *Ten Days to Die.* New York: Doubleday & Company, Inc., 1950.

PAYNE, ROBERT. *The Life and Death of Adolf Hitler.* New York: Praeger Publishers, Inc., 1973.

SPEER, ALBERT. *Inside the Third Reich.* New York: The Macmillan Company, 1970.

STEVENSON, WILLIAM. *The Bormann Brotherhood.* New York: Harcourt Brace Jovanovich, Inc., 1973.

TREVOR-ROPER, H. R. (editor). *The Bormann Letters.* London: Weidenfeld & Nicolson, 1954.

————. *The Last Days of Hitler.* 3d ed. New York: The Macmillan Company, 1966.

Trials of War Criminals Before the Nuremberg Military Tribunals. Washington: U.S. Government Printing Office, 1951–52.

WHITING, CHARLES. *Skorzeny.* New York: Ballantine Books, Inc., 1972.

WILLIAMS, WYTHE AND VAN NARVIG, WILLIAM. *Secret Sources.* New York: Ziff-Davis Publishing Company, 1943.

DOCTOR GOEBBELS
by Roger Manvell
and Heinrich Fraenkel

Joseph Goebbels was possibly the most dangerous and intelligent member of the Nazi hierarchy, not excluding Hitler himself. Without Goebbels' flair for propaganda and spectacular organisation Hitler might never have come to power. As founder of the Reich Chamber of Culture, the Gauleiter of Berlin and the architect of modern totalitarian propaganda, Goebbels has a claim to be the most evilly portentous figure of this century.

The book includes much new information, both from personal interviews and from hitherto unpublished material making this the best documented biography yet written. In its thoroughness and lucid organisation it is unlikely to be rivalled for a very long time.

'Serious work of research . . . much previously unknown material . . . fascinating.'

Sebastian Haffner, **Observer**

'Enthralling . . . certainly the best of any (books on Goebbels) that have yet appeared.'

Ewan Butler, **John O'London**

NEW ENGLISH LIBRARY

GÖRING
by Roger Manvell
and Heinrich Fraenkel

Hermann Göring: Hitler's Deputy, founder of the Gestapo,
Marshal of the Luftwaffe, and Maecenas of the Third
Reich, has always been viewed as a character of immense
and baffling contradictions. Brutal in action but good-
humoured in society, megalomaniac in his display of
wealth, he was nevertheless the man whose intelligence
and charm did much to make the Nazis seem respectable
and their policy plausible during the days of appeasement.

In this outstanding study the authors have used the
impressions of those who knew Göring, as well as the
mass of public records available, to present a unique
portrait in depth of this extraordinary man – and reveal
him as a leader corrupted through opportunism, moral
cowardice, and self-indulgence.

'This is 20th-century biography at its best.'
Books and Bookmen

'This . . . massive and masterly biography . . . will hold
its own for many years as a standard work.'
Times Literary Supplement

NEW ENGLISH LIBRARY